TRIUMPH
TWINS &
TRIPLES

NITON PUBLISHING

TRIUMPH TWINS & TRIPLES

The 350, 500, 650, 750 Twins and Trident

Roy Bacon

Published by Niton Publishing
P.O. Box 3, Ventnor, Isle of Wight, PO38 2AS

© Copyright Roy Bacon 1995

First published in 1981 in Great Britain by Osprey Publishing Limited, 12–14 Long Acre, London WC2E 9LP Member company of the George Philip Group

All rights reserved. Apart from any fair dealing for the purpose of private study, research, criticism, or review, as permitted under the Copyright, Designs and Patents Act, 1988, no part of this publication may be reproduced, stored in a retrieval system, or transmitted in any form or by any means, electronic, electrical, chemical, mechanical, optical, photocopying, recording, or otherwise, without prior written permission. All enquiries should be addressed to the publisher.

ISBN 1-903088-38-0

Printed by
I.R.Best International Corporation
Kaohsiung
Taiwan

September 2007

For
Mercian Manuals Ltd
353 Kenilworth Road
Balsall Common
Coventry
CV7 7DL

Original edition:
Editor Bacon, Roy

Contents

Foreword by C. E. 'Titch' Allen   6
Acknowledgements   8
1 Early twins   10
2 The start of the line   20
3 Military mounts   34
4 Postwar, pre-unit   44
5 The Grand Prix   66
6 Unit construction   74
7 After Meriden   100
8 The Trident   108
9 The scooter twin   118
10 The OHC twin   126
11 Competition   132
12 Specials   144

Appendices
1 Specifications   152
2 Colours   177
3 Engine and frame numbers   181
4 Model recognition points   183
5 Production flow chart   184
6 Carburettor settings   187
7 Prices   189

Foreword by C. E. 'Titch' Allen

No single designer and no one design can have had so much influence on the development of the motorcycle as Edward Turner and his Triumph Speed Twin of 1937.

By its instant success, this machine changed the shape of motorcycles for three decades, and more, and signed the death warrant of the traditional big single.

While Triumph twins and triples still abound it will be difficult to evaluate their precise contribution to motorcycle history because they arouse such strong emotions. Nostalgia may now replace competition success in the Triumph mystique but it is still difficult to be truly objective.

I certainly cannot be objective because I still recall, as if but yesterday, the thrill of riding one of the first Speed Twins in 1938, a machine so smooth, so flexible and yet so joyously fast after a lifetime of thumping singles and indifferent multis, that it was not so much a milestone in motorcycle development as a breakthrough into a new dimension.

Historians may well decide that the Speed Twin was the first machine to satisfy both the enthusiast and the man in the street by its unique blend of performance with docility, and silence; its widespread adoption by police forces throughout the world supports this view.

It was a *Triumph* for Great Britain. It added at least twenty more years to its domination of world motorcycle markets and was a personal *Triumph* for Edward Turner, who more than any other of his time had the knack of knowing not what the average motorcyclist would like in his dreams, but what he could afford to buy in the showroom, and moreover what the manufacturer could make at the price and show a profit.

Between 1938 and 1958 Turner led the world of motorcycle fashion with cosmetic innovations like the nacelle headlamp, the parcel grid, the 'bath tub' rear enclosure ... gimmicks, if you like, which avoided expensive major design changes. He was taking design towards styled enclosure with cleanliness and weather protection when the pendulum of fashion suddenly swung back to the reactionary café racer, or pseudo racer, and this was not Turner's scene at all. His good work in gaining public acceptance of the Triumph motorcycle as quiet and unobtrusive, with smooth, flowing lines, was destroyed by a rash of stark race replicas attractive to enthusiasts but an anathema to the 'man in the street'.

From then on Triumph leadership began to wane and one senses that Turner, soon to retire, was disillusioned by the caprice of fashion. However, the Twin was not yet defeated, reaching new heights of triumph with the Bonneville race and record successes. Then came the Triple.

With hindsight it seems logical that adding a cylinder to a well-tried design would be a good way of obtaining the extra performance the market demanded, but no one had done it before and yet it succeeded beyond expectation. Almost alone it fought a dramatic rearguard action for the British motorcycle industry against the advancing army of oriental fours.

Roy Bacon has done his homework well. He has avoided rumours, speculation and legends and stuck to facts so that the reader can make up his own mind about the place of the Triumph twins and triples in history. And the restorer of Triumphs will be overjoyed to find at last a book which details the smallest changes in specification from one year's production to the next.

C. E. 'Titch' Allen
Ibstock,
Leicestershire.
October 1980

Acknowledgements

This third edition of *Triumph Twins & Triples* completes the story of the machines built in Coventry and at Meriden. It touches on the rebirth of Triumph under John Bloor and the interim period when the twins were built in Devon by Les Harris. It does not cover the Hinckley models which do appear in my *Triumph* title in the Legends series (Sunburst Books) and in my *Illustrated Triumph Motorcycle Buyer's Guide* (Niton Publishing).

Note that this book uses calendar years for the changes so may not totally seem to agree with the above titles or my *Triumph Twin Restoration* and it is they which should take precedence as to detail data.

This is always the most difficult part of the book to write as one tries to say thank you to all the people who have given information, help and advice during its production. Without that help it could not have been done and I am very grateful to all.

To Titch Allen for his kindness in writing the Foreword. Bob Currie, who answered my many queries on finishes and specifications by return of post. Amal for data on carburettor settings. Tony Cooper of TMS who now owns the Trisolastic, the camshaft triple and the Thunderbird Three in a very interesting collection. Chris Mason of Italjet for data on the Grifon. Charles and Moo Ivory and their autojumble stand for a sought-after magazine. Tim Parker who edited the book and gave me help and advice during its preparation.

Finding pictures for this type of book would be impossible without the help of the motorcycle magazines who once more kindly let me forage in their files. *Motor Cycle News, Motor Cycle Weekly, Motorcycle Sport* and *Which Bike?* provided most of the pictures. My thanks go to the respective editors: Bob Berry, Mick Woollett, Cyril Ayton and John Nutting. From some 600 pictures the 165 finally used were chosen with difficulty and all returned to their homes after use.

Some pictures used had the stamp of a freelance photographer on them and in every case I have tried to make contact to clear the copyright. If by chance my letter failed to reach you or I have unknowingly used an unmarked print, I can only apologise.

A special thank you must be made to S. R. Keig, the Isle of Man photographers who took my list of needs, telephoned me to check a point or two and came up with just what I wanted.

The freelance photographers and agencies whose pictures were used are: Cecil Bailey, M. Carling, Jim Greening, Keith Lee, Nick Nicholls, Donald Page, Publicity Designs, F. Reynold, Thompson of Coventry and P. J. Worden.

Finally I must thank the National Motor Museum at Beaulieu for a needed picture and the Triumph Engineering Company for the use of some of their sales material.

I hope you will all find the finished result acceptable.

Roy Bacon
Hampton, Middlesex
January 1981

Note This updated edition was prepared to include the closure of Meriden and the continuation of the Triumph story in Devon.

November 1985

1 Early twins

Crankshaft from the 1913 twin. Forged in one, with skew gear for camshaft drive. Split big ends and 180 degree throws

The Edward Turner design of 1937 is the definitive four-stroke vertical twin, and every subsequent engine with two upright cylinders owes something to the Triumph for at least a part of its ancestry. The Triumph Twin was the first to be built in any numbers and, because the Second World War came along when it did, it won a head start over all the other firms whose reply to the Speed Twin should have appeared late in 1939 but was forcibly deferred for six or seven years.

However, although the Speed Twin of 1937 is the true starting point of the Triumph Twin story, the company had some previous knowledge of that engine layout, their earliest experience being in 1909. For their first trials they used an imported Bercley engine of 616 cc. This was an advanced design for the time with mechanically operated side-valves, a three-bearing 360-degree crankshaft and a cross-flow head with inlet and exhaust valves placed fore and aft of the engine. The Bercley engine also featured a built-up crankshaft with the crank pins formed with the half shafts and carrying plain big ends. These extended into heavy flywheels and were secured by nuts pulling up the shaft tapers. The two flywheels were joined by a short shaft secured in the same way, which passed through a central crankcase web. This provided the centre bearing and was clamped by the crankcase halves.

In August 1913 Triumph announced their own

engine, which followed the lines of the Bercley but with some very fundamental changes. The capacity was 600 cc and the side-valves were still placed fore and aft of the engine, but it used a 180-degree crankshaft, which was a one-piece forging running on two ball races. Split big ends were used, and the caps dipped into the oil in the sump for lubrication. The crankcase was split horizontally on the centre line of the main bearings and was cast in aluminium. Its top half carried the camshaft, which ran on ball races, was positioned at right angles to the crankshaft and thus ran fore and aft in the engine. It was driven by a large skew gear machined on the centre web of the crankshaft. By giving this gear a large helix angle it was possible to obtain the required reduction ratio, although the crankshaft gear was larger in diameter than the camshaft one. The cams were positioned at each end of the shaft and operated the valves through adjustable tappets with fibre caps. At the rear of the camshaft a further skew gear drove the magneto.

The two cylinders were cast in one with their cylinder heads and had air spaces between the cylinders and the valve pockets. The block was in cast iron and was secured to the crankcase by four studs.

A large external flywheel was fitted on the left side, drilled and plugged with lead to balance the engine, while the other end of the crankshaft

The Val Page 650 cc twin with Triumph sidecar attached being tested by 'Ambleside' of The Motor Cycle **with Harry Perrey in the chair. September 1933**

carried a chain sprocket. This drove a three-speed bottom-bracket gear. The machine was fitted with a kickstarter on the right lower chain stay and this rotated the belt rim a quarter turn when depressed.

The engine did not go into production and the outbreak of war in 1914 was suggested as the reason. As remembered, the problem was vibration, and with the type of crankshaft used

Early twins

650 cc engine and gearbox unit cut-away for exhibition and training use to show some of the internal details

together with the flywheel fitted this seems a likely explanation.

Twenty years passed by before another vertical twin came from the Triumph factory. In 1932 Val Page had left Ariel to join Triumph and in 1933 two prototypes of the new twin, known as the model 6/1, appeared in a rally. One ran solo and the other pulled a sidecar and both were powered by the new engine. This was not Page's first experience of the vertical twin, for while with Ariel he had built a 250 cc twin with 360-degree cranks by assembling one crankshaft from the original 500 cc Ariel Square Four with the cranks in line and having a special camshaft made. The experiment was carried out in the two rear cylinders of the four and the resultant machine ran very well. Ariel did not take the matter further due to their commitments with singles and the four, but when Page moved to Triumph he remembered this work and so can be said to be the father of the modern twin, although it was to take Turner to make the result a bestseller.

The new machine had a straightforward vertical twin engine of 646 cc with overhead valves and a 360-degree crankshaft. The design was advanced with gear primary drive and semi-unit gearbox, but was also massive in construction. The crankshaft had a stroke of 84 mm and was a one-piece forging incorporating three bobweights, one at each end and one in the middle. These were supplemented by a flywheel housed in the nearside primary drive case and mounted inboard of the drive gear up against the drive side ball race main bearing. The crankshaft ran on two mains and was housed in a vertically split crankcase, which was extended down as a dry sump, with a compartment to carry the lubricating oil. This was filled through a cap situated in front of the cylinders on the right side of the crankcase.

The cylinder casting was one-piece with a pushrod tunnel cast in at the rear between the two bores. These were of 70 mm diameter and contained conventional solid skirt pistons with three rings and small valve cutaways in their crowns. The pistons were attached to steel connecting rods with split big ends using white metal bearings and the crank pins were of massive proportions.

The cylinder heads were separate and each spigoted to the barrel. The outer pairs of holding-down bolts also located a bracket on each side of the head and between these ran the rocker spindles. Each rocker was spring loaded with a washer placed between it and the bracket, and was fitted with a ball-ended pin at its inner end and an adjuster at its outer. The adjusters had square ends and were locked with nuts. The rockers were grease lubricated with nipples screwed into the left end of the spindles and were part enclosed. This was done with a horizontally split pair of alloy castings. Both located on the centres of the rocker spindles and held the rockers apart. They bolted to each other with 10 small fastenings, the lower one enclosing the pushrods down to the cylinder head level. The upper one enclosed the rockers except for the outer arms and adjusters, which protruded through suitable slots.

The cylinder heads carried the overhead valves at an included angle of about 90 degrees, with the sparking plugs splayed out between the valves in the side of the hemispherical combustion chamber. The valves ran in pressed-in guides and were closed by coil springs retained by conventional means. Hardened valve stem end caps were fitted. The exhaust ports were round in section and splayed out and down, while the inlets were fed by a cast, Y-shaped inlet manifold fixed by studs and nuts and carrying the Amal carburettor. A type 75/014 of $\frac{7}{8}$ in. bore was used, mounted at an angle of seven degrees downdraught. It was fed by a bottom feed type 64/079 float chamber on the left and no air cleaner was used.

The valves were operated by unequal-length pushrods, which ran down the tunnel in the barrel casting to locate on flat-faced tappets mounted in a single housing located at the bottom of the tunnel. The camshaft lay below the tappet feet in the upper part of the crankcase behind the crankshaft and ran on two ball races. It was gear driven from the crankshaft by a train on the right side, the half-time pinion driving a similar-size idler, which drove the camshaft gear. This in turn drove the Lucas magdyno mounted behind the engine and all four gears were enclosed by an alloy timing cover retained by nine screws.

The magneto was a conventional Lucas twin-cylinder instrument of the time, with manual advance and retard, and carried the dynamo strapped to it and gear driven from it.

Lubrication was dry sump with the plunger oil pump driven from an eccentric in the timing gear and housed in the cover. The oil was pumped through a cooler and filter fitted behind the gearbox before being fed to the crankshaft at the timing end and to the intermediate timing gear bearing. A pressure valve opened at 60 psi and surplus oil lubricated the rest of the timing gear.

The power output was 25 bhp at 4500 rpm and this was transmitted to the gearbox by a pair of double helical gears. This primary drive was fitted with a four-lobe, cam-type shock absorber on the engine shaft. The use of double helical gearing made for quieter running without the usual problems of the side loads induced by normal helical gears, but would have been very expensive to gear cut and not easy to assemble. Alignment is critical, otherwise the loading is taken by one set of gear teeth only.

The clutch was a conventional multiplate device with four springs operated by a lever and pushrod through the gearbox mainshaft. The gearbox was bolted to the rear of the crankcase and contained four speeds. Top gear was 1:1, as the box had the typical English layout of the time with gearbox sprocket behind the clutch and running concentric with it. Due to this the engine

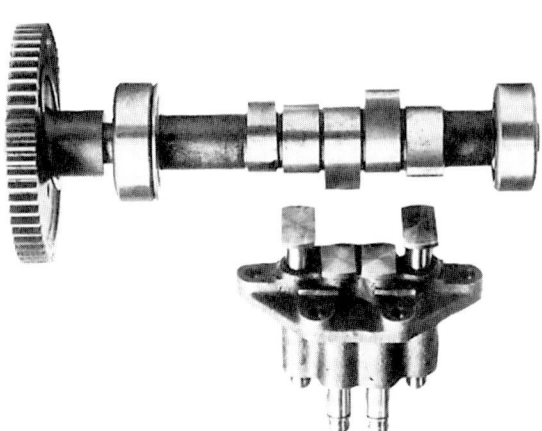

Camshaft with ball races it turned in and flat faced tappets in their housing. The cam on the left was an eccentric which operated the plunger oil pump

View of 650 cc twin bottom half with mag-dyno in position. Oil filler at front and neat timing drive gears

rotated 'backwards' to the normal way. Gear-changing was by a hand lever with the change gate fitted to the right-hand side of the petrol tank with first at the top of the gate and fourth at the bottom. The hand lever connected to a vertical rod which linked to a lever on the rear of the gearbox. A kickstarter was fitted to the box endcover, which also carried the filler for the lubricant.

The engine and gearbox assembly was mounted in a massive duplex cradle frame with four fixing points and a head steady. The frame was rigid and the front girder forks of equally massive proportions, for the machine was primarily intended for sidecar use. The brakes were both of 8 in. diameter and interconnected so that operation of the pedal applied both. The brakes could also be locked on, using a ratchet device, for parking. The front brake was on the right with a torque arm to the backplate (which also carried the speedometer drive box), while the rear brake was on the left and the drum incorporated the sprocket.

Mudguards were of generous proportions and

One-piece cylinder barrel with separate heads each of which spigoted into place. Hemi-spherical combustion chambers, flat top pistons and mildly splayed exhaust ports

the rear stay of the front one doubled as a front wheel stand. A rear stand was also provided. Exhaust pipes swept down on both sides of the machine to tubular silencers with tail pipes which extended to the rear number plate. A toolbox was fitted beneath the saddle, and on the mudguard behind this was mounted a rear carrier. Headlight and horn were both carried on the girder forks, with the speedometer at the top of the fork. The other instruments, along with the lighting switch, were all contained in a tank-top panel. The tank was nicely styled with the rear part angled off to match the line of the upper chain stays as was common with several Triumph models about that time, although it did give a vintage flavour to the saddle-tank style.

As the new model was intended for sidecar use a special sidecar and chassis were designed to match it, with most of the chassis effectively hidden by the body. This was the work of Harry Perrey, a top-class trials rider and salesman with a flair for publicity, and it was he who had ridden the sidecar at the rally. Before the rally the machine, in both solo and sidecar form, had covered many laps at Brooklands at high speed and after it Perrey undertook an ambitious test to promote the machine and attempt to win the prestigious Maudes Trophy.

His aim was to cover 500 miles at Brooklands in 500 minutes using the sidecar outfit and, as a prelude to this high-speed test, to ride the outfit in the International Six Days Trial, which was held in Wales in September in 1933. He duly carried out the first part of this programme, losing five marks in the trial and winning a silver medal. The machine was returned to Coventry, stripped and examined for wear and, as everything was in order, it was reassembled and driven down to Brooklands.

The test run started at 8 am and for the first three hours fog restricted visibility and the average speed remained at 56 mph. However, as the fog lifted so the speed crept up, and riders Perrey, Tim Robbins and Len Crisp circulated at the required rate. The passengers carried were Syd Slader and Bob Holliday and with just three minutes left the Triumph completed the 500 miles.

The run had not been without incident for, apart from the fog, at one point the outfit suddenly slowed and ran rough. A quick investigation showed that one of the valve stem caps had vanished and despite all the spares they had there were no valve caps. The Triumph was sent out to circulate at 50 mph, everyone crossed their fingers and prayed that the pushrod would stay put, while Perrey dashed into Weybridge and tried to buy valve caps. He could only find some for a Norton, but one fitted adequately and the Triumph was back on song again. It could in fact do about 80 mph with its light sidecar, which was fast motoring for the time. For this exploit the company was awarded the Maudes Trophy.

Triumph were not to rest on this particular laurel and, looking round for further promotion, noted that *The Motor Cycle* had offered a trophy for the first British multicylinder machine of under 500 cc to cover 100 miles in an hour on British soil. Their earlier trophy for the first rider to achieve this feat on any machine had been won by Bill Lacey in 1928, so they had put up another one to encourage multis. This had not been won, although several firms and individuals were preparing machines.

The only place where the attempt could be made was Brooklands, then the home of many very clever rider/tuners who could turn the track's assets and defects to their advantage. All, however, had to contend with the severe bumps and the regulations requiring the use of silencers.

Triumph elected to try for the trophy using the new twin reduced in capacity. The stroke was shortened slightly to 80 mm and the barrel casting machined to a 63 mm bore, which gave a capacity of 499 cc and allowed the use of parts from the 250 cc single, which was of the same dimensions. To obtain the power needed the engine was run on alcohol fuel and supercharged. To withstand the added loads the crankshaft was increased in size and run on roller bearings with the drive side extended and supported by an outrigger ball race in the primary drive cover.

This cover was special anyway as the Zoller blower was mounted behind the cylinder and driven by a splined coupling from a gear meshed with the clutch gear. The primary drive case was extended up to support this gear and the coupling was adapted from the quickly detachable rear hub. The supercharger ran at two-thirds engine speed with a delivery pressure of 7 to 10 psi and had its own oil tank and pump for lubrication. It was fed by an Amal mounted behind it and the mixture was compressed by 7·5:1 pistons.

With the blower occupying the space normally used by the magneto, this was moved to a position in front of the cylinders and driven from the camshaft, the drive being enclosed in an

Front view of engine with side covers off. Note exposed valve gear with boss for valve lifter cable, also fins on spark plugs

alloy case with a cover retained by nine screws.

The engine was lubricated by an oil pump of increased size and produced 46·7 bhp at 4600 rpm on the bench. To deal with the power the gearbox mainshaft was stiffened up and run on roller bearings and an additional friction plate was added to the clutch.

The complete unit was housed in a standard frame with the seat tube bent slightly to clear the intake system, but the forks were from the 5/10 model, a racing version of the standard 500 then sold by the firm. A special 6-gallon tank was fitted

The supercharged engine with special cover enclosing the drive to the blower. This is the final road version

with a rear-mounted saddle, rearward footrests and the compulsory Brooklands silencers.

Attempts by other firms to win the trophy began in May 1934, and it was clear that the New Imperial would soon succeed, for they lapped at 103 mph before being stopped by a minor fault.

A few days later the Triumph was at Brooklands for its first real run as a complete machine with Tommy Spann in the saddle. He quickly began circulating around the 100 mph mark, but all too soon was back in the pits for new plugs and a minor correction or two. More laps and the Triumph seemed ready to go.

From the standing start Spann did a lap of 92·57 mph and then circulated at a steady 104 mph for a while. Then his speed dropped to 100, and in came the Triumph running on one cylinder only. This was a fairly fundamental problem, for the magneto just was unable to keep the engine firing under the conditions. It was not helped by the direct coupling of the blower to the cylinder head with no reservoir tank at all and this gave rise to poor mixture distribution between the cylinders and made the engine choke if the throttle was opened abruptly.

On August 1 the Triumph was back at Brooklands with some improvements and lapped steadily at 105 mph, so looked set for another attempt. However, New Imperial were there on the same day and Ginger Wood ran their vee-twin round to cover 102·21 miles in the hour to take the trophy.

The reason for the blown twin vanished instantly, but it made one final appearance on the road in 1935 when used as a test bed by McEvoy for supercharging experiments. The blower pressure was raised to 15 psi, while the compression ratio went down to 5·5:1 and the engine ran on petrol. The lack of an intake mixture reservoir was dealt with by running an induction pipe right round the cylinder head before it reached the inlet ports, while the Brooklands cans were changed for conventional tubular silencers.

In this form it was reported to have extremely good acceleration, but nothing further was heard of it, and of course the Val Page twin was shortly to be superseded itself.

Despite all the good publicity attending the Maudes Trophy win and the attempts at Brooklands the machine was not a great success. Certainly it was massive enough to be reliable, although hindsight indicates two areas of weakness.

Ground clearance was suited to sidecar-use, not solo, and the whole machine was solid to the eye. It was also expensive to make, with many special items not common to the rest of the range. Family pressures often made a small car preferable, but if that was outside your budget then a single-cylinder sidecar was your mark, not a twin, while if you could afford the twin the temptation was to buy a bigger and more glamorous vee-twin, not something that looked so large and heavy. The handchange did not help either, as footchange had become common by 1934. Only in its final year did the Triumph have this fitted—and then only as an option, using an external mechanism bolted to the top of the gearbox that was untidy. The long pushrods made for noisy valve gear, which did not help much either.

Solid the twin was, but the conservative motorcycling public did not buy, so it was quietly allowed to drop as the curtain began to rise on the archetype Triumph Twin that really founded the line.

Left **Front cover advertisement used on** Motor Cycling **dated 2 January 1935. Footchange has replaced the hand lever, same sidecar as before**

2 | The start of the line

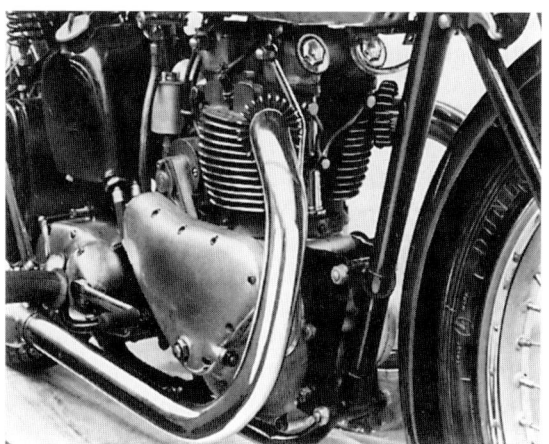

The Speed Twin engine as featured in the original announcement in *Motor Cycling* in August 1937

If Val Page was a gentleman in manner who became a brilliant designer by experience, then Edward Turner was a designer with flair who became a manager and director by ambition and ruthless determination.

Turner had been trained in a hard school, having run his own motorcycle shop in the 1920s and built a machine of his own design in 1927. This brought him to the notice of Jack Sangster, whose family had been in control of Ariel since the turn of the century and who took over the Ariel motorcycle business when the original concern fell into financial difficulties in 1932.

Turner's own machine was a 350 cc single with an overhead face cam operating the valves, but he had other, more ambitious, design aims to build a four-cylinder engine with the cylinders arranged in a square. Sangster liked the idea, so Turner joined Ariel in 1928. So was born the Square Four, in its original form a light and very fast 500 with overhead camshaft operation of the valves. Turner also worked on the Red Hunter singles, a range that became renowned over nearly 30 years for their classic single-cylinder styling and their toughness under hard conditions.

Val Page had joined Ariel in 1925 and designed a new range that had taken the company to the front of the industry, but even his brilliance could not hold back the effects of the Depression. He moved on to Triumph and the Model 6/1 twin, while Turner continued at Ariel.

In 1936 Sangster purchased the Triumph

motorcycle business and moved Turner to it as chief designer and general manager with a brief to rationalize the model range and run the firm efficiently. Turner moved fast and autocratically to reorganize the firm, rearrange production and sales and introduce three sports singles to the range. These were derived from existing models and demonstrated Turner's flair for styling and his uncanny knack of sizing up what the public would accept and, most important of all, actually buy.

The singles were of 250, 350 and 500 cc, all with overhead valves, and were fitted with chromium-plated petrol tanks with top and side panels in silver sheen lined in blue. The headlamp shells were also chromium plated and for 1937 high-level exhaust systems were fitted. The lines and the rocker spindle support plates were very similar to those of the Ariel Red Hunter, but Turner's ace was the name given to his models, Tiger 70, 80 and 90, giving an indication of top speed and their nature. It was an inspired move and the machines sold well, while in 1937 Harry Perrey devised another hard test which once again brought the coveted Maudes Trophy to Triumph. In the same year Freddie Clarke set the all-time 350 cc Brooklands lap record at 105·97 mph, using a modified Tiger 80 running on dope.

Amidst all this reorganization, Turner was also designing the machine for which he will always be best remembered, and, in their issue of July 29, 1937, *The Motor Cycle* announced the 'New Vertical Twin Triumph'. *Motor Cycling* followed up in their issue of August 4 with a description and another line drawing which included some further information.

The model T emphasized a design characteristic that Turner shared with that great Guzzi engineer Giulio Carcano, a passion for lightness and making things small and simple. The new twin engine was in fact lighter than the single cylinder Tiger 90 unit and its crankcase width was slightly less. Its concept was devastatingly simple, for it was really a single in all but its two cylinders. The two camshafts were placed in logical positions and driven by the simplest means, so only the absence of pushrod tubes above the timing cover gave any indication that the engine was not a twin-port single.

The design was based on a simple, vertically split crankcase, cast in aluminium, which carried the crankshaft on two substantial ball races. The crankshaft was built up from three parts, a central flywheel and two single stampings, each of which formed a crank, bobweight and mainshaft. Machining of both was nearly identical, only the mainshaft ends varying. The inner flange of each stamping was ribbed to better support the crankpin, and these flanges spigoted to the flywheel. The three sections were bolted together with six bolts to provide the 360-degree crankshaft layout that Turner favoured. Its use gave even firing intervals, so allowing a standard magneto to be used, an even exhaust note, which was very important at that time, no carburation bias problems and some reduction in the out-of-balance loads, although vibration problems would eventually become more acute as engine speeds rose from the 6000 rpm of 1937.

The crankshaft design made the use of connecting rods with split ends automatic and the rods themselves were light-alloy forgings in RR 56 alloy, itself an excellent bearing material which could be run directly on the crankpin. The rod cap was however made of manganese-molybdenum steel with a tensile strength of 80 tons/sq in., later changed to a 100-ton nickel-chrome steel, and incorporated a central rib and the two fixing studs. The cap was white metal lined and retained by two castellated nuts locked with split pins.

Speed Twin launch in 1937 at Earls Court and the start of a new format for motorcycle engine

Drive side of the original Speed Twin engine with unfaired boss on chaincase. This was changed for the first production machines

The rods were of H section with bronze small-end bushes and carried conventional solid skirt pistons with two compression rings and one oil control ring. Small valve cutaways were provided in the flat tops that gave a compression ratio of 7·2:1 and the pistons ran on hollow gudgeon pins retained by wire circlips. The bore was 63 mm, which, combined with the 80 mm stroke, gave an actual capacity of 498·76 cc, the engine dimensions being those of the Tiger 70 single and the blown 500.

The cylinders were a one-piece iron casting which, viewed from above, had the appearance of a figure 8 with the valve pushrods in the sides of the figure. Cylinder finning extended right round each bore, those between the two being joined. The block was attached to the crankcase halves by six studs with nuts.

The cylinder head followed the same outline as the barrel and was also a one-piece iron casting. It employed an eight-bolt fixing and the two bores were both spigoted up into the heads with a cylinder head gasket fitted round the spigots. The head casting contained wells for the valve springs and the valves were set at 90 degrees to one another.

The exhaust ports were splayed out, but the inlets lay parallel to each other, while the sparking plugs were fitted in the sides of the combustion chamber, so angled out to each side of the engine.

The valves ran in long cast-iron guides pressed into the cylinder head and were controlled by dual coil valve springs retained by a collar and cotters. Each valve was fitted with a hardened end cap and the lower ends of the valve springs were supported by a washer.

The valve rockers were contained in two separate rocker boxes cast in a heat-treated light alloy. Each contained two rockers on a common spindle with thrust washers and coil spring washers to prevent wear and cut out noise. The spindles were drilled for oil, which was fed into them from the right ends. Each rocker carried a ball end on its inner arm and an adjuster with lock nut on its outer. A small gasket was fitted between each rocker box and the cylinder head and each box was held by six fastenings. Two of these were the inner head bolts, two were smaller bolts on the same line across the engine, and the other two were studs which passed through holes in ears cast on the front and back of each valve well and which were held by nuts.

Access to the valve adjusters was via four screw caps with hexagon bosses on them as used on many modern machines. The snag with the Triumph ones was a tendency for them to unscrew and many were the devices produced to stop this from occurring.

The camshafts were mounted high in the crankcase, inlet behind and exhaust in front of the crankshaft. They ran in bronze bearings and the two cams were formed close together either side of the centre line of the engine. Both cams were of the same shape and in fact the camshafts were interchangeable. Above them and fitted into the cylinder base were tappet housings, each retained by a single screw and carrying two tappets.

Each pair of pushrods was very neatly enclosed in a plated tube that fitted between the tappet housing at the bottom and the rocker box at the top. Both tubes were waisted for most of their length to promote air flow between the cylinders and were sealed at both ends with a rubber ring. Thus the whole of the valve gear was totally enclosed, something not always done in 1937.

The camshafts were driven in a simple way by a train of gears, the crankshaft pinion engaging with a single idler gear which meshed with gears on the ends of each camshaft. These gears were retained by large nuts, that on the inlet incorporating an off-centre pin used to drive the twin-plunger oil pump mounted immediately below it in the timing chest.

Dry sump lubrication was used, as was common at the time, and the two plungers of the pump were moved up and down by a sliding block driven by the off-centre pin. The pump fed oil at some 50 to 60 psi to the big-end bearings

Exploded view of the pre-war Triumph Twin engine with mag-dyno mounted behind crankcase on the platform provided. Built up crankshaft, plain big-ends and simple construction used for so many years

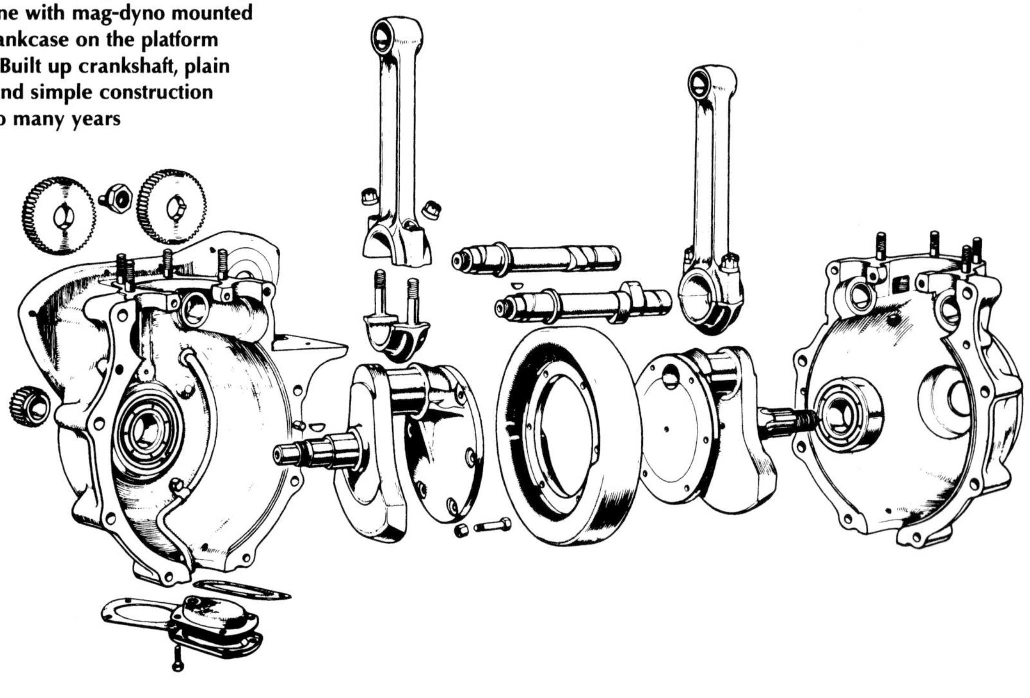

via a bush in the timing cover and drillings in the crankshaft. An external pipe was taken from the front of the timing cover at crankshaft level and ran straight up in front of the cylinder and just to the left of the right-side exhaust port. This pipe connected first to the exhaust rocker spindle, via a banjo fitting held in place by an acorn nut, and then to the inlet one. A second pipe ran up to the oil gauge carried in the petrol tank top, a feature most self-respecting machines had at that time to stop their owners worrying about oil pressure. In fact the Triumph was satisfactory at a figure as low as 15 psi.

The oil from the rocker spindles drained into the valve wells and these were themselves drained by external pipes connected to the pushrod tubes. The drains from the exhausts were from the front of the cylinder head, but those from the inlets were attached at the sides of the casting. This arose because the exhausts were splayed, and so for once Edward Turner had to use two different parts rather than the same item twice, as he much preferred to do. Once in the tubes the oil drained down to lubricate the tappets and cams, below which the crankcase was formed as a trough to hold some oil in the camshaft area.

All the oil eventually drained to the bottom of the crankcase, where a small sump was formed in the castings with a mesh filter secured by a plate held by four bolts. The mesh located on a pipe attached to the inside of the timing-side casting by one clip and this pipe ran up and back round the main bearing housing to the point where the oil pump was mounted. Thus the oil was scavenged from the crankcase and returned to the external oil tank.

The magdyno was mounted behind the cylinders and driven by a gear which meshed with the inlet camshaft gear. The magneto sat on a platform cast with the timing-side crankcase and was sealed to the back of the timing cover, which extended back to enclose the drive. The whole of the timing gear train was enclosed in a single alloy cover, so was readily accessible. The dynamo was strapped to the magneto and gear-driven from it. Both items were of Lucas manufacture.

A single type 6 Amal carburettor of $\frac{15}{16}$ in. bore was fitted to an induction manifold bolted to the cylinder head, which gave the instrument a small downdraught angle. It was fed by a bottom-feed float chamber attached to its right side. This was supplied by copper pipe from a single petrol tap fitted to the rear of the tank on the right side.

Separate exhaust pipes and silencers for each cylinder were fitted, each pipe being clamped to its exhaust port by a finned clamp ring and sweeping down and back to its tubular silencer, which was clipped to it. The silencers were attached to the chain stays and the complete system looked very similar to the then conventional twin-port single style.

Power output of the new engine was given as 26 bhp and figures from the power curve at the time were quoted as 14 bhp at 3000 rpm, 19·1 bhp at 4000 rpm, 23·6 bhp at 5000 rpm, 24·3 bhp at 5200 rpm, 24·5 bhp at 5400 rpm, 25·5 bhp at 5600 rpm and 25·2 bhp at 6000 rpm. This power was fed through a cam lobe shock absorber mounted on the crankshaft to the four-speed gearbox by a single-strand primary chain. As the engine was so compact it was able to use the same chain line as the Tiger 90 without any need to be offset to one side. The primary drive was enclosed in a very smart, polished aluminium-alloy chaincase with a single hole in the outer for pouring the oil in and checking the primary chain tension. This tension was adjusted by moving the gearbox back and forth and the clutch and box were Tiger 90 items. The clutch had cork inserts, so ran well in oil provided the correct SAE20 grade was used. Engine oil caused clutch sticking and drag.

The clutch ran on twenty $\frac{1}{4} \times \frac{1}{4}$ in. free rollers, the actual length of these being slightly undersize. These rollers ran on a hub taper bored and Woodruff-keyed to the gearbox mainshaft. The rollers were supported on one side by a flange on the hub and on the other by a free thrust washer. The chainwheel, with clutch drum riveted to it, ran on them and was held in position by the clutch centre, which splined to the hub and was itself held by a nut, washer and lockwasher. The centre carried four bolts inserted from the rear, and once the five steel and four inserted plates had been assembled the pressure plate with its hardened centre button was added and the four spring cups, springs and clutch nuts were screwed to the bolts. These items locked together by suitable pips and tags, so no additional locking was necessary. All four nuts were initially screwed in so their tops were flush with the screw ends and then adjusted in or out so that the clutch ran true when lifted and spun.

Clutch operation was by a single long pushrod through the gearbox mainshaft. This carried a hardened tip at the right end and was pushed by a lever mounted in the gearbox end cover. This lever was in two sections, the first external to the gearbox with a vertical arm and a pivot shaft running fore and aft in the casting. This was carried in two lugs and between them was fitted a short lever which was locked to the shaft with a cross-bolt. This lever carried an adjustable grub screw with locknut which bore on the end of the pushrod end-piece. Externally the lever was pulled by a cable whose outer was held by an adjuster screwed into a lug on the top of the gearbox. This adjuster was on the outer side of the lug for access and fitted with a locknut. The end of the inner cable and top of the operating lever were enclosed with a neat rubber cover.

The gearbox was of conventional English type of the time with the output sprocket carried on a sleeve gear through which ran the mainshaft carrying the clutch. Thus top gear was a direct 1:1 ratio and the other three involved two pairs of gears on main- and layshaft. The layshaft was mounted below the mainshaft and ran on bronze bearings, as did the mainshaft in the sleeve gear. The sleeve gear and the right end of the mainshaft were supported by ball races.

The gear ratios were selected by sliding the

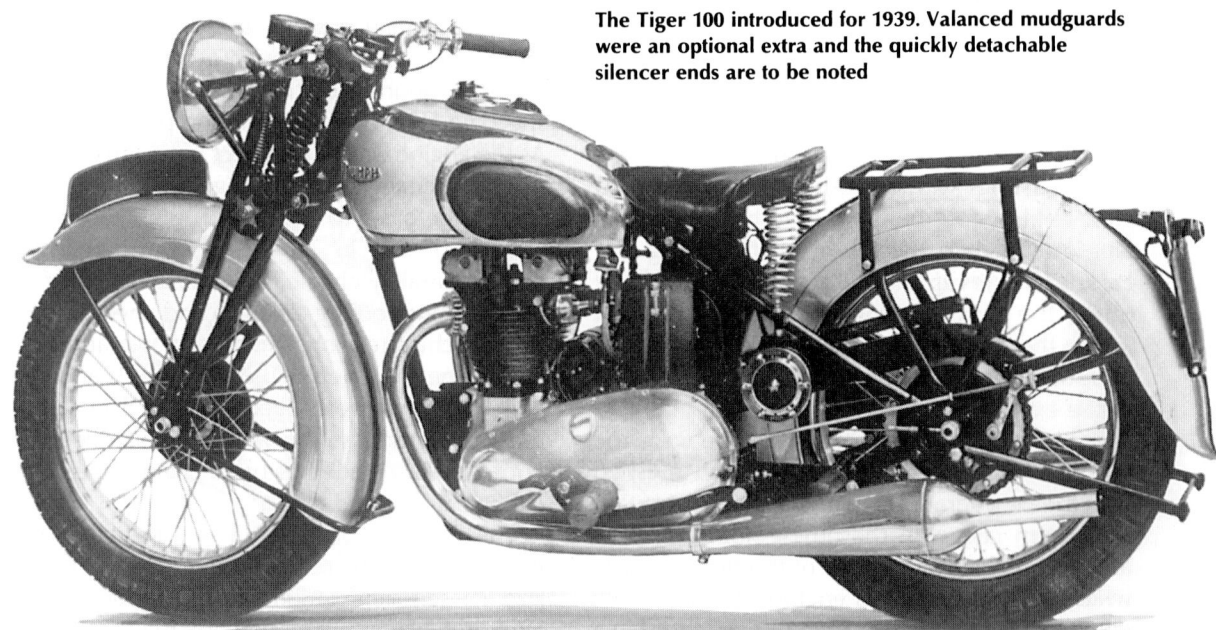

The Tiger 100 introduced for 1939. Valanced mudguards were an optional extra and the quickly detachable silencer ends are to be noted

1939 Tiger 100. Finished in the classic Tiger style with a potential to match its name

two centre gears on each shaft as a pair, the layshaft ones being moved for first and second, and the mainshaft ones for third and top. As two gears had to be moved each time, and in fact four on the change from second to third, the gearbox did not represent the best of designs, but was to prove adequate.

The gears were moved by two selectors, each of which was formed to encompass two gears while allowing them to run at different speeds. The selectors were mounted on a rod positioned in front of the gearshafts and were in turn moved by a flat circular cam plate pivoted in the front face of the gearbox casting. This was located by a spring-loaded plunger contained in the floor of the casting and geared to a quadrant pivoted on a pin laying in the same plane. This carried a small external pointer which indicated on a scale which gear was engaged. The quadrant was moved one gear at a time by a positive stop mechanism that engaged with its outer end and the mechanism comprised two spring-loaded plungers contained in a small lever. This lever was keyed to the inner end of the gear pedal shaft and was centred by two compression springs. The action of the spring-loaded plungers was controlled by a fixed U-shaped plate attached to the inside of the gearbox outer cover.

The gears and shafts were carried in an aluminium casting with lugs for mounting on top and bottom, and closed by an end cover on the right side. This supported the gear shafts, selector rod and the quadrant pivot, and outboard of it on the mainshaft was fitted the kickstart gear. This ran freely on the shaft and was spring loaded against a collar, which it drove via a face ratchet, the whole assembly being held by a nut that clamped it up against the shaft bearing.

The kickstart gear was turned by a quadrant gear attached to the spindle which carried the kickstart lever locked in place with a cotter pin. The kickstart was returned by a clock spring wound round the spindle with its outer end located on a pin and its inner on a spline. This assembly and the gear change were both carried in the outer cover and both spindles were also supported by the inner one. The outer cover also carried the clutch lever and access to this was by a screwed cap which was also the filler cap for the lubricant.

Both foot controls were fitted with rubbers and the gear lever was splined to its shaft so that it could be moved round to suit the rider.

The whole gearbox was attached to the frame by a pivot bolt passing through the lower lug and an adjuster arrangement attached to the top. The actual adjuster bolt lay above the gearbox and its end was located in a socket in the back of the saddle tube. It carried a screwed cross-bar and when the bolt was turned the bar pulled on plates bolted to the top gearbox shell lug, which extended forward with slotted holes in their ends. These plates were clamped to a lug on the saddle tube to complete the gearbox mounting.

Final drive was by chain on the left side, this being covered on both its runs by guards. Gear ratios were variously quoted as 5·23, 6·28, 9·05 and 13·3:1 (*The Motor Cycle*), and 5·0, 6·0, 8·65 and 12·7:1 solo, with sidecar ratios of 5·8, 6·95, 10·0 and 14·7:1 (*Motor Cycling*).

The remainder of the machine was Tiger 90 for all practical purposes and with the slightly lighter engine mounted in the same place as the single the weight distribution remained the same. The frame was a full cradle built up from forged lugs with tubes brazed into position and had a main loop formed from single top, down and saddle

tubes with duplex rails running under the engine. The rear end was rigid and the two pairs of chain stays were joined by cross tubes. Naturally sidecar lugs were provided, as no self-respecting machine went without this feature in 1937.

The front forks were girders, and here Turner's eye for line and style put the front wheel in just the right place for appearance. Later knowledge indicated that a steeper fork angle would have improved the handling at the expense of cramming the wheel and mudguard back into the frame. Turner made sure it looked right and sold. The girders themselves were of tubular construction with friction dampers built into the forward ends of the lower links, and a single barrel-shaped fork spring was used to give variable-rate springing within the rather restricted movement of the forks. A steering damper was fitted as standard with the friction disc at the lower end of the steering column and the pressure plate located onto the frame, while the load was applied by a knob at the top of the column. A clip held this in its set position.

Both tyres were given as the same size in *Motor Cycling*'s report, but both their photo and those in *The Motor Cycle* indicate that the latter's data were correct, with the front a ribbed 3·00 × 20 and the rear a 3·50 × 19 with block tread. Wheels were of course wire spoked and equipped with steel rims. Both brakes were of the single leading-shoe type and worked in heavily finned brake drums of 7 in. diameter. These were bolted to the hubs and this construction allowed the use of equal-length spokes on both sides of the wheel. The front brake was on the right of the machine and cable operated with an adjuster located by the fork damper, while the rear brake cam lever was directly connected by a rod to the brake pedal on the left. The front hub also incorporated the drive for the speedometer angle box screwed into the brake back plate.

The mudguards followed the wheel outline closely, the front being supported by two stays, the rear one of which could be hinged down to act as a front stand. The front number plate was flat with a curved front edge. The rear mudguard was bolted to the chainstay cross members and was also supported by a pair of stays at the rear and an inverted triangular loop stay on each side. This attached to the frame just above the rear wheel spindle and was curved to match the mudguard along its upper edge. The rear number plate was carried by the mudguard and it, and the tail section of the mudguard, could be hinged to assist rear wheel removal, this feature being an optional extra.

A sprung saddle was provided, pivoted at its nose, but there was no pillion pad or footrests. The rider's footrests were positioned that stra-

The Speed Twin as it would have been in 1940 with few changes from its inception. Eight stud barrel and the front number plate bead are most noticeable. Chrome plated headlamp

tegic 2 in. behind the saddle nose that all riders of rigid-frame machines know gives a very comfortable ride, as your legs act as highly efficient shock absorbers and you rise and fall over the bumps as in horse riding. Under the saddle was fitted the control box for the dynamo and on the right the oil tank of 5 pints capacity. This was closed by a cap fitted with a cross lever which locked the cap when screwed down and released it when turned the other way. In those days only real racers had quick-filler caps. The oil tank breather was neatly taken into the top of the saddle tube so that any residue would drain away out of sight even if it was aimed at the rear tyre!

The petrol tank was of $3\frac{1}{2}$ gallons capacity with the same type of cap as the oil tank and its two halves joined at the front with a U-tube. It carried a tank-top panel, another common feature of the time, and this contained an ammeter, an oil pressure gauge, the lighting switch and an inspection lamp with wander lead. The two instruments were illuminated when the lights were on. The main instrument, the speedometer, was carried on the top of the forks, where it could be directly driven from the front wheel.

The electrical system was very straightforward with just a headlight housed in a painted shell, with chrome rim, tail light and an electric horn mounted from the left saddle spring mounting. The 6-volt battery was mounted on the left side beneath the saddle and on the right in the corner formed by the chainstays was a triangular toolbox. This was not the most helpful of shapes, but at least the rear chainguard carried a tyre pump.

The controls were straightforward with the footchange and kickstart levers both on the right and rear brake pedal on the left. The handlebars were rubber mounted and adjustable over a wide range of positions. They carried twistgrip, front brake lever, clutch lever, air and magneto controls, and the horn push and dip switch.

The weight of the model T was given as 353 lb, so it would not have been too difficult to get up onto its rear stand, and its wheelbase was quoted as 54 in. The finish and price were not fixed at that time, but the photographs show a dark-coloured machine except for the petrol tank, which is chromed with light-coloured panels surrounded by a dark line with the Triumph name in a very light colour. The kneegrips were not enclosed by the lining, which was shaped to follow their front edges.

In the middle of August the complete range for 1938 was announced and a few minor changes were incorporated into the twin along with the rest of the range. The most noticeable were styling points, with the petrol tanks being equipped with all-metal Triumph badges, which were screwed to their sides. The primary chaincase cover was re-cast, with the shock absorber housing faired back in a style that was to last into the 1950s, and this gave a much improved line to the machine in comparison to the original lump that hid the mechanical parts. The tank-top instrument panel was changed from a metal pressing to a moulded Bakelite construction and a new twistgrip was fitted. This incorporated a spring-loaded plunger, which prevented the throttle closing under return-spring pressure, a useful feature when signalling a right turn before indicators became universal some 30-plus years later. Finally, the quickly detachable rear wheel was made available as an option and the finish confirmed. This was the famous amaranth red, which was applied to frame, forks, mudguards, toolbox and oil tank, together with the minor clips and stays that made up the cycle parts. The petrol tank was chrome plated with red, lined, side and top panels, while the wheel rims were also chromed with red, lined, centres. The exhaust system, minor parts and headlamp rim were finished in chrome, but at first the shell was painted, changing to all-chrome as production began.

The price of the machine was only £5 more than the Tiger 90 and the new twin in fact weighed 5 lb less.

On October 20, 1937, *Motor Cycling* published the first road test of the new model, now called the Speed Twin. The machine's registration number was CKV59. Their rival, *The Motor Cycle*, came out a day later and their test machine was CVC750. Both tests were extremely complimentary, reporting exceptional performance and a very pleasant ride. In fact the machines proved capable of over 90 mph with the rider prone and with a tail wind *The Motor Cycle* managed 107 mph on one run, very rapid for any road-equipped 500 cc machine. Acceleration was well above the class norm and the machine was flexible enough to run down to 12 mph in top gear. The vibration aspect was touched on lightly, but one machine fractured the angle bracket supporting the front end of the fuel tank. Oil leaks were confined to the rocker box to head joint on one machine and the rear of the primary chaincase on the other, but both were very slight smears. Fuel consumption was of the order of 65 mpg or more when motoring briskly, and with 60 mph in second and 80 mph in third the testers put up some fast averages over the rather indifferent roads of the times. The fully equipped weight was given as 365 lb, and the price including speedometer as £77 15s. 0d.

So the Speed Twin went on sale and was an immediate success. The reasons for the success lay in a combination of the styling, engineering, performance, price and name and there is no doubt that Turner had got the equation right. In some ways the Page twin was a better engineering job, but the Turner twin looked small, compact and light, so fitted in with the contemporary twin-port single image. It also had speed and style to appeal, was as easy to maintain as a single and was only a few pounds dearer, giving the lie to those who claimed that multis were complex and expensive.

The design was right and had no real weakness to give it a bad name in the early months. The only problem that did occur was with the six-stud fixing to the crankcase and a few machines either pulled off or broke the cylinder casting. A classic case of designing light and only strengthening up the parts that need it.

By the autumn of 1938 the fault had been corrected and the cylinder flange was much more robust and held down by eight studs. This was the major change for 1939, but the exciting news was the introduction of a sports version, which, with typical Turner flair, was named the Tiger 100.

The new machine did not have or need many changes. The compression ratio was raised to 8:1 with forged slipper pistons and the ports and internals were polished. For a further £5 an aluminium bronze cylinder head was also available. The finish of the new machine matched the other Tiger models with a chromed petrol tank with silver sheen panels lined in black. The rear of the tank was recessed slightly at the sides to keep the kneegrips in to a comfortable width. The mudguards were also finished in silver, black lined, and the frame and forks were black. Wheel-rim finish copied the

350 cc Tiger 85 for the 1940 range. Mainly 500 cc cycle parts but Tiger 80 forks

tank, while the headlamp shell was chromed. It was advertised at £80 and sold at £82 15s. 0d with speedometer. An added bonus was that the silencers were formed as megaphones with end caps and tailpipes and these could be removed for competition work. In this form the machine was capable of well over the 100 mph mark.

Both twins incorporated minor changes for 1939, the noticeable one being a chromed bead surround for the front number plate, a Triumph feature that continued for many years. Braking efficiency was improved and the fork geometry changed slightly, while positive lubrication of the rear chain was provided by a leak valve in the back of the primary chaincase.

Turner was never one to rest on his laurels and, while the rest of the English industry was thinking about and designing a 500 cc twin, he was laying down a new machine to be announced in the autumn of 1939 for the 1940 range. This was a smaller brother for the Tiger 100, a 350 cc twin finished in exactly the same livery and called the Tiger 85.

While the appearance was the same, there were differences to both engine and cycle parts. The rocker boxes were cast integral with the iron head and closed with alloy lids. The head and barrel were held down by a two-part fixing, which held the barrel down with through bolts and the head with set screws that screwed into the bolts.

In the bottom half the crankshaft was still in three parts, but assembly was simplified by extending the crankpin of each outer part into a hole in the central flywheel. These extended pins were then secured by two cross-bolts acting as clamps. The cycle parts were mainly from the 500 cc twin, but with the petrol tank and front brake off the Tiger 80. The weight came out at 360 lb.

The Tiger 85 was to be announced along with the rest of the range in September 1939, but the war broke out and it was cancelled. What did go out that week was *The Motor Cycle* with a headline on all the covers of 'New 350 cc British Twin' and, in a few cases, also containing the article, before they stopped the presses and changed the type.

Before that occurred, however, Triumph, in March 1939, staged an attempt on the Maudes Trophy once again. For this the ACU selected two 500s, a Speed Twin from a Biggleswade dealer and a Tiger 100 from one in Sheffield. They were checked over at the factory and then set off from Coventry to visit John O'Groats, Land's End and Brooklands. Because of snow in the north of Scotland the route was shortened slightly to 1806 miles and this was covered at an average speed of 42 mph. Once at Brooklands the two machines were given a six-hour run with Ivan Wicksteed and Dave Whitworth on the Tiger 100, which averaged 78·5 mph, and Freddie Clarke and Allan Jefferies on the Speed Twin. This averaged 75·02 mph, and its best lap was at 84·41 mph, while the Tiger 100's was at 88·46 mph. No major mechanical problems occurred, the only trouble being that the oil pipe to the pressure gauge on the Speed Twin fractured at Brooklands and was hammered flat to prevent the oil pumping out. Also at Brooklands the Tiger 100 picked up a nail in its rear tyre early on and lost nearly five minutes while the wheel was changed and the Speed Twin had one plug stop firing late in the attempt, thought to be due to running low on fuel and thus overheating. Other factories attempted to win the Maudes that year and it was not until November that Triumph knew they had won it, but by then it was of little account.

Brooklands had been the scene of another success for Triumph in 1938. Ivan Wicksteed and Marius Winslow had become friends at school and began a partnership as rider and tuner in the early 1930s. It was successful and at the 1937 Show they asked Edward Turner for his opinion of their idea to blow the new twin. Turner's reply was short, 'A very logical conclusion. Good afternoon, gentlemen.' Undismayed the pair bought a Speed Twin and began work on it. It ran in a race in March 1938 and lapped at over 107 mph unblown, so then the blower was added and the problems began.

Most of the difficulties centred on the mixture strength and induction bias, for they were groping in the dark to quite an extent, but they also hit a basic structural snag when the barrel cracked off at its bottom flange. The solution was proposed by Titch Allen, who suggested fitting a nut and bolt between the head and the tank rail and screwing these apart until the tube bent. It caused some amusement at the time, but was tried, cured the problem, and the same idea is still in use today on many of the Triumphs raced in vintage events.

Finally, the twin was raced and lapped at 111 mph, but still with mixture problems, for it seized on one side. A new induction system and further trials moved the lap speed up to 121·47 mph and Dunlop insisted on the use of track tyres. They were fitted and the handling was so bad that the machine could not be used on the outer circuit. The standard wheels went back with road-racing tyres and on October 8, 1938, Wicksteed made his run for the 500 cc lap record during the BMCRC Hutchinson 100 race day. It then started raining so, rather than wait for their scheduled time, they pushed the machine to the line between races. One warm-up lap and then a flying lap to take the record at 118·02 mph, a record to stand for all time.

Edward Turner made amends for his earlier brusque manner by heavily advertising the success and providing the pair with a new Tiger 100 engine with special crankshaft for the blower drive sprocket. This ran into the same mixture bias problems, but covered the half-mile on the Railway Straight at 124 mph. Its steering was dreadful with the special track tyres fitted. Then the war came.

Towards the end of 1937 an event occurred that was to have a considerable effect on Triumph's sales and image over the years. The Metropolitan [London] Police Force decided to increase the size of their motorcycle force, which had been run down. To this end they purchased one or two examples from seven different makes in February 1938 for assessment. The Triumph was not among these but, luckily for them, two machines were returned in March and replaced by a single Speed Twin. This proved so suitable for their myriad duties that it was decided to replace the existing machines with Triumphs as the stock became due for renewal. By the middle of the year two dozen Triumphs were in use, the forerunners of the thousands that the police force in London were to use over the years.

This and many other matters had to be shelved, however, while a war was fought, but the twin had its part to play in this also.

An early 350 cc twin fitted into Speed Twin cycle parts. The smaller twin had the rocker boxes cast in one with the cylinder head, a different head and barrel fixing, and a built up crankshaft using clamps to hold the crankpins in the central flywheel

3 Military mounts

When war broke out in September 1939 the British Forces had a motley collection of motorcycles at their disposal, a mixture of 500 cc side-valve M20 and 16H singles, together with a whole variety of impressed civilian machines. These were used until they failed and many machines of that period had to be destroyed on the retreat to Dunkirk.

Most of the Triumph twins went that way, as did a batch of 350 cc side-valve Nortons, unique for the firm and unique in that they were very light, with alloy used for head, barrel, handlebars

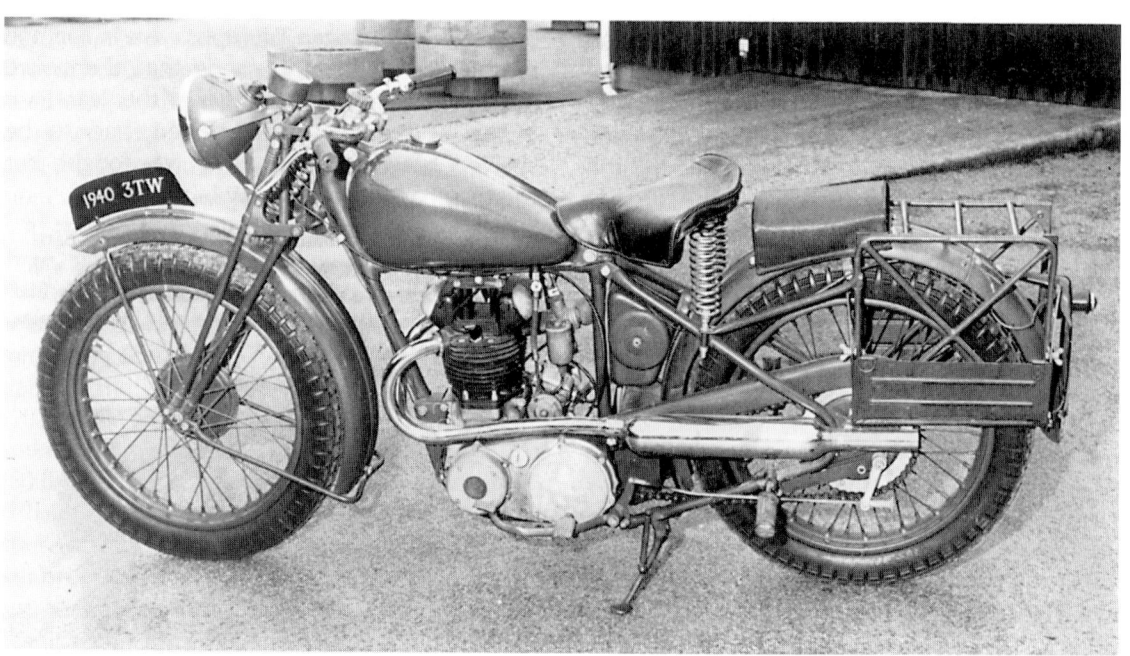

Wartime 3TW based on the Tiger 85 engine with alternator, three-speed gearbox and built to a target weight of 250 lb. Iron head and barrel used due to aluminium shortage

and levers. This was all done to meet a Ministry of Supply specification that asked for a capacity of over 250 cc and a weight of less than 250 lb.

While other firms produced prototypes to meet this specification, Edward Turner cut through the development time by modifying the Tiger 85 curtailed by the outbreak of war. The engine was thus a 350 cc twin with overhead valves and had a three-speed gearbox attached to it to give unit construction, this being driven by a duplex primary chain. The engine was an all-alloy unit with dry-sump lubrication and fed by a single carburettor, producing 17 bhp at 5400 rpm. It featured a Lucas alternator in the timing chest, this being the first time such a device had been used on a motorcycle, but retained the magneto in its usual position. Some models had the alternator housed in the primary chaincase.

The engine and gearbox were housed in a light, rigid frame with the fuel tank forming part of it. Girder forks were fitted and the machine was fully equipped with headlamp, speedometer, saddle and rear carrier and it weighed in at 247 lb. It was type coded the 3TW, and as the first machines had most of the power above 3000 rpm and were so light, they were fast, fun but not totally suitable for the War Office.

A heavier flywheel and a slightly smaller carburettor sobered the performance and the twin was so obviously better than the alternatives that the contract was Triumph's. Due to the shortage of aluminium, later prototypes had an iron head and barrel, increasing the weight to a still acceptable 263 lb.

Sadly all plans for the 3TW vanished when the Coventry factory was destroyed in the blitz in November 1940, and for the duration Triumph built 3HWs, a 350 cc overhead-valve single based on the pre-war machine.

While working from temporary premises in Warwick another military twin was designed and built to compare with the 3TW. This was the 5TW, a 500 cc twin, but with side valves. This machine was designed by Bert Hopwood and made its first appearance in 1942.

The engine was based on the usual Triumph dimensions of 63 × 80 mm and the crankshaft, rods and pistons all followed the Speed Twin design. The camshaft was positioned across the front of the engine and was driven by a chain that ran from engine sprocket to camshaft and then back to the dynamo fitted in the normal magneto position behind the engine. This ran at engine speed and incorporated a contact breaker and automatic advance and retard. Coil ignition was used and the system was referred to as dynamotic lighting and ignition.

The timing chain was tensioned on the return run to the engine sprocket by a sprung blade and the camshaft sprocket was secured with a nut with offset pin, which drove the twin-plunger oil pump mounted in the timing chest. This layout of timing chain, camshaft position, tensioner and oil pump was a direct copy of the Ariel Square Four layout without the front cylinders.

Military mounts

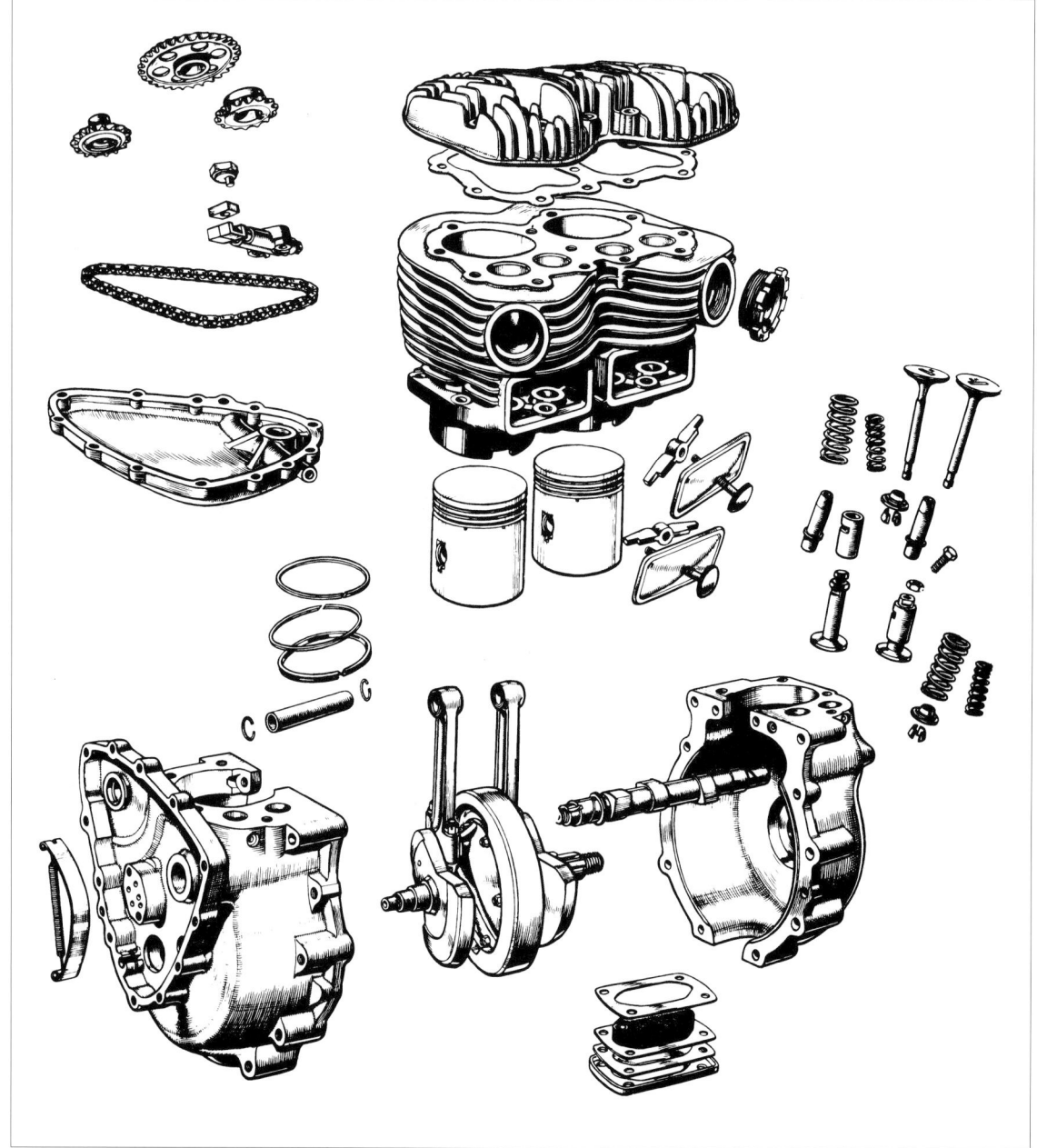

The first of the 500 cc side valve twins, the 5TW. Speed Twin type crankshaft but chain drive to camshaft and oil pump. Dynamo fitted in normal magneto position with points and advance unit. Carburettor at rear of block

The complete 5TW machine with four-speed gearbox and the new telescopic front forks. This model was not put into production but led to the later TRW

The camshaft operated four flat-faced tappets working in separate guides fitted in a line across the two halves of the crankcase, in front of the cylinder. The tappets had the usual screw adjusters locked with nuts. Access to them was via openings in the front of the cylinder casting, each being closed by a cover held in place by a single screw and cross-bar.

The cylinders were in one cast-iron block, this material being used only because of the shortage of aluminium. The four valves were shut by dual valve springs and these were retained by normal collars and cotters. The block was deeply spigoted into the crankcase and the exhaust ports splayed out slightly from the front corners. The ports were threaded and the exhaust pipes retained by screwed rings with C-spanner slots.

The inlet passage began at the rear of the block and passed between the cylinders to reach the valves, so aiding cylinder cooling at the expense of warming up the incoming charge. The induction passage changed to an oval section between the bores, but reverted to round at either end.

The cylinder head was also a one-piece iron casting and was held down on its gasket by nuts fitting studs in the barrel top. The compression ratio was 5:1.

This engine was fitted with a four-speed gearbox and most of the cycle parts were from

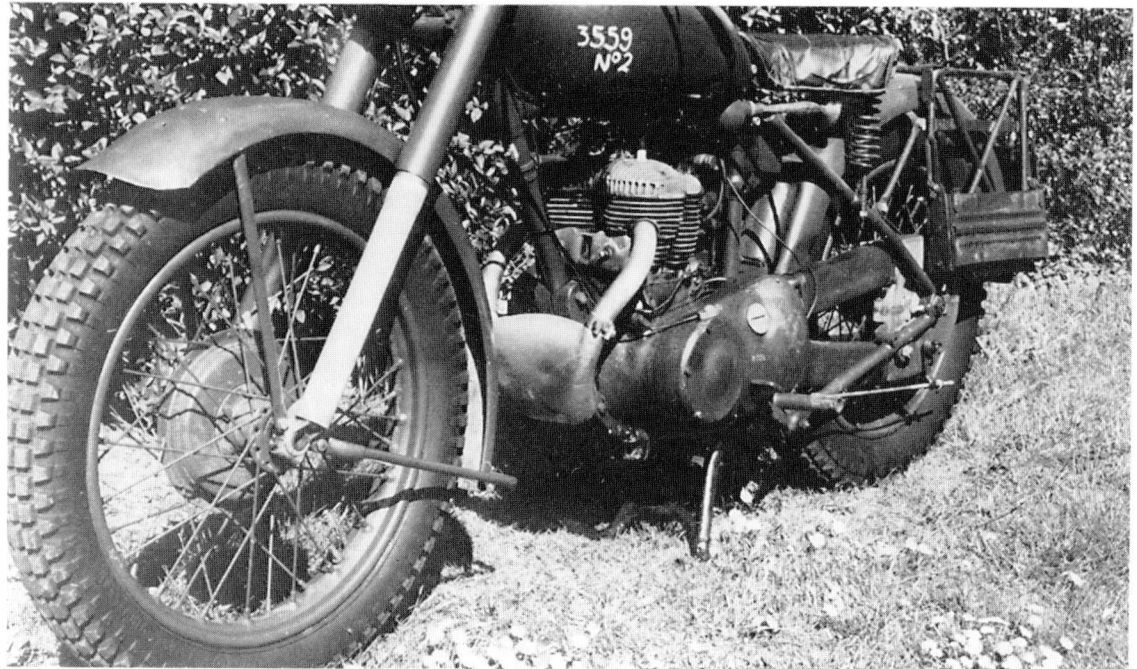

the pre-war machine. The one aspect that was new was the adoption of a telescopic front fork for the first time on a Triumph. The whole machine weighed 330 lb and its wheelbase was 52½ in.

This machine also did not go into production, but provided further data which was to be of use later. The Ministry of Supply still liked the idea of a machine designed specifically for military use and, taking heed of the two Triumphs, its new specification called for a 500 cc twin-cylinder engine. Performance had to better 70 mph and 80 mpg at 30 mph. Weight was limited to 300 lb and other requirements included braking from 30 mph in 35 feet, a laden ground clearance of 6 in., the ability to ford 15 in. of water, an inaudible engine at a half-mile range, the ability to climb a 1 in 2·24 gradient at 4 mph and to be able to stop and restart on that gradient.

In July 1946 the Triumph answer was on view together with a Douglas at a military vehicle exhibition. The Triumph was based on the company's experiences with both earlier machines and was a 500 cc twin with side valves in front of the engine. It followed the lines of the 5TW in respect of general layout, although the exhaust ports were splayed out and angled down much more. The bottom half was generally as before, but the camshaft drive reverted to the normal Triumph design, using gears with a large idler between crankshaft and camshaft gears also driving the BTH magneto, used in place of the coil ignition system.

The carburettor shown at the exhibition at Chertsey was a type 6 Amal with float chamber on the left, and the exhaust pipes both fed into a box mounted in front of the frame in front of the crankcase in what must have been a highly vulnerable position. From the lower right corner of the box an exhaust pipe ran back at low level to the silencer.

The engine had an AC generator attached to the crankshaft and housed in the primary

Left **Prototype TRW with gear driven camshaft, three-speed gearbox and fully enclosed rear chain**

Bottom **Production TRW with coil ignition and distributor mounted behind crankcase**

Below **Line drawing of 500 cc side-valve engine installed in period frame. Specialist carburettor**

chaincase. The gearbox was a separate unit with only three speeds and its end cover was different from the normal units. The filler cap was replaced by a small cover secured by two screws and the speedometer drive was taken from the gearbox shaft, not the front wheel. The final drive chain was fully enclosed, each chain run being encased in Rubberoid tubes clamped to the rear half of the primary chaincase at the front and to a light-alloy casting enclosing the rear sprocket. This was split horizontally on the wheel spindle line for assembly.

The engine and gearbox were installed in a rigid frame with a head steady connected from the down tube to the cylinder head. The petrol tank continued to act as a frame member and to this end had a square-section member running through it. A further frame tube ran back beneath the tank, connecting the down tube to the top of the saddle tube. The front forks were telescopic and carried headlamp and speedometer. The remainder of the machine followed usual Triumph lines modified to suit the specification and with various parts in alloy to reduce weight. This move was successful, for the prototype of what became known as the TRW weighed in at 280 lb, well below the required figure.

Unfortunately for Triumph, by this time the war was over and the military had a great surplus of motorcycles so was not interested in buying. However, two years later, in 1948, the TRW emerged in its final engine form and, while few were sold to the British Army, other branches of the military, both at home and abroad, bought enough machines to keep the line going into the 1960s.

What Triumph did was to build what became known as the Hybrid. This used the 500 cc side-valve engine together with as many parts as possible from the commercial production machine to keep costs to a reasonable level.

In its final form the TRW engine followed many of the lines of the prototype with a simple, vertically split crankcase carrying the crankshaft and gear-driven camshaft at the front of the engine. The crankshaft was, however, a development from that first tried in the Tiger 85 and subsequently used in the postwar 350. It was of a different form, although still built up from three major parts. The design allowed the use of one-piece connecting rods with plain big ends by clamping the crankpins to the central flywheel. The outer webs were forged in a 3 per cent nickel steel with an integral half shaft and crankpin which extended at a slightly reduced diameter into a hole in the flywheel. A bush was trapped between the two crankpins to prevent loss of oil pressure and the webs of the flywheel were slit. Once assembled, two cross-bolts with nuts were fitted, and when tightened these clamped the flywheel to the crankpins. Alignment was assisted by a close-tolerance hole in the two web cheeks and the flywheel.

The crankshaft ran on a drive-side ball race with a plain timing-side bush. The camshaft was carried in two bushes and driven by an idler meshed with the crankshaft gear, this idler also driving the magneto. It was thought surprising that this was retained when an alternator was fitted to the end of the crankshaft in the primary drive case, but at the time the design was laid down the alternator was in its infancy.

The cylinder block was an alloy casting with the two liners pressed in and the valve seats cast in pairs. It incorporated a number of vertical webs in the finning to remove any tendency for them to ring and followed the lines of the prototype with regard to the ports. The valve chest was at the front and pressed-in guides were located by a cross-pin, which prevented the tappets from turning by bearing on flats machined on them. The tappets carried screw adjusters with serrated heads and these were locked by a spring that engaged with the tappet and the underside of the head. A special tool for adjusting the valve clearances was provided in the tool kit. The valves worked in phosphor bronze guides and were closed by single coil springs retained by collars and cotters. The valve chest was sealed by a one-piece cover held by two nuts and this incorporated the valve lifter mechanism and the engine breather.

The compression ratio was 6:1 and the pistons were conventional, with solid skirts and three rings, two compression and one scraper. The cylinder head was a one-piece sand casting fitted with a gasket and secured by 12 studs and nuts.

Lubrication was dry sump with the oil circulated by the standard Triumph twin-plunger pump driven by an offset pin on the camshaft gear nut. The usual gauze filter was fitted to the underside of the crankcase with an internal pipe connecting to the scavenge pump.

The carburettor fitted, after some experiments with Amal and SU, was a Solex type 26 WH-Z,

The ministry men rode the TRW in the Scottish as a practical test. This is a magazine trial of one machine

and the exhaust pipes were siamezed into a single low-level system with silencer on the right.

The cycle parts of all the TRWs were basically those that were current at the time of manufacture. The early machines, built in the late 1940s, thus had many parts from the TR5 Trophy model, this being the most suited to the needs, including rigid frame and telescopic forks, although the nacelle headlamp shell was retained, four-speed separate gearbox and Trophy wheels. The military needs added various special items, but these were all of a bolt-on nature and did not affect the basic parts. In this guise the machine came out at 340 lb, more than originally specified, but still acceptable for many years.

In 1953 *Motor Cycling* road tested a TRW, which by that time had lost the magneto and, like the Speed Twin, was equipped with coil ignition and a distributor fitted in the magneto position. The wheels were both of 19 in. diameter, although the rear one still carried a 4 in. section tyre for the cross-country work envisaged. Machine weight was down to 320 lb and so, with a power output of nearly 17 bhp, acceleration was adequate and top speed about 74 mph. The brakes were good and comfort acceptable, as the effect of the rigid frame was offset by the fat rear tyre and good saddle. Handling was good both on the road and off it. Complaints concerned the rear stand, which flapped about over the rough, and the chrome, which rusted rapidly. The standard panniers were sited too far back and rattled, but the smart green finish stood up to the weather well. There was little chrome in fact as wheel rims were painted, so the main problem was the exhaust system.

Army use of the TRW continued right up to 1969, when the Royal Corps of Signals finally changed over to ohv 500s based on the Tiger 100 but fitted with low-compression pistons, milder cams and a Monobloc carburettor.

Three years earlier Triumph won a substantial order at the Dutch show, but this was for a 350 cc machine based on the unit construction model. It had been designed as a replacement for the TRW and was similar to the road machine, but was finished in a drab green colour and was fitted with a Solex carburettor. It had been demonstrated in Scandinavia and tested by British Forces. It was fitted with a short seat, a siamezed exhaust system, light mudguards and heavy-duty tyres on both wheels.

Another side of the military story began in 1943, when the Air Ministry wanted an easily transported generator set. The required output was 6 kilowatts and the unit had to be self-contained and capable of being lifted easily by two men. The dynamo was no problem, but no obvious engine was to hand. So the Ministry of Aircraft Production spoke to *The Motor Cycle* and the result was that Edward Turner agreed to design an engine and produce the complete generator set except for the dynamo. He approached the task with his usual energy and in three months tests were being made, while in six, production had begun.

The basis of the engine was of course the Speed Twin, but few parts from the motorcycle engine would fit the generator unit. The whole layout was in fact turned round with the timing gear on the opposite side to normal relative to the induction and exhaust pipes, so the two camshafts were effectively reversed and the magneto driven from the exhaust one.

The head and barrel were both cast in a silicon aluminium alloy and both had inserts. Those in the head were a high-expansion iron forming the valve seatings and the plug boss, while the cylinder liners were formed with integral lobes for threading to take the cylinder-head bolts. In both cases the alloy was then cast round the inserts. The block was of a square form and carried two small bosses on each side to take the screws holding the cooling fan cowling in place. The fan, in magnesium alloy, was fitted to the end of the crankshaft and its centre incorporated a driving dog for the cranking handle used to start the engine.

The fan shifted some 400 cubic feet of air per

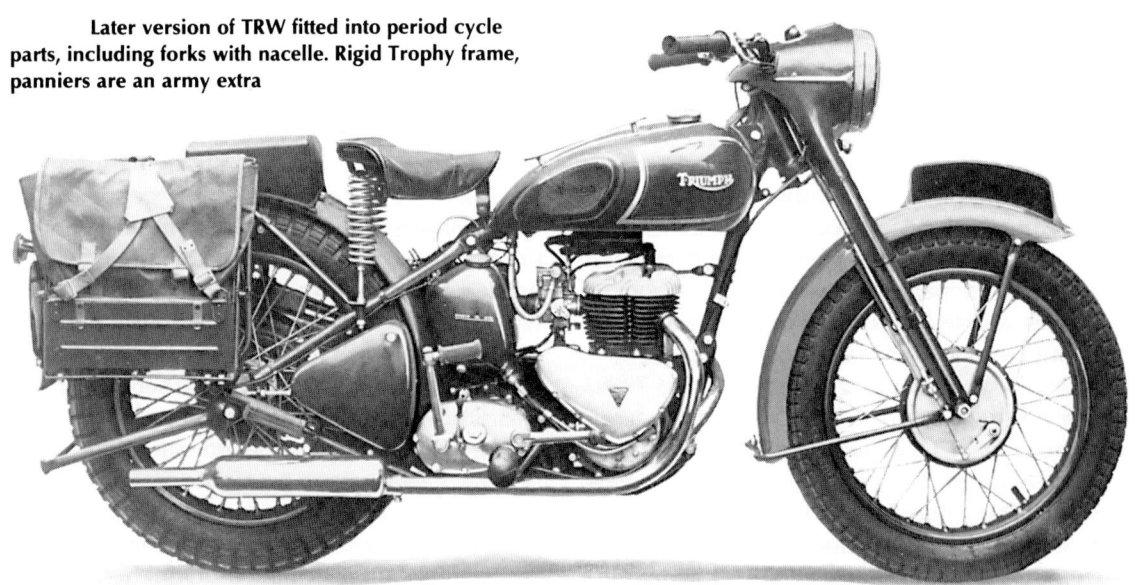

Later version of TRW fitted into period cycle parts, including forks with nacelle. Rigid Trophy frame, panniers are an army extra

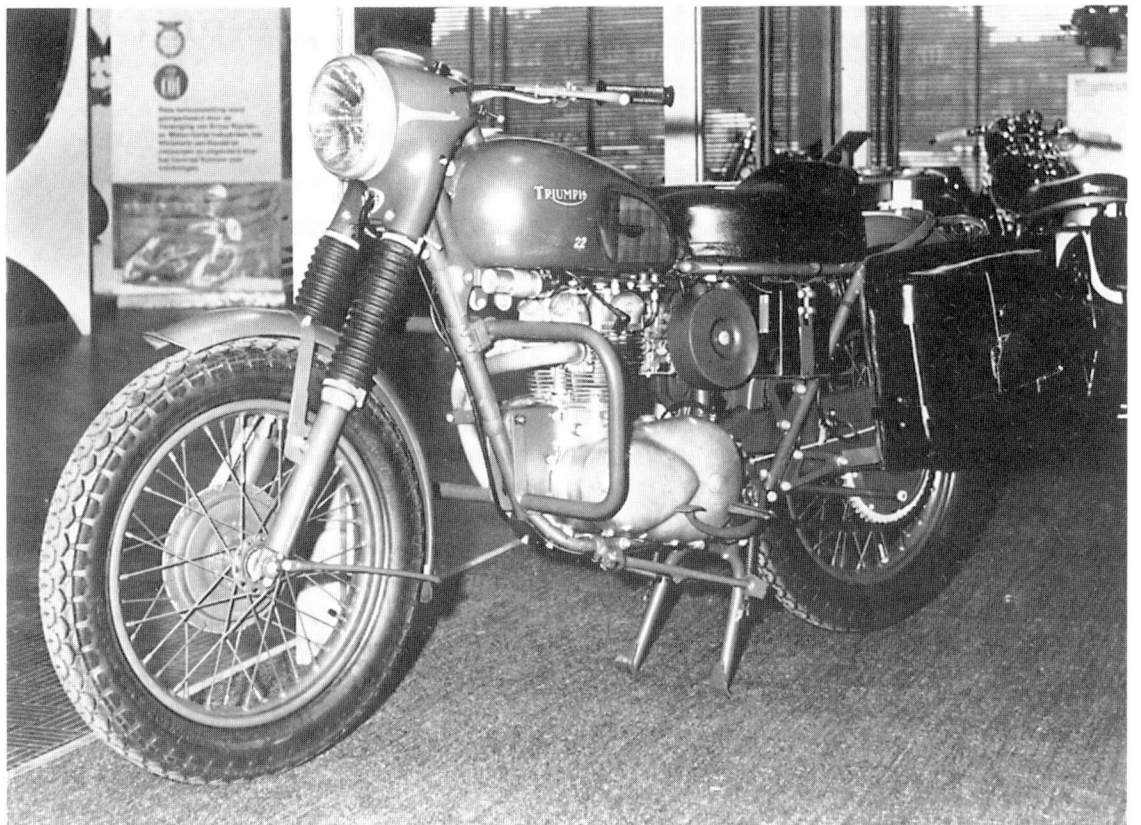

Military machine with unit construction engine, panniers, single seat and big air cleaner

minute at the normal running speed of 4000 rpm, and over half of this was ducted over the engine to hold the cylinder-head temperature below 120°C at all times. A duct fed the remainder of the air to the dynamo, where it passed through vents in the body.

Cooling of the lower half of the engine was assisted by the use of an oil pump of nearly twice the capacity of that fitted to the Speed Twin engine. The oil was passed through a Vokes fabric filter on its return to the oil tank, which was of 5 pints capacity and incorporated in the base of the fuel tank of 3 gallons capacity.

The engine was connected to the dynamo by a flexible coupling and inboard of this was a ratchet mechanism. This came into use if a cover plate was removed and a kickstart crank and quadrant fitted as an alternative means of starting.

The engine was controlled by a governor device which held its running speed well within the plus or minus 5 per cent required and this was driven by the inlet camshaft pinion. It was connected to a dashpot and the updraught Zenith carburettor fitted, which was equipped with a Vokes air filter.

The whole unit measured $30\tfrac{1}{2}$ in. long, $23\tfrac{3}{4}$ in. high and $17\tfrac{1}{2}$ in. wide. It weighed 175 lb dry and was used all over the world by the RAF.

It also gave birth to the Grand Prix and the Trophy as described later.

4 | Postwar, pre-unit

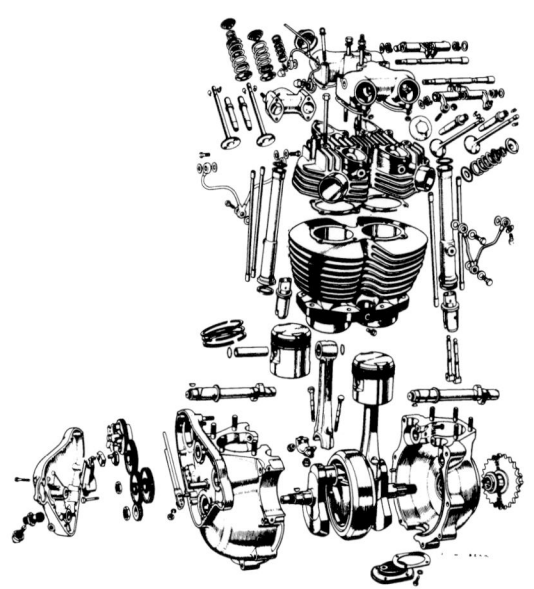

Exploded view of postwar Triumph Twin engine with separate dynamo in front of crankcase and magneto bolted to back of timing case

At the end of the Second World War enormous adjustments had to be made at the factory. Everyone was very tired after six long, hard years of worry, bombs, rations and overwork. Materials and plant were in very short supply, the government cry was as ever for exports and the entire factory, now located at a new site at Meriden, just outside Coventry, had to be reorganized to produce civilian twins in place of military singles.

Edward Turner lost no time in doing this and in a very short period Triumph were back in production with old favourites and a new model. The two 500 cc twins, the Speed Twin and the Tiger 100, reappeared with minimal changes, the most noticeable being the fitment of telescopic front forks. Other changes were to the electrics, with the dynamo moved from its mounting on the magneto to a cradle on the front of the crankcase. In this position it was gear driven from the exhaust camshaft gear and the timing case was extended forward to enclose the drive.

Within the engine the lubrication system was modified to remove the external drain pipes connecting the valve wells to the pushrod tubes, internal drillings taking over this function. The rocker box lubrication was taken from the scavenge return line, so ensuring a steady supply of warm oil, an improvement over the earlier arrangement. A timed engine breather was fitted at the left end of the inlet camshaft and driven by it.

The new front forks were based on those

developed during the war and gave a total movement of 6·25 in. with hydraulic locks at both ends of the travel to prevent a mechanical clash occurring. They were hydraulically damped in both directions and the tubes slid on a lower bush of mild steel, white-metal coated, and a Tufnol upper bush. Felt rings acted not as oil seals but as reservoirs of oil to keep the stanchions lubricated. Three alternative fork springs were provided for 350 cc solo, 500 cc solo and 500 cc sidecar. The adoption of the new fork reduced the unsprung weight from 21 lb 7 oz to 6 lb 2 oz, a very substantial change, and still allowed the handlebars to be adjusted while retaining the steering damper.

The wheels and brakes remained as before, with the front suitably adapted to suit telescopic forks. Due to the much-increased fork travel the front brake cable was carried down the fork leg through a steel tube, which slid in a guide mounted on the upper part of the fork. The front wheel was reduced in diameter to 19 in., but the tyre section increased slightly. With the adoption of the new forks the speedometer drive moved to the rear wheel.

The new addition to the range was a 350 cc

1946 model 3T, similar to 500 cc twin but with significant design changes to the engine construction. A much liked machine

twin based on the wartime 3TW and was known as the model 3T. It was intended that a sports version, the Tiger 85, would also be produced, but apart from a few prototypes this was not to be, due to production problems.

The new machine was to all intents a Speed Twin with a smaller engine, but that item was in no way a straight copy of the 5T. It combined features from both the 3TW and the TRW in its own unique way, although much of the design and a good few parts were from the 500.

Engine dimensions were 55 × 73·4 mm to give a capacity of 349 cc and the compression ratio was 7:1. The lower half of the engine was laid out as the Speed Twin, but used the TRW form of crankshaft construction with clamped crankpins and one-piece connecting rods. Unlike the 500 it ran in a bush on the timing side, but retained the drive-side ball race. The top half of the engine followed the same lines as on the larger engine except that, as on the 3TW, the rocker boxes were cast in one with the iron cylinder head. The valve clearances were adjusted in the same manner and enclosure achieved with a single cover for each pair of valves, this being retained by a large knurled nut.

The remainder of the machine was essentially Speed Twin with the gearing lowered by fitting the sidecar engine sprocket, a slightly smaller fuel tank and a rear tyre of the same size as the front.

Motor Cycling reported on the 3T in 1946 and found it to be capable of returning high cross-country averages. They timed it at 74 mph with speeds of 68 and 55 mph in third and second, while it returned nearly 80 mpg. Problems in handling were minimal, although the machine was found to be sensitive to front tyre pressures and needed a touch of steering damper to check pitching on high-speed corners with ripples in the surface. The brakes were excellent, in fact the rear was if anything too good and could lock the wheel. Complaints were minor, although the rear chain oiler feed from the primary chaincase proved sensitive to adjustment and the mudguards could have done with deeper valances.

Above **The postwar 3TU with economy engine and gearbox, disc wheels and gigantic mudguards. Never put into production and of poor performance**

Left **Early 1950s Trophy model with die-cast head and barrel, tank top grid but no nacelle and old style tank finish**

Edward Turner also conceived another 350 cc twin with better weather protection for what was to become the scooter market in later years. He sought to build a machine that was cheap both in purchase price and running costs with a modest performance. The result was the 3TU, which was built as a prototype but never reached production.

The machine contained a number of unusual features both in its engine and its general make-up. At first sight the engine was an ohv twin with vertical valves operated by pushrods contained in tubes behind the block. Closer examination showed that this car practice extended to the cylinders being cast in one with the upper half of the horizontally split crankcase. The rocker box was just an alloy box with detachable lid bolted to the separate one-piece head. The plugs were at the front of the engine, the single carburettor at the rear and the exhausts splayed out from the front corners. A single alloy casting completed the underside of the engine and the timing side was a masterpiece of simplicity. It contained a train of gears which drove up to the rear camshaft and onto the dynamo. This train also drove the oil pump and a car-type distributor housing containing the points, which pointed half forward from the top of the case. The crankshaft was built up from two cast-iron sections and had plain big-end bearings with shells. The rods had split ends and were steel stampings.

Lubrication was by dry sump and the transmission based on the prototype TRW unit with three-speed gearbox. The whole unit was fitted into a rigid frame with undamped telescopic front forks and equipped with enormous mudguards and pressed-steel wheels with fat tyres. The rear mudguard extended into the wheel centre totally enclosing the upper half of the wheel, and on the left was extended forward to act as a massive chain guard. The rather strange appearance was enhanced by the styling of the single silencer carried on the right and the shiny black finish.

Test riders of the time found the machine too slow to get into trouble in crosswinds and it retained too much of the motorcycle to have made any real impact on the forthcoming scooter scene. It was not perhaps one of Turner's best ideas and, in practice, the firm was far too busy producing the conventional machines to bother with a utilitarian model. In fact in a few years the 350 cc twin was to be dropped under production pressure and a side-valve 750 cc twin intended for sidecar use only reached prototype form for the same reasons.

With all the problems that beset production at that time Triumph made the sensible decision to continue the range unchanged into 1947, with the addition of a prop stand as an extra. The range nominally still included the Tiger 85 at that time and, in September 1946, it was also announced that the spring wheel would become available as an extra. This device had been seen in competition earlier in the year and was designed by Turner to provide rear suspension with the minimum of unsprung weight, minimum additional weight and cost, and the ability to fit to the existing rigid frame.

The sprung hub dated back to pre-war days and had first gone onto the road in an experimental form in 1938. A patent had been applied for in 1939 and it was originally intended to incorporate it in the range in 1941.

Essentially it comprised a large-diameter hub which turned on ball races carried on a square-section guide member built up from two castings bolted together. This member was slightly curved and slid on a close-fitting block incorporating the fixed wheel spindle that was attached to the frame and was located to hold the block and guide member in the vertical. Thus the guide member could slide up and down on the block and carried the rotating wheel. The block curvature kept the rear chain in constant tension and substantial springs were fitted inside the guide member, one above and two below the wheel spindle. These were under very heavy compression and the halves of the member have a stern warning cast into them. Without the special equipment, casual dismantling releases the springs like bullets and is very dangerous.

The hub was completed with seals on the spindle and the brake back plate, which floated freely on a boss and was located by a torque arm and a short link to the frame. The brake was of 8 in. diameter.

The design was certainly ingenious and met most of its criteria. The increase in overall weight was 12 lb and the sprung hub would fit straight into any frame dating back to 1938. In practice the lack of damping and very small

Rear of 1947 model Tiger 100 fitted with sprung hub. Typical finish and straight sided, not barrel shaped saddle springs then used

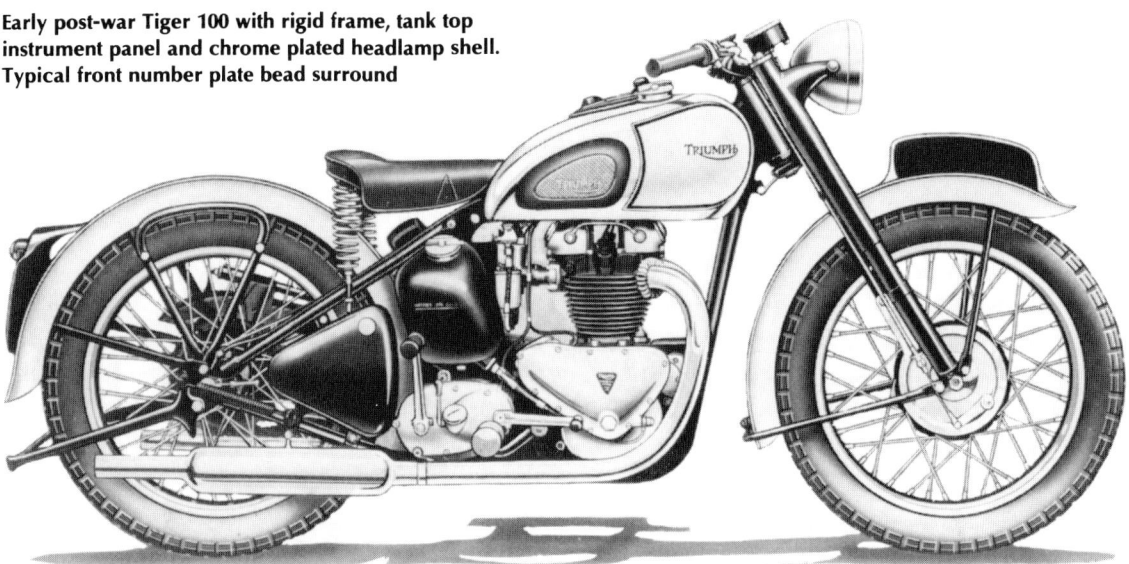

Early post-war Tiger 100 with rigid frame, tank top instrument panel and chrome plated headlamp shell. Typical front number plate bead surround

wheel movement, which was so constrained by the design concept, showed that the improvement was of a limited nature and the handling something of an acquired taste. In 1946 demand far exceeded supply, as enthusiasts managed with rigid frames and saddles over the cobbles and tram lines.

Throughout 1947 and most of 1948 production was the name of the game, so changes to machines were minimal. A spring-loaded choke control, which could be pulled down and locked for starting, was fitted to the carburettor, and the prop stand was introduced in two forms to suit all machines in the Triumph range from 1937 onwards. It cost £1 5s. 0d.

In August 1947 *The Motor Cycle* road tested a Speed Twin fitted with the sprung hub and reported it as well-nigh faultless. Actual performance was 84 mph in top with figures of 43, 61 and 78 mph coming up in the gears. Fuel consumption tests were carried out at constant speeds and ranged from 58 mpg at 60 mph to 94 mpg at a steady 30 mph. Acceleration, braking and handling were all favourably commented on and the engine was oil-tight throughout the test.

It was perhaps typical of the early Speed Twin and reflected the high popularity the make enjoyed. The twin's image, appearance and sound all contributed to this and it met the challenge of other twins from other firms one by one, overcoming them all. The Triumph always had an eager manner that appealed to the public. It took a while to loosen up, for it seemed that the crankshaft had to wear the mains enough to allow it to whip. Once this state was reached it flew. It also vibrated in patches, but had calm spots in between where the rider could relax before he followed the engine into the next period of vibration and its succeeding calm. This way of performing was typical of the Triumph twin and one of its best sales features, for riders loved it and its sporting feel and image.

In October 1948 the range for the next year was announced and a number of changes were introduced. The most noticeable were the deletion of the tank-top instrument panel and the introduction of the headlamp nacelle. This was fitted to all three road models and completely enclosed the top of the forks and handlebar mountings, the bars emerging

Postwar, pre-unit

1948 Speed Twin with separate headlamp; already the model was 10 years old and soon to receive a styling facelift

through rubber grommets. The top of the nacelle carried the speedometer, with extended trip return control, ammeter, lighting switch and ignition cut-out button. The headlight unit was set in the front of the nacelle and the horn fitted below the light, slots being provided to let the sound out. As the handlebar fixing had been cleaned up, the opportunity was taken to clean up the bars themselves. The horn button was screwed into the bar and its wiring thus concealed, while the dipswitch was attached to the back of the front brake lever clip. The click action twistgrip was changed to another type with an adjustable knurled knob. The handlebars continued to be fitted with their traditional extra-long rubbers with the Triumph logo moulded into them.

With the top of the fuel tank now clear of instruments it was provided with four tapped holes and, as an extra, a chromium-plated parcel grid was offered, this being very popular.

The oil pressure gauge was dropped as it caused considerable confusion to owners and trouble for the factory, who had to calm down riders worried that their engine was no longer producing the 50 psi it had managed when new.

In its place came a tell-tale plunger fitted in the pressure release valve on the timing cover. At the same time a small change was made to the breather duct and all models were fitted with the same type of oil tank.

With the adoption of the sprung hub the speedometer could no longer be driven from the rear wheel. A drive point was therefore taken from the end of the gearbox layshaft, and this method was adopted for all models.

A Vokes air cleaner was added next to the battery and connected to the carburettor with a rubber hose, and the choke control replaced by an air lever fitted on the top of the left upper chain stay under the saddle.

The dynamo was changed to the larger 60-watt type and the rear mudguard tidied up by running the rear light cable through the centre beading. The guard fitted to the 500 cc road machines could be removed from the upper chain stays rearwards to assist rear wheel removal.

A month later, in November 1948, an addition to the range was introduced at the Earls Court show. This was the TR5 Trophy model based on the machine that the works team had been riding in trials. These had included the 1948 ISDT, where the three team riders won gold medals and the team award, hence the model name.

The Trophy was instantly successful among clubmen, who could use it during the week and for their weekend sport in trials, long-distance events and even club-level speed meetings. The engine was based on the Speed Twin, but with the light-alloy cylinder barrel and head from the generator engine, still with the cooling shroud bosses in the rather square fins. It was fitted with standard camshafts, low-compression pistons and a single carburettor to produce a modest 25 bhp at 6000 rpm.

Most of the other parts were stock Triumph twin items, but the frame was special, with short down-tube and boxed-in front engine plates. Duplex tubes ran under the engine and back to the rear wheel, but the wheelbase was shorter than standard and the engine a tight fit in the frame.

The exhaust system was siamezed, with the pipe from the right cylinder curving round tightly to join a common system that ran along the top of the primary chain case to a single tubular silencer mounted just above wheel spindle height.

The machine was supplied fully equipped with dynamo and quickly detachable headlamp connected to the wiring with a multipin plug and socket. Most had a pillion pad and rests and the weight was 304 lb. All were fitted with a progressive throttle that lifted the slide slowly at first but quickly at large openings.

Very soon a whole range of parts was made available to enable owners to ring the changes on pistons, gearing and camshafts, and the light and easy-to-handle Trophy was seen in all forms of motorcycling.

The standard machine was good for over 80 mph and in ISDT tune with 7·5:1 pistons they ran up to near the 100 mph mark. At the other end of the scale the works trials engines were detuned and on 4·5:1 pistons to give them punch at low engine speed. When introduced the Trophy sold for £195 11s. 8d, with the sprung hub as an option.

In this manner the Triumph range continued into 1949, still ahead of their rivals, but beginning to come under pressure from their USA distribu-

The 350 cc twin of 1949 with nacelle but no parcel grid on tank top. Engine retained its design differences from the 500

tors for more capacity. In competition events in America the Tiger 100 was having to be more and more heavily tuned to keep in front, and this made it less tractable and more fragile. An increase in capacity would give the Americans not only the power they sought but also far more mid-range torque, making for ease of riding and a less stressed engine. In the end Turner agreed and, in September 1949, the Thunderbird was launched in a dramatic high-speed demonstration.

The new machine was listed as the model 6T and the engine design relied heavily on the 500 cc twin. The engine dimensions were 71 × 82 mm, which gave a capacity of 649 cc, and the compression ratio was 7:1, although for the US market, with its better fuel, a ratio of 8·5:1 could be used. In its detail design the new engine followed the old in most ways, although there were minor differences.

In the bottom half crankshaft construction was the same, but the big-end caps were retained by separate bolts with ground location diameters and locknuts. The cap was still white-metal lined and the rods forged in alloy, a combination that was to prove good for 100,000 miles. The crankshaft ran in a double-lipped roller bearing on the timing side, but retained the ball race on the drive. The remainder of the lower half of the engine followed the 500 cc twin engine practice.

The head, barrel and valve gear were also very similar with eight studs holding down the barrel and eight bolts the head. The detail parts were sized to suit the increased capacity and the original external oil pipes connecting valve wells in the head to the pushrod tubes reappeared. The head and barrel were no longer spigoted and a solid copper gasket was used.

The result was 34 bhp at 6300 rpm, with a big increase in mid-range power.

The engine was fitted into Speed Twin cycle parts which had some changes for the 1950 season. The most noticeable of these was the adoption of painted fuel tanks to replace those with chrome and lined panels. It was suggested that the chroming process could affect the weld seams and that the sea journey to America encouraged rust. In fact there was a shortage of nickel at the time, so chrome plating was kept to a minimum.

The colour adopted for the Thunderbird was a blue-grey of steely hue that was applied to all the painted parts. The tank was relieved by four horizontal chrome-plated bars that ran forward from the kneegrip to the front of the tank and carried the Triumph logo. They used the same theme for their stand at Earls Court, backlit with fluorescent tubes—another Turner idea. Chrome was restricted to the exhaust system, usual small items and the wheel rims, which had their centres painted in the blue-grey colour.

A less noticeable change adopted at the same time was a redesign of the gearbox to give easier engagement of the intermediate gears. On the 650 the clutch had an extra plate and on all machines the speedometer drive was taken horizontally from the gearbox.

The demonstration launch was held at the Montlhèry track near Paris, and the scheme was to take the first three machines off the production line, ride them to the track, cover 500 miles at over 90 mph and ride them back to Meriden. This was not in fact attempted without practice and the Thunderbirds went to Montlhèry for secret trials wearing silver Tiger 100 tanks. The riders covered the 500 miles at over 95 mph, but found the limiting factor was tyre wear if they laid the machine over for the banked circuit. After less than 400 miles the tyre was down to the canvas on one side, so they had to change their riding style to keep the machine more upright. Keeping to a steady speed was also none too easy, but they solved this by setting the throttle cable slack so they could get the speed they wanted with the grip against the stop.

The machines were fitted with sprung hubs for the test and the horns were removed. Changes from the 6T specification amounted to the fitting of Dunlop racing tyres and KLG racing plugs, 25-tooth sprockets on the engine shaft in place of the standard 24-tooth ones, and footrests on the chain stays to give some degree of rider comfort.

Number 1 machine set off at 9.15 am with Alec Scobie aboard and promptly lapped at 94 mph, so was slowed a little to 91 mph. Seventeen minutes later Bob Manns went out on number 2 and after a further interval Jim Alves took number 3 onto the track. After 1 hr 17 min Scobie was signalled in and the machine was refuelled and checked over. Len Bayliss took it over and it was circulating again 1 min 36 sec later. In turn Manns handed over to Allan Jefferies and Alves to Scobie, for the riding was shared between five men.

Up to 1 o'clock all proceeded well, but then Bayliss on number 3 coasted into the pits out of fuel with the tank split. Fifteen minutes were lost while a new tank was fitted and refuelled, and this stop meant that a non-stop 90 mph average was no longer possible for that machine. The same machine had one more unscheduled stop when Allan Jefferies pulled in with transmission noise, which proved to be the lower chain guard adrift. Soon afterwards the first machine completed its 316 laps and was signalled in. With the others home the timekeepers completed their sums and announced that machine number 1 had completed the 500 miles in 5 hr 32 min 11·9 sec at an average of 90·30 mph, including stops, and a running average of 92·23 mph. The figures for the other machines were; number 2, 5 hr 29 min 55·26 sec, 90·93 mph, 92·48 mph and

Above **Tiger 100 with twinseat, as it was called, all-alloy engine, nacelle and sprung hub. New tank style adopted from 1950**

Below **1950 model 3T with dynamo, nacelle and new tank style. Parcel grid was so popular that it became a standard fitting**

number 3, 5 hr 48 min 32·7 sec, 86·07 mph, 92·33 mph.

With the test concluded the handlebars of the machines were dropped and each machine did a flying lap at over 100 mph, the exact speeds being 100·71 mph for number 1 ridden by Scobie; 101·78, number 2, Baylis and 100·71, number 3, Manns. The machines were then serviced and ridden home.

The whole range was shown at Earls Court in October and all the road machines featured the new tank style, only the Trophy retaining the chrome plating. A further small change was the adoption of barrel-shaped saddle springs on all models.

During 1950 the sprung hub was modified in several ways, the most important of which was a change from the original cup and cone bearings to conventional ball races with integral oil seals. The location of the moving parts was also modified along with the brake back-plate mounting to improve life.

Later that year *The Motor Cycle* road tested a Thunderbird both solo and with a Watsonian Avon sidecar attached. The test machine was fitted with the sprung hub and a new addition to the range of extras, a twinseat. In solo form the machine gave a zestful performance with a top speed around the 100 mph mark and speed in the gears limited by valve float to 45, 61 and 90 mph. Acceleration was such that very high average speeds could be achieved across country aided by good handling and excellent brakes. Although the low-down carburation was not completely satisfactory, slow-speed riding in traffic was exceptionally easy, aided by the low weight. Starting was positive, although it did require some effort on the kickstarter and the engine remained completely oil-tight. With sidecar fitted and a suitable adjustment to the gearing the outfit proved capable of over 70 mph in both third and top gears.

In November 1950 the range for 1951 was announced with news of a new head and barrel for the sports 500s and a racing kit of parts for the Tiger 100. Both the new engine components were gravity die cast in aluminium alloy and this allowed the cylinder fins to be closely pitched. The head had inserted valve seats in cast iron and its holding-down bolts screwed into plugs in the barrel made of the same material. The better cooling resulting from the increased fin area, and the use of aluminium, allowed the compression ratio of the Tiger 100 to be increased to 7·6:1. The exhaust ports were also splayed out in the same manner as on the iron engine. A larger inlet valve was fitted and the internal breathing improved, which all resulted in an increase in power to 32 bhp. The external drain pipes connecting to the pushrod tubes reappeared on all models except the 3T.

The Trophy was also fitted with the new head and barrel, but had low-compression pistons to keep its 6:1 ratio. The exhaust pipes had to be redesigned to fit the new head and on all machines a new front brake with cast-iron drum was used. Filler caps were all changed to simple quarter-turn types and speedometer dials in the nacelle-equipped models were changed, bringing the more used 30 to 70 section to the top or front of the instrument. Larger-bore petrol taps were adopted to avoid any possibility of fuel starvation at speed, and the five-plate clutches given reduced-rate springs.

The Tiger 100 was fitted with the new twinseat as standard, with the toolbox moved to a position just below it and above the upper chain stay, and it was for this model that the racing kit was sold. The kit was very comprehensive and included a pair of high-compression pistons with various ratios available, racing camshafts, racing valve springs and twin carburettors with all the attendant pipes and cables, these instruments being supplied from a remote-mounted float chamber. A rev-counter drive was obtained by using the dynamo fitting and gearing the right angle box to the exhaust camshaft. Megaphones were supplied along with new exhaust pipes. The cycle parts were just as comprehensive and included a larger-than-standard oil tank together with more suitable handlebars, footrests, folding kickstart and a number plate. These either fitted to standard lugs on the frame or to additional ones, which were incorporated on all new Tiger 100 machines.

All the parts were available separately, along with close-ratio gears, alloy mudguards and a range of sprockets.

Paintwork of the range changed little, the only model to be affected being the Thunderbird, which altered to a slightly lighter shade of blue with a polychromatic finish. All machines were supplied with the parcel grid as standard and most came with the new dualseat except the Trophy, which continued with the pillion pad.

So the twin rolled into the 1950s very popular with its owners and its makers, for it sold in large numbers both in England and abroad. Nor did it stop there, for that one trial with the London police before the war had resulted in sales all over the world to nearly 70 different forces by 1951. In fact it was so successful, and production was so stretched with the 500 and 650 cc machines, that the 3T had to be dropped from the range. In several ways it was the odd man out and, as the cheapest in the range, would have been the least economic to make, but it had made many friends and a good few riders mourned its passing.

Late in 1951 the Thunderbird received a change of carburettor with an MC2 from the SU range being fitted in place of the original Amal. This required a change of induction manifold, a modification to the frame, and a learning period for owners, as few motorcyclists had any experience of this type of unit. Otherwise the range continued unaltered except that wheel rims were either chromed or plated depending on the nickel supply situation at any time.

In the middle of 1952 Triumph held a fuel economy run over a 10-mile road circuit using a Thunderbird. The machine was fitted with a type EB needle in place of the normal M9 to give a leaner mixture at small throttle openings, a raised top-gear ratio of 4·24:1 and tyre pressures of 35 psi. Five laps of the course were covered at 30 mph with different riders, two from the press, Ginger Wood of SU, Tyrell Smith of Triumph and

The 1951 Tiger 100 fitted with the racing kit. Two carburettors, open exhausts, remote float, larger oil tank and modified controls

Edward Turner. The overall consumption was 155 mpg, which showed what could be done if you tried.

Later the same month readers of the specialist press noted that one of the Triumph machines prepared for the ISDT selection trials used a TR5 frame with the 650 engine squeezed in. A foretaste of what was to come.

In August *The Motor Cycle* road tested a Tiger 100 and gave it a good write-up, as was the custom of the time. The performance was 92 mph in top with figures of 41, 60 and 85 mph in the gears. Acceleration was extremely brisk and braking first class. In the handling area a slight tendency to roll on fast, bumpy corners was reported. Riders of that era knew that this meant that at over 65 mph the machine would begin to weave on a corner and could get quite exciting. Similarly, comments that the gear change was best carried out leisurely and that bottom gear would not engage silently when at rest were noted. Most of the latter problems arose because the clutch would not free very well, and this fault plagued Triumph for some years. Fortunately most people learnt to live with it, just as they accepted the Triumph up-for-up gear pedal movement, at that time at variance with most other machines.

Late in 1952 a change was made to the Speed Twin that had a number of repercussions on

Top **Tiger 100 with twin carburettors from race kit. Float chamber normally to left of oil tank but battery intrudes on road model**

Above **Speed Twin with alternator, coil ignition and inacessible distributor in old magneto position**

Left **Thunderbird engine fitted with an SU carburettor in place of the earlier used Amal. Dynamo still on this machine from 1952/53**

other parts of the machine. This was the adoption of the Lucas crankshaft-mounted alternator, which necessitated changes to the crankshaft and chaincase, the movement of the shock absorber to a new clutch centre, a new wiring harness with different switches and the substitution of a rectifier for the voltage control unit. The same system, along with coil ignition, was adopted for the Thunderbird within a short time, but the other machines in the range continued with their dynamo for the rest of the 1950s.

For 1953 the racing kit for the Tiger 100 was dropped, but in its place came the Tiger 100c, this being effectively the same thing but built as new for competition work. Thus the machine was fitted as standard with racing camshafts, twin carburettors and the large-capacity oil tank, although supplied fully equipped for road use with silencers and electrical equipment. All the parts from the racing kit were available, including alternative pistons and close-ratio gears.

The result was a competitive clubman racer, as Vic Willoughby proved by following one as it was built at Meriden and then riding it to MIRA for speed tests and on to Snetterton, where it proved to have ample performance, reaching the final of its two events. For club meetings it was a potential winner.

In October 1953 a sports version of the Thunderbird was first seen at the Paris show and featured many changes. The model was called the Tiger 110 and was the first Triumph twin to be offered with swinging fork rear suspension. This was controlled by Girling units with pre-load adjustment and the opportunity was taken to clean up the design by combining oil tank, air cleaner, battery case and toolbox into one assembly above the gearbox. The seat was new and of the stepped twin-level type, while the valanced rear mudguard was supported by extensions of the rear sub-frame.

The engine was based on the standard 650 cc unit, but had high-compression pistons, different camshafts, modified ports and a larger carburettor. The result was 42 bhp. To cope with this the front brake was enlarged to 8 in. while a quickly detachable rear wheel was available as an option.

Finish was a new shade of shell blue sheen for petrol tank and mudguards, with the remainder of the cycle parts in black. Styling remained as before with the four horizontal bars on the tank.

The result was a very fast and tractable machine with a maximum speed of well over 110 mph. In tests it consistently ran at 113 and 114 mph, and with a larger main jet managed 117 mph on more than one occasion. In the gears speeds of 93 mph in third and 70 mph in second were reached, truly impressive for a single-carburettor twin. It also proved to have a very flexible engine, which made for fast but easy riding on all roads. Fuel consumption was an impressive 65 mpg over a full test, but excluding high-speed runs. Brakes were good and the new seat gave a comfortable ride.

At the end of 1953 the T100c was dropped from the range, but the Tiger 100 gained the swinging-fork frame and the 8 in. front brake. By the start of 1955 all the twins were fitted into frames with swinging-fork rear suspension and the sprung hub had been laid to rest.

During 1955 a further change was made to the engines with the introduction of bigger main bearings. These engines are easily recognized by the additional bulge on the timing side under the case and the change-over continued for some while. At the same time the design of the big ends was changed and conventional shell bearings fitted. This later design of crankshaft will fit the earlier engine, but requires the use of a rather rare bearing, whose dimensions suit the needs but result in it being a little overloaded.

Other changes for 1955 included an increase in compression ratio to 8:1 for the Tiger 100 and a similar change to the TR5, which raised its power to 33 bhp at 6500 rpm with the aid of a hotter camshaft. The Trophy also received a slightly larger petrol tank and a change of rear wheel size to 18 in.

Near the end of the year the range for 1956 was introduced and, for the sports 650 cc engine, a light-alloy cylinder head was announced, being known at Meriden as the Delta head. It was designed to dispense with the external oil drain pipes, with the oil draining directly into the pushrod tubes which ran from crankcase to the underside of the cylinder head, not the rocker boxes. The new head was die-cast with cast-in valve inserts and redesigned rocker boxes and its use allowed the compression ratio of the Tiger

Alternator model Speed Twin with key-operated ignition switch in headlamp nacelle. Fitted with sprung hub and stands for both wheels

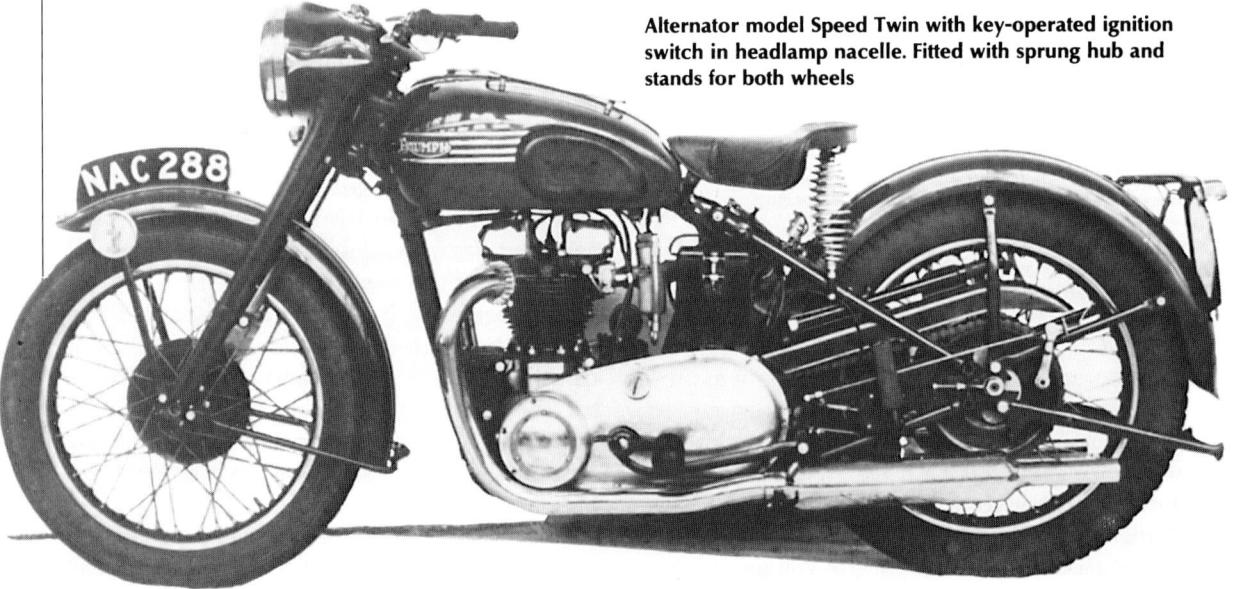

Top **First version of Tiger 110 with swinging fork frame, cleaned up centre area and stepped level twinseat. Modified 650 cc engine**

Above **ISDT version of Trophy in swinging fork frame for the 1954 Army team. Note nail catcher on front mudguard—considered essential then**

mounting was changed to improve its insulation from vibration and a chrome styling flash added along its top seam. A minor change on the 500 cc models was the reduction of spigot height of the barrels into the heads. Thus new heads would not fit earlier barrels, but the reverse was allowable as the change was only from $\frac{3}{16}$ in. to $\frac{1}{8}$ in.

During the year the Tiger 110 was tested by *The Motor Cycle*, reaching 94 mph in third and 101 mph in top under adverse conditions. It proved to have a scintillating performance, although the high compression ratio did call for sensible use of the manual advance and retard lever. Handling was light and the riding position very comfortable except for really fast motoring, when a less upright stance would have helped. The brakes worked well, especially from high speeds, but some oil leaked from the gearbox onto the rear tyre during performance testing.

In contrast, *Motor Cycling* tested a Thunderbird with a Garrard single-seat sidecar attached.

110 to rise to 8·5:1. An added feature on the big Tiger was the ventilated front brake with air scoop and exit formed in the brake back plate.

It was joined by a new model, the TR6 Trophy, which used the 650 cc engine with its new cylinder head in a trial bike form with small petrol tank, detachable headlamp and large-section rear tyre. The road machines continued with a number of minor changes and improvements such as the redesign of the steering-head lug, the incorporation of sidecar lugs to the frame, adjustable lock stops and a new horn-mounting grille. The forks were improved to prevent bottoming under heavy braking, and electrical changes brought the horn push and dipswitch onto the left bar as a single unit. The petrol tank

Classic Alex Oxley cartoon advertisement from 1955, one of a brilliant series all based on the same theme. An earlier theme series ran from 1947 on similar lines

Postwar, pre-unit

It ran up to just over 70 mph, but this was also its cruising speed if the rider wished, while it could potter along very quietly in both town and country.

For 1957 there was a change of tank motif and finish, with a full-width front hub being fitted to the Speed Twin, Thunderbird and Trophy models. The new tank badges carried the company name on a chrome-plated grille on the tank side. A plated band ran from the ends of the grille back to the kneegrip, so the styling of the tank sides was effectively split into two.

This allowed the adoption of two-tone finishes to the tank and the two Tigers were the first machines to have this option listed, the colours

Left **1955 Speed Twin with Amal Monobloc carburettor and new style primary chaincase. Note access to points**

Below **Tiger 100 modified for production class racing using some race kit items. Big front brake with air scoop and vent**

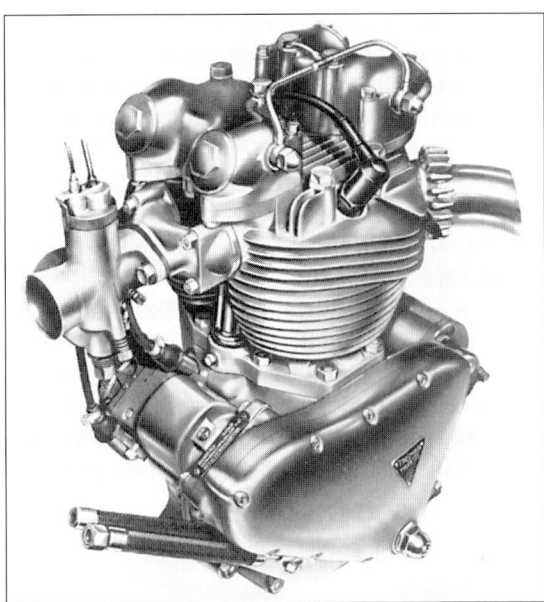

Above **The 650 cc sports engine as used in 1956 with die-cast alloy cylinder head, raised compression ratio, modified rocker boxes and revised oil drainage. Fitted with magneto and separate dynamo but only one carburettor**

Below **650 cc Thunderbird in 1957, still with SU carburettor, nacelle and iron head but with new petrol tank styling, swinging fork frame and coil ignition**

being ivory top and blue lower with matching mudguards in ivory with a gold-lined, light blue centre strip. Over the years many variations were used to capitalize on the idea for the complete range.

Mechanically the Tiger 100 benefited from a new cylinder head, made from the Delta head casting, but with twin splayed inlet ports and screwed-in adaptors locked with large nuts and carrying 1 in. Monoblocs. The larger Trophy model was fitted with the 8 in. front brake.

The machines also carried a new transfer reading 'World Motorcycle Speed Record Holder', which referred to the 214 mph achieved by Johnny Allen at Bonneville Salt Flats in 1956. In fact this record was disputed by the FIM due to the timing gear used, and a legal wrangle went on for several years. Everyone, however, fully believed that the streamlined Triumph had achieved the speed stated and the machine was shipped over to be run and shown on British TV and exhibited at the 1956 Earls Court show standing on some genuine Utah salt!

Early in 1957 a new 350 cc unit construction model was announced fitted with a one-piece

rear enclosure over the rear wheel. The model is described in a later chapter, but the enclosure, or skirt, or bathtub as it became known, was to affect the styling of the pre-unit models before these were phased out.

In April 1957 *Motor Cycling* road tested the Tiger 100 fitted with the optional splayed head and twin carburettors, and it proved good for 105 mph, with 92 coming up in third and 76 in second. It was doing 8400 rpm for the last speed, nearly 2000 rpm above its peak power engine speed. With a dry weight of 385 lb and a free-revving engine it was both fast and frugal, with consumption figures in the order of 75 mpg being recorded except during speed tests. One of its nice features was a new roll-on centre stand, which had been developed for the police models and was available as an option. Handling and braking were also well liked and the magazine had no problems with the machine.

For the 1958 range some of the style of the 350 cc unit twin was used, as the larger road twins were fitted with deep-section front mudguards without the forward stays. They also received steering locks, and both Tiger models and the TR6 had full-width front hubs still with the 8 in. brake. The most controversial change was made to the gearbox with the adoption of the 'Slickshift' gearchange. This gave a semi-automatic clutch operation with movement of the gear pedal in either direction acting on the clutch-lift mechanism in the gearbox end cover to free the clutch. Thus if you pressed the gear lever to make sure it was home, or held it down when you changed gear, the clutch freed. It was not a very popular device and took some getting used to. In fact a good many owners removed the appropriate parts and reverted to normal clutch operation, as they could not get on with the new arrangement. It remained, however, for several years.

Early in 1958 came the tuning aid for which the American market had been crying out—a twin splayed port head for the 650 cc engine. This brought the power to a point where both the original built-up crankshaft and the six-plate clutch were beginning to wilt under the strain. The result was a new crankshaft forged in one piece with a central cast-iron flywheel which was threaded over the outer crank cheek, pressed into place and located by three radial bolts screwed through the flywheel periphery into the crankshaft.

In August 1958 the Speed Twin and TR5 Trophy were dropped from the range to make way for a unit construction 500, and the following month the 1959 range was announced, with all models being fitted with the new crankshaft. At the last moment a new machine

Top **1957 Tiger 100 with splayed inlet ports and two carburettors fitted to screwed in adaptors. Big, ventilated front brake**

Above **Geneva Show in 1958 with the new 350 cc unit construction machine surrounded by its forebears in Tiger 100, Tiger 110 and touring model forms**

was added to the list, destined to become one of motorcycling's legends, the T120, called the Bonneville to commemorate the speed records set up on the salt flats. In its essentials it was the Tiger 110 with the splayed head and twin carburettors without air filters, and the 1959 version was the only one to be built with the headlight nacelle. It had touring handlebars and was finished in tangerine and pearl with black cycle parts. As well as the two Amals it also had a higher compression ratio, so produced 46 bhp at 6500 rpm, and from the start had a normal clutch lift without the 'Slickshift' device.

The Bonnie was the pinnacle of the original Edward Turner design, being no larger than he thought was reasonable for a 360-degree parallel twin with no special counterbalancing. Other makes and other designers stretched their twins, and oversize kits from specialist suppliers boosted the Triumph to 750 and even 850 cc, but Turner did not. In his view 650 cc and 6500 rpm are about the limit before vibration and wear become problems and spoil the machine for the rider. He also kept his machines light and easy to handle so they were pleasant to ride, and of simple construction so they were easy to maintain all over the world. Their endearing strength is borne out by the large number that

Right **The Tiger 100 in its 1959 form with the splayed cylinder head and two carburettors. Front brake without ventilation**

Below **1959 Tiger 110 fitted with the standard cylinder head. Iron barrel and much disliked Slickshift clutch operation worked by gear pedal and dropped fairly quickly**

came to dominate vintage racing in the late 1970s, most running on dope fuels with high compression ratios, very fierce cams and high engine speeds.

In the middle of 1959 the Tiger 100 was replaced by a unit construction derivative, so the

Above **Line drawing of 1959 TR6. Fitted with new crankshaft, full width hubs, gaitered front forks and block tread front tyre**

only non-unit engines that remained in production were of 650 cc capacity and the long line of 500 cc engines had come to an end after 22 years.

In September the changes for the next year were announced and the 650s all received a new swinging fork frame with single top and saddle tubes joined by duplex down tubes passing under the engine. The sub-frame was bolted on and the fork pivoted on a pin fixed in a lug on the saddle tube. New forks were fitted to the new frame along with a new petrol tank, while the wheels were changed to 18 in. diameter on the Thunderbird. This machine and the Tiger 110 were both fitted with the rear wheel enclosure as used on the unit construction models and similar style mudguards. A new exhaust system was also fitted. The two Tiger models retained their magneto ignition, but the charging system was changed to an alternator with the appropriate modifications to the primary drive and the electrical system. The Bonneville kept its sports mudguards and the headlamp was made quickly detachable, so the nacelle was discarded while the new Trophy tank stayed at 3 gallons capacity.

Late in the year *The Motor Cycle* tested the Bonneville and reported it to be very fast with tremendous acceleration and an acceptable thirst of 52 mpg. The new floating brake shoes worked really well and handling was first class, being heavier than usual for a Triumph. Adverse comments were few and concerned the rather uneven idling, the heavier-than-usual twistgrip operation, and the siting of the light switch under the dualseat. Other points were that the steering damper knob unscrewed itself and the oil filler

The Bonneville, the ultimate Edward Turner 650 cc vertical twin. This is the 1960 model

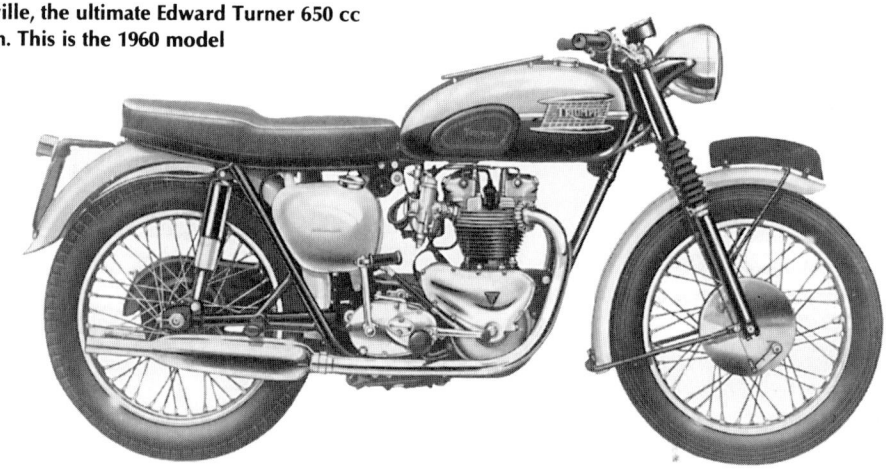

cap allowed lubricant to seep out, although the engine itself was oil-tight.

In September 1960 the Trophy model was discontinued, but reappeared again in February 1961. Changes to the other models for 1961 included a modified frame with a lower tank rail added to prevent any recurrence of breakages and at the same time the steering-head angle was altered. Finally, the Thunderbird was fitted with the alloy head and the compression ratio was increased slightly to 7·5:1. The brake shoes were all changed to the floating type with the Thunderbird front increased to 8 in. diameter and the gearing of that model and the Tiger 110 lowered. The Bonneville was fitted with a 3-gallon tank and a timing cover was made available with an inbuilt tachometer-drive gearbox, which was driven off the exhaust camshaft.

While the Trophy model had reappeared early in 1961 it was really in a totally new form as a single-carburettor version of the T120, so was far removed from the early TR5. In its new style it had all the fittings of the Bonneville, so really took the place of the earlier sports 650 cc model in its first form. The Tiger 110, now with rear enclosure, was dropped in August and the following month the Trophy was renumbered the TR6 S/S. At the same time the Thunderbird finally lost the Slickshift gearchange and gained a siamezed exhaust system with new silencer. The Bonneville received a number of minor changes, as the power brought various problems to light, and one of the more notable was a change in the balance factor and an increase in flywheel weight.

Finally, in October 1962 the 650 cc engine was launched in unit construction form and so the original 1937 layout had run its course, as all the models now had engine and gearbox as one. However, the basic concept of a 360-degree parallel twin with two camshafts continued on.

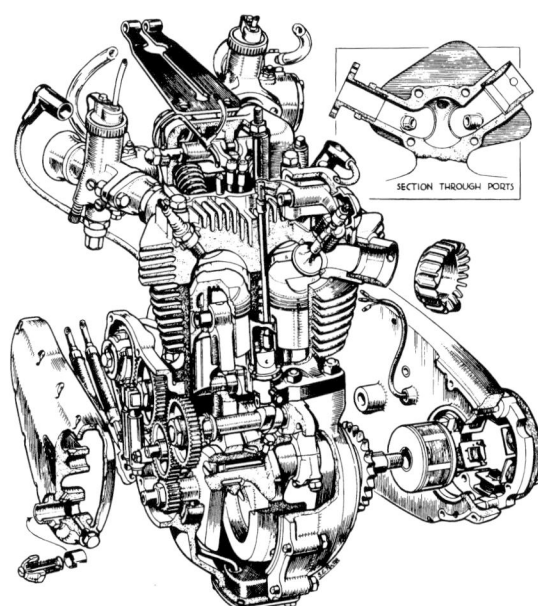

Above **Partially exploded and cut-away line drawing of the 650 cc Bonneville engine in 1961. Inset shows the splay of both inlet and exhaust ports**

Right **1961 Tiger 110 with bathtub and deeply valanced mudguard. Not liked by all but gave a smooth clean look to the machine**

5 | The Grand Prix

The Grand Prix engine with the famed cowling bosses on the barrel casting. Two carburettors on special inlet manifold. Coarse pitch fins

Triumph did not make road-racing machines, Triumph built reliable motorcycles for Mr Average to ride 20,000 miles off the end of the production line with minimal maintenance. So believed Edward Turner, and only twice did he let the firm waver in this belief. Once was in 1938, when Wicksteed broke the Brooklands lap record, and the other occasion was just after the war, when Ernie Lyons persuaded him to provide a quick engine for road racing.

Lyons had been successful in his native Ireland on grass tracks and short circuits, but few races can have been as hard as talking Turner into a racing machine programme. Somehow he managed this, and the result was an instruction to Freddie Clarke to see what he could produce in the development shop.

Freddie was a tuner of no mean ability, so was well suited to this task. He had ridden at Brooklands and held the all-time lap records for the 350 cc class, for which he had used a Tiger 80 running on dope, and the 750 cc class. The latter was at over 118 mph, and for it he had used a 500 cc twin bored out to 502 cc and supercharged.

The basis of the machine for Lyons was a Tiger 100 modified to give as much power as could be obtained using the poor-quality petrol then available. To the basically standard bottom half was added the light-alloy cylinder head and barrel from the generator unit, which gave a good starting point.

The ports were bored out and separate inlet

manifolds made to carry two Amal carburettors, both fed from a single float chamber suspended to the left of the oil tank. The compression ratio was raised using pistons with bigger crowns, and these had fairly large valve cutaways on both sides. Due to the layout of the generator unit the head casting had both inlet and exhaust ports parallel to one another and, perforce, the racing engine had to use the same arrangement.

The valve gear was based on standard parts, but considerably lightened and freed off for minimum friction. The rocker boxes were stock, but the head sat on a solid copper gasket and a very careful hand was required to tighten the head down evenly.

The lower half of the engine was very basic Triumph, although, as with the ports and combustion chambers, the parts that mattered were highly polished. These included the crankshaft, which was the normal built-up one, although it did run on roller main bearings. The connecting rods were heavier than normal, but still forged in RR56 light alloy, and for this engine the rod caps were also formed in the same

The first one: the Triumph used by Ernie Lyons to win the 1946 Manx Grand Prix and so found the line

material. Thus they ran direct on the crankpins. Such a bearing is very good but also very easily damaged by any particles in the oil, so a full-flow Vokes oil filter was fitted into the oil supply line to the engine. It was external and positioned on the right engine plate between engine and gearbox.

Full-race camshafts were fitted with much-extended timing and the Lyons engine used solid alloy pushrods in place of the standard tubular steel ones. The tappets were hard chromed and worked in guides made from RR56. Ignition was by a BTH racing magneto and a rev-counter drive replaced the normal dynamo and was driven from the exhaust camshaft gear.

Lubrication was dry sump with the usual Triumph twin-plunger oil pump driven from the inlet camshaft. A larger-than-standard oil tank was fitted in the usual place below the seat and was closed by the screw-action cap which passed as a quick filler at that time. The rockers were fed from the scavenge return in the normal way.

Separate exhaust pipes and megaphones were fitted, each pipe being secured to the cylinder head by a ring nut screwing into it. The nuts were machined with slots for a 'C' spanner to tighten them. The pipes were clipped to the front engine plates and had the megaphones welded to them. These were of a fair size and terminated in a rolled lip, which would have prevented them from splitting. Each was attached to the frame chain stay by a braced bracket welded to the megaphone.

The cycle parts of the machine were based on Tiger 100 items and the gearbox was a Triumph four-speed unit with close ratios, a reversed gear pedal and no kickstarter. It was driven by an exposed primary chain with only a very light guard over the top chain run. Chain lubrication was from the engine breather, whose outlet pipe was pointed at it, and a drip feed. The clutch ran dry and retained the usual four springs and the engine-shaft shock absorber was fitted. The rear chain was not guarded.

The frame was the stock rigid one using existing or added lugs to support such parts as the rear-mounted footrests and rear brake pedal. Telescopic front forks were fitted along with the new sprung hub. Although this had a limited movement and was not damped it was better than nothing at all. The sheer size of the sprung hub dictated the use of an 8 in. brake in it and the front matched it with an experimental single leading-shoe brake of the same size. The machine had light mudguards and the rear one carried a racing pad behind the saddle, while the fuel tank was without kneegrips or recesses and was finished in Tiger 100 silver. The usual controls, racing plates and a rev-counter completed the machine.

Right **Don Crossley at Quarter Bridge on his way to win the 1948 Senior Manx GP. Some consolation after the TT**

Below **Drive side of the Grand Prix showing the flimsy chainguard and rather remote float chamber mounting. Pipes and trumpets are in one**

The Grand Prix

Above **Bob Foster before the start of the disastrous 1948 TT when all the Triumphs retired**

Right **Ken Bills in the 1948 TT. Fifth on lap 4 but retired at the Bungalow**

The first outing for the new machine was the Ulster Road Race held in August 1946. Entries for this were curtailed by the travel restrictions then in force, but Lyons managed to get the Triumph to the line for the race. It was not a successful debut, for he was forced to retire after a few laps. However, this was due to using up all his racing plugs and the cause was simply too low a setting for the fuel level. Between plug changes the Triumph motored very well, which gave him confidence for his next race, the Manx Grand Prix.

In practice his times were none too quick because he toured over the sections he thought he knew to spare the engine, as so few parts were available if it gave trouble. The evening before the race the engine had to be stripped for a check, but while the work was in hand the front mudguard from a Tiger 100 was fitted, which was to be a great help during the race.

The race was held in poor weather conditions which began damp and became steadily worse, with both mist and rain for the riders to contend with. Lyons started number 12, and just after Craig-ny-Baa took the lead on the road only to

find a large black dog on the circuit in front of him as he came out of Brandish. A spectator jumped down, grabbed the dog and hurled himself and dog over the bank to clear the road, but the incident threw Lyons completely off line for Hillberry, which was taken standing on the footrests. As the weather became worse Lyons seemed to go faster and was never headed, winning the six-lap race in just under three hours and finishing in pouring rain. On the last lap the down tube of the frame broke just above the engine mounting and the rev-counter packed up.

Lyons went on to put up the fastest time of the day at Shelsley Walsh later that year and the factory was inundated with requests for a replica of his machine. In the end Edward Turner bowed to the pressure and agreed that 50 would be built on the lines of the Manx winner, using the Tiger engine with generator castings. He also agreed to David Whitworth riding on a semi-works basis in 1947 and this was quite successful, for his twin won on its first outing at Cambre in July. He went on to more success both at home and in Europe, continuing this the following year.

In February 1948 the racing twin was shown to the press with the name 'Grand Prix' and followed the lines of the Lyons machine very closely. The standard compression ratio was set at 8·3:1, although pistons were available to give 8·8 for better-quality petrol and 12·5 for dope. The engine internals were polished and the exhaust pipes were $1\frac{1}{2}$ in. in diameter. The solid alloy pushrods and roller mains from the prototype were fitted, but the whole accent was on using standard or slightly modified production parts, only changing where this was easy to do. The primary chain oiler was taken from the oil return pipe and incorporated an adjuster to meter the feed. The engines ran on mineral oil not castor, but the larger oil tank was retained. The carburettors were standard type 6 of 1 in. bore and ignition by racing magneto with manual control. An 8000 rpm counter was fitted and the safe engine speed was quoted as 7600 rpm. Power output was 40 bhp at 7200 rpm, sufficient to push the machine along close to 120 mph on its standard gearing.

The gearbox was based on the standard unit equipped with close ratios, but also had the shafts and gears made in a higher-grade steel and modified engagement dogs to speed up the gearchange. Unlike the Lyons machine, a gear-pedal linkage was fitted with the pedal pivoted in the kickstart spindle boss in the gearbox end cover and linked to a short, downward-pointing gear lever. The clutch had four Ferodo-lined plates and five plain ones.

The cycle parts followed the lines of the prototype closely with the frame constructed from forged lugs, scarfed for lightness, and high-quality tubing brazed together. The telescopic forks were standard, as was the sprung hub used at the rear. The front brake was 8 in. in diameter and its steel drum with cooling fins was machined from a solid billet. An alloy back plate was used without any air scoop.

Both wheels had Dunlop light-alloy racing rims and tyres with the front 1 in. larger than the 19 in. rear. Light-alloy mudguards were fitted and a steering damper, saddle and mudguard pad completed the machine. The wheels were balanced and the exhaust-pipe nuts wire locked to small holes drilled in the block.

The petrol tank was produced from the standard dies, but the kneegrip recesses were omitted, so increasing the capacity slightly. Its finish was silver sheen and the weight of the complete machine was 310 lb.

So the eager road-racers took delivery of the twin and by June Edward Turner was regretting the entire affair. That year nine Triumphs entered the Senior TT and seven came to the line, with riders of the calibre of Frith, Foster, Bills, Moule and Willoughby among them. Vic only made it to Quarter Bridge on lap 1 and gradually, one by one, they all retired. It was little consolation that Don Crossley won the Manx and Freddie Frith at

Shelsley, while Whitworth continued to collect places in the European classics, for in 1948 it was the performance in the TT that counted above all else.

In the autumn the doyen of road testers, Charles Markham, rode the Crossley Triumph at Ansty, a short-lived postwar airfield circuit. He was impressed by the machine's speed, handling over the bumps and the brakes.

So further batches of Grand Prix machines were built, all on the same lines as the first, and the model continued in the maker's lists. It was never to be in the front rank of racing machines, but filled a gap at the time with something that many an aspiring road-racer could cut his teeth on. It also showed that a competitive machine could be built simply and be easy to maintain.

In its day, the Grand Prix was faster than the average Manx Norton and also weighed a good deal less, so accelerated well. The engine was none too reliable if it was run up to the red line all the time and it required plenty of work to keep it in tune. The engines would go to 8000 rpm, which was a high speed for a long-stroke engine at that time, but at that point anything could happen and often did. The results were usually spectacular, with crankcases splitting and shedding parts in all directions.

The machines made a wonderful noise, very appreciated in those days of fairly low-revving singles, as the only racing multis seen then were the AJS Porcupine and the rare vee-twin Guzzi. The Triumph handling was good, but not as good as that of the contemporary garden gate Norton, so was well below the Featherbed standard that was to come. However, the machines were competitive in national and club races at a time when the only alternative was a Manx or a special, often using a JAP or pre-war engine.

Various sources indicate that between 150 and 200 Grand Prix machines were built and a good number went for export, for they won races worldwide. Not many now remain, for the engines lent themselves to being cannibalized for other ventures and the remainder of the machine was either discarded or modified.

The model remained in the catalogue into 1950, but by the end of that year had been dropped in favour of the racing kit. This had the advantage, for the factory, of absolving them from warranty or other problems, no matter how much the owner over-revved the engine.

Even Edward Turner could forget business once in a while.

Below **Cylinder head parts and pistons from the David Whitworth machine used in 1947**

Bottom **Grand Prix in full flight at a Vintage race meeting. Reverse cone megaphone not original**

6 Unit construction

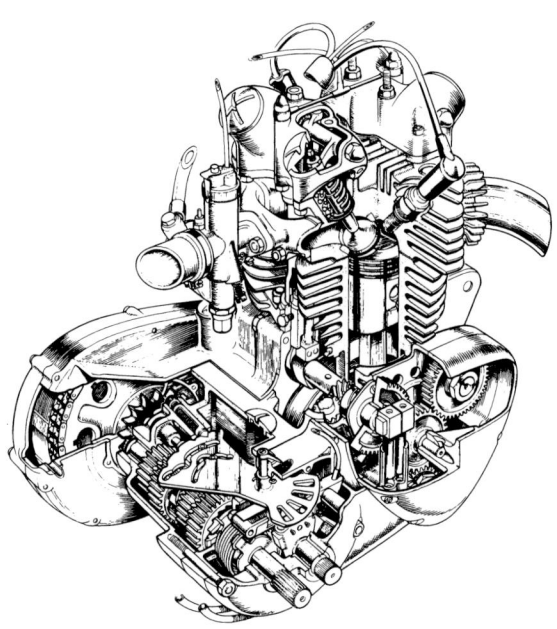

Line drawing of 350 cc model 21 engine launched in 1957. Unit construction with gearbox

Early in 1957 Triumph announced a new machine with a twin-cylinder engine, which revived their interest in the 350 cc class. The new model was called the Twenty-One to celebrate the twenty-first birthday of the Triumph Engineering Company and the useful fact that in the USA a 350 cc engine falls in the 21-cubic-inch class.

The new engine was said to be of unit construction, and so far as it had fixed primary drive centres, it was. However, its method of construction bore little relation to that used by the Japanese in later years for unit construction four-strokes, where engine, gearbox and primary drive shared the same oil and the crankcase was split along the horizontal centre line.

The Triumph engine followed the Turner precept in many ways, with forged crankshaft, flywheel retained by three radial bolts as on the 650 cc engine, and two separate camshafts gear-driven from the crankshaft. The inlet drove a timed rotary breather. The connecting rods and pistons followed normal Triumph practice with split big ends, bolts with location diameters and three piston rings, two compression and one scraper.

The top half of the engine was equally conventional, with a cast-iron barrel, painted silver to match the alloy head, held by eight studs with pushrod tubes in front of and behind it locating on the tappet blocks at the bottom. The cylinder head was aluminium alloy with cast-in valve-seat inserts and screwed-in exhaust pipe adaptors. The rocker boxes were separate and the detail parts followed the lines of 1937. Duplex valve springs were fitted and the four inspection caps lost their hexagons and gained two large slots. They still came off unless locked by one of many means devised by owners.

It was in the crankcase that the design was new. The left case half was extended back as the inner wall of the primary chaincase and taken across over the gearbox sprocket. Access to the sprocket was by means of a detachable circular plate held by six bolts and containing an oil seal in its centre.

The right crankcase half was more complex, for it comprised the case half with the gearbox shell in one. The case was machined much as before with holes for the camshaft bushes, mounting face for the oil pump and bosses for pressure-relief valve and sump filter. The gearbox section was open on the right with the left wall machined for the sleeve gear bearing and a needle race fitted behind it to support the layshaft. The gearbox section protruded past the case centre line and incorporated the rear mounting lug for the complete unit. It had a filler plug in its top and a combined drain and level in the base of the standpipe design, where the pipe was hollow to give the correct oil level while its removal drained the gearbox.

The crankcase carried a timing-side plain bush and a drive-side ball race for the crankshaft to locate on, with the usual internal scavenge pipe connecting sump to oil pump. The timing side was completed with a triangular-shaped cover under which were the timing gears and oil pump. Ignition was by coil with a car-type distributor mounted behind the right cylinder and skew gear driven from the inlet camshaft. The distributor contained a single pair of points, the condenser and a two-lobe cam. It could be rotated in its housing to set the ignition timing and incorporated an advance-and-retard mechanism.

The carburettor was a single Amal Monobloc fitted with an air filter and mounted on a separate induction manifold. Two separate exhaust pipes and silencers were used, the pipes being fixed to the ports with finned clamps.

An alternator rotor was fitted to the left end of the crankshaft, with the stator mounted on studs screwed into the crankcase. The alternator leads were taken through a sleeve in the primary chaincase inner wall. Inboard of the rotor the primary-drive sprocket drove a duplex chain connecting to a four-plate clutch with shock absorber centre. The clutch had four springs and was of normal Triumph design. The primary chain had no tensioner or means of adjustment.

The gearbox had four speeds, with input and output on concentric shafts, but the layshaft was positioned behind the mainshaft, not beneath it. The selector rod and camplate lay above the shafts, the plate pivoting on a pin in the roof of the gearbox inner end cover. With this construction the assembly of shafts, gears and selector mechanism could be put together on the bench and fitted to the shell as a single unit.

Unit construction

The outer cover was shaped to blend in with the crankcase in front of it and carried the gear-change pawl mechanism, the gear pedal, the clutch worm and a bearing for the kickstarter spindle. This last item worked on the layshaft bottom gear, which had an internal ratchet. The kickstarter pawl engaged with this to start the engine and was held out of mesh by a plate when not required. Final drive was by chain on the left.

Lubrication of the various parts was quite separate, with the engine using the familiar twin-plunger pump driven from the inlet camshaft and a dry sump system. The gearbox and primary chaincase were both separate and each had its own filler plug, level and drain. The rocker gear was lubricated from the scavenge return line to the oil tank and the pressure valve and indicator were fitted in the front of the crankcase forward of the timing case.

The frame of the new machine was straightforward, with a single down tube and single top

Below right **Tiger 100A in 1961 with nacelle and ample front mudguard. Parcel grid still in use**

Below **The model 21 plus windscreen, apron and legshields to supplement the bathtub**

Bottom **1960 model Tiger 100A with unit construction engine and bathtub enclosure**

tube. This curved down at the steering head and then ran back parallel to the ground, but at tank rail level until it turned down to form the single saddle tube. The lower ends of down and saddle tubes were joined by duplex engine rails. The rear sub-frame was separate and bolted into position, while the swinging fork for the rear wheel pivoted on a pin clamped in a lug attached to the saddle tube. Wheel movement was controlled by two Girling units with pre-load adjustment.

Front forks followed normal Triumph practice, with a nacelle fitted to carry the headlamp, instruments and switches. Both wheels were of 17 in. diameter with 3·25 in. section tyres and had 7 in. diameter brakes. The front hub was a full-width unit, but the rear was not. A quickly detachable version was also available as an option and either type incorporated the speedometer drive. Both brakes were single leading-shoe type.

The most striking feature of the new machine was its styling, with much of the rear half enclosed. This was done with two steel panels which joined at front and rear on the centre line, the joint being covered with a rubber strip. The panels were also supported by the seat loop of the sub-frame and fastened to its tubes. The nose of the enclosure picked up on the rear tank bolt. The front mudguard was much larger than usual to balance the styling and provide good weather protection and only required a single mounting stay at the rear in addition to its attachments to the front forks. Both front mudguard and enclosure were ribbed along their edges for strength and rigidity.

The dual seat was matched to the rear enclosure and hinged on the left. When raised it disclosed a tool kit, with each item located in a

Unit construction

recess in a moulded rubber tray, and also gave access to the battery, oil tank filler cap, ignition coil and rectifier. The seat could be locked down with an anti-theft catch to protect the contents. The very tidy lines were enhanced by the fitting of an extra-deep chain-guard that reached down to the fork tube, supplemented by a guard on the lower run welded to the underside of the brake torque arm.

Inevitably the rear enclosure became known as the 'bathtub', for it was very reminiscent of the old-fashioned hip bath, inverted.

The all-over finish was a metallic silver grey with chrome-plated brightwork, and the weight was 340 lb. With a power output of 18·5 bhp it could run up to the 80 mph mark, but its true metier was as a quiet, clean tourer and commuter. In this it was very successful, being comfortable and easy to ride with no vices or problems. It went on sale at a basic £175, which, with purchase tax, increased to £217.

One or two changes were incorporated during the year, with the fuel tank being modified to take the luggage grid fitted as standard on the other twins. The frame had further lugs added, which allowed a prop stand to be fitted and provided mountings for panniers. The finish also changed, with the frame being painted black and the remainder of the machine shell blue, while its name 'Twenty-One' continued to adorn each side of the bathtub in metal script.

In September 1958 the 350 became known as the model 3TA and at the same time a 500 cc version, the 5TA, was introduced to take the place of the original Speed Twin. The new model was nearly identical to the 350, having a larger bore of 69 mm but the same stroke. Apart from head, barrel and pistons it was the same machine with raised gearing, a slightly fatter rear tyre and different paint. The finish was the traditional amaranth red; in fact it could hardly have been anything else. The old name continued, with 'Speed Twin' on the sides of the bathtub, and the machine weighed in at 350 lb dry.

Early in the new year *The Motor Cycle* published a road test of the 500 and reported favourably. Although still a little tight it proved capable of over 85 mph, while returning 75 to the gallon over give-and-take conditions. Acceleration was brisk, handling characteristically light and the suspension a touch on the hard side. The brakes were good and the engine consumed one pint of oil in 600 miles.

For the 1960 season the 500 cc engine was fitted with a primary-chain blade tensioner. This was rubber faced and adjusted by a threaded pull rod which was accessible from behind and below the chaincase. Also new was a sports version of the 500 cc model, which replaced the pre-unit machine and continued the well-known name, being typed the Tiger 100A. This was fitted with special cams, a higher compression ratio of 9:1, a five-plate clutch and different silencers. Ignition was by an energy transfer system, with two of the alternator coils linked directly to the ignition coil so that it could work with the battery flat or even removed. It was to prove critical of points and timing settings. Finish was all black except for the lower section of the petrol tank, which was painted ivory.

Tested by *Motor Cycling* in early 1960 the Tiger ran up to 95 mph with the wind and 77 mph against it with brisk acceleration. Fuel consumption came out at 76 mpg over 500 miles and the brakes worked well. Servicing procedures were checked over and found easy to do, with most points very accessible.

In September 1960 the changes for 1961 were announced and at first sight seemed minimal. However, they did in fact include a change of steering-head angle and fully floating brake shoes on all twin-cylinder models. The Speed Twin had its gearing lowered a shade, and the 3TA was fitted with the primary chain tensioner used on the larger engine. The Tiger engine was given a change of camshaft and an increase in carburettor size. For police use the 350 was also available with an electric starter fitted to the

1961 Tiger 110 with sleek enclosure but pre-unit engine and magneto ignition

front of the crankcase and driving through the timing gear—in effect a reverse of the pre-unit dynamo drive. The installation was extremely neat, with the starter lying in holes formed in the front engine plates, with its supply cable running down and under the crankcase.

September 1961 brought news of the 1962 models, and the main change in the unit construction machines was to the sports 500. The Tiger 100A was replaced by the Tiger 100SS, which had changes to both engine and styling. The bathtub was replaced by a much abbreviated version cut off along a line running from the rear of the gearbox to the top suspension unit mounting. The headlamp nacelle went as well and was replaced by a chrome-plated separate shell mounted on lugs from the fork shrouds. With this change the ignition and light switch was moved to a position just below the dualseat nose on the left side panel. The forks themselves acquired gaiters and the wheel sizes went up to 19 in. front and 18 in. rear. Sports mudguards were fitted.

The engine was fitted with redesigned camshafts and its output quoted as 34 bhp at 7000 rpm. Ignition was by coil, the energy transfer system having been dropped and a siamezed exhaust system connected to a low-level tubular silencer.

The other two machines also had siamezed exhausts and all used a new design of silencer in which inlet and exhaust pipes were coaxial, not offset as before. The steering damper was no longer fitted, RM19 alternators replaced the earlier arrangements and a new method was adopted to attach the clutch cable to the arm at the gearbox. This allowed the cable to be changed without taking the end cover off the box, as had been necessary before.

Motor Cycling road tested the new Tiger 100SS late in 1961 and managed a lap of MIRA at 96 mph with a best speed of 98 mph. They also managed to achieve a consumption of 82 mpg over 500 miles despite considerable fast road work. The brakes worked well, although heavy use did promote a slight touch of fade. The handlebar ends sloped down slightly and this caused some aches in the wrists, but otherwise

Unit construction

comfort was good. The moulded rubber toolpan had been replaced by a tool roll squeezed in by the oil tank and replacement was not easy. Frequent use was likely to short out the main electric supply wire, so in all this was not an improvement.

The magazine followed this up with a Speed Twin test early in 1962 and had the machine fitted with a fairing. This made it even more suitable for fast cruising, and high speeds failed to distress the engine. Handling remained satisfactory even in gusty conditions, and the brakes worked as well as ever.

Right **The unit construction 650 cc engine for 1963. This is the Thunderbird with one carburettor**

Below **Tiger 90 for 1963 with partial rear enclosure and points in timing case**

1963 model Bonneville with separate headlamp shell. A classic motorcycle

In July *The Motor Cycle* reported on the 350 cc model and rode it hard enough over 900 miles to put the consumption figure at 66 mpg. It also used two pints of oil, but the figures included performance testing and considerable 70 mph cruising. Maximum speed was 82 mph, but the machine was quick and nimble with good brakes, so could put up fast averages. Vibration was minimal, occurring between 55 and 60 mph, but otherwise was of no consequence.

In October 1962 the 3TA was joined by a sports version called the Tiger 90. It made its debut at the Paris show and followed the general lines of the Tiger 100SS in its styling with separate headlamp and partial rear enclosure. The engine was based on the existing 350 cc twin, but had bigger inlet valves, a sports camshaft, a 9:1 compression ratio and a larger carburettor. The ignition system was also revised, with the distributor being replaced by a twin contact breaker assembly mounted in the timing case with the cam driven from the end of the exhaust camshaft. Twin coils were rubber mounted to the frame tank rail. A siamezed exhaust system was fitted and separate light and ignition switches on the left enclosure panel.

Other changes to the 350 and 500 cc models were the adoption of a three-vane clutch shock absorber and a miniature Lucas rectifier. The Tiger 100 was fitted with the contact breakers in the timing case, but the touring models continued with their distributors and also reverted to twin exhaust pipes and silencers, although the siamezed system was still available as an option. All had new-style rocker caps with knurled edges, which were locked with spring blades.

The major change to the 650 cc twins was to unit construction of engine and gearbox. The detail design used followed that laid down by the Twenty-One, with the gearbox carried in the right crankcase half and accessible without disturbing the engine. Much of the inside of the engine was unchanged, but a new light-alloy cylinder head with increased fin area was fitted and the fins were extended to the sides of the rocker boxes. With a new head the opportunity was taken to place the fixing bolts on a wider spacing and to add a ninth one between the cylinders. As with the Tiger 90 engine, ignition was controlled by twin contact breakers housed in the timing cover, with their cam driven from the exhaust camshaft.

Unit construction

Primary drive was by duplex chain with a slipper tensioner, and the clutch was redesigned and operated by a ball-and-ramp mechanism. The gearbox followed normal Triumph practice and had the layshaft fitted below the mainshaft, with the operating camplate pivoted on the casting wall in front of the two shafts. A conventional positive stop gearchange was fitted and the layshaft ran on needle rollers and drove the speedometer cable.

The new engine unit was fitted into a new frame with single down tube and bolted on sub-frame. The swinging-fork rear suspension was controlled by two units and at the front the Triumph telescopic forks were fitted.

The unit construction 650 was produced in three forms, the most docile of which was the Thunderbird, fitted with a single carburettor. Alone among the big twins it retained the nacelle headlamp, but its bathtub was abbreviated to the partial enclosure of the smaller sports twins. The Trophy and the Bonneville were very similar, but the Trophy only had one carburettor and a siamezed exhaust system while its companion had two of both. Both machines were fitted with gaiters on their front forks.

The Motor Cycle conducted a quick test on the Bonneville and found that the change to unit construction had not affected the way in which the engine delivered its power. Low down, the tickover was fast because the test machine was fitted with the energy transfer ignition system that was an American market option. It limited the automatic timing range, hence the fast idling and a tendency to kick back when starting.

Handling was excellent up to 100 mph, and only above this speed could any weaving be detected. That problem was already under Doug Hele's eye for attention. The riding position was comfortable, but some vibration got through to the handlebar grips. There were no oil leaks, but the exhaust pipes turned blue rather rapidly.

Motor Cycling replied with a Tiger 90 test, and in poor conditions recorded a mean speed of 89 mph at MIRA, so the model was aptly named. They returned an overall consumption figure of

The Speed Twin with unit construction engine, still with distributor for 1963

68 mpg, so must have used the acceleration to good purpose. Despite the power being mainly at the top end of the scale the engine proved to be very tractable. So it was equally at home in town.

Motorcycle Sport also rode the new sports 350 for an hour and liked it. Performance was good, but the front brake a little disappointing, while the front fork was deemed to have a stiff action.

During the first half of 1963 an agreement was made between Triumph and Mitchenall Brothers, who produced the Avonaire dolphin fairing for all the models. This fitted well to the twin range and was matched to the bathtubs and partial skirts on the machines fitted with them.

About this time sales manager Neale Shilton christened the police specification 650 the Saint, from its ability to 'scoop (or stop) anything in no time'. The police model was the latest in the long line stretching back over the years and was based on the Thunderbird without the skirt and fitted with a single seat. They could be, and were, fitted with radio equipment and emergency gear for coping with both accidents and crime.

The Motor Cycle had one on test during the year and listed the modifications fitted. Aside from the chassis, the engine had the Bonneville inlet camshaft and a different Monobloc and air cleaner. Smaller-diameter exhaust pipes connected to extra-large silencers and the generator was to the high output specification. Wide gearbox ratios were fitted along with a lowered top gear, so the machine was equally at home trickling along in a procession as it was accelerating fiercely to a maximum around the 100 mph mark. Just the job for police work, and it could have been equally nice for fast touring.

During 1963 *The Motor Cycle* had three other Triumph twins on test, the first being the Tiger 90, for which they confirmed the earlier findings, with easy cruising at 75 mph, a good gearbox and excellent lights. The horn earned a debit as it

ISDT preparation in 1963 with air bottle, tank top bag and qd features

Unit construction

had a weak note and the stop lamp switch jammed on, so flattening the battery. This, however, really did prove that the emergency ignition system worked.

The 350 was followed by a Thunderbird with an Avon sidecar, the machine being fitted with the siamezed exhaust system. The outfit proved good for 76 mph, with plenty of low-down urge available to pull the chair along. The horn was considered too quiet and the rear chain needed

Right **A detail from the 1964 Trophy machine. Twin electric switches and drip tray over air cleaner to keep water at bay**

Bottom **The super-sports Thruxton Bonneville fitted with many optional parts as standard. Here making its debut at Earls Court 1964**

attention every 400 miles. Apart from this, maintenance was no problem, although rear wheel removal would have been awkward as no centre stand was fitted.

Following this the magazine had a solo Thunderbird to test, not the previous one less sidecar, and this proved good for 104 mph, but had the same poor horn as the other machines. All told it produced just the type of performance expected from it and what owners had become used to expecting from Triumph. The weight was still only 374 lb as tested with some petrol in the tank so, with 34 bhp available, it could hardly do other than offer high-speed, low rpm, easy-on-the-rider cruising. Brakes and handling were up to the power, so the result was a very satisfactory motorcycle.

The changes for 1964 centred on styling and new front forks, which were fitted to all the twins. The bathtubs disappeared from the 3TA and 5TA, which adopted the partial enclosure from the more sporting machines and in turn these lost their enclosures completely.

On the smaller twins the camshaft-driven contact breaker became standard on all models, the clutch operation was modified and a magnetic speedometer fitted in addition to the new forks and rubber mounting of the oil tank. All now had two separate exhaust systems, that of the Tiger 90 having smaller-diameter pipes.

The sports 650s received slightly larger inlet valves and carburettors, together with the new-style speedometer. An induction balance pipe was fitted to the Bonneville, while the Thunderbird was changed to 12-volt electrics and fitted with new slotted-skirt pistons to reduce running clearances. All 650s had the footrests raised and mounted to the rear of the engine plates above the exhaust pipes and changes to the crankcase breather timing. Scavenging was improved by changes to the sump filter and drain plug.

In January *Motor Cycling* road tested the Speed Twin and summed it up as a fast and flexible multi, just as they had in 1937. It ran up to nearly 90 mph and returned a respectable 76 mpg on some fast journeys. They found the new forks were of limited movement and, although the machine handled well, it could be tiring on long runs. Curiously the speedometer was illegally slow at 30 and 40 mph and only at 80 mph did it read fast—by one-tenth of an mph.

Motor Cycle had a Bonneville on test a little later that year and ran it up to a maximum of 112 mph, while finding it quiet and unobtrusive in town. It was comfortable, it handled and the brakes worked, no wonder it was so popular in the early 1960s.

The remarks about the forks bore fruit, for they were further modified for the 1965 season, along with the rear brake. The front mudguards of the touring models were made smaller and more sporting and on the smaller machines the petrol tank was rubber mounted. The 350 cc models received a new cylinder head and all engines had the flywheels machined with a slot to enable top dead centre to be located. This was done with a plunger that slid in a housing screwed into a tapped hole in the crankcase. Suitable dimensioning gave tdc when the pin dropped in and

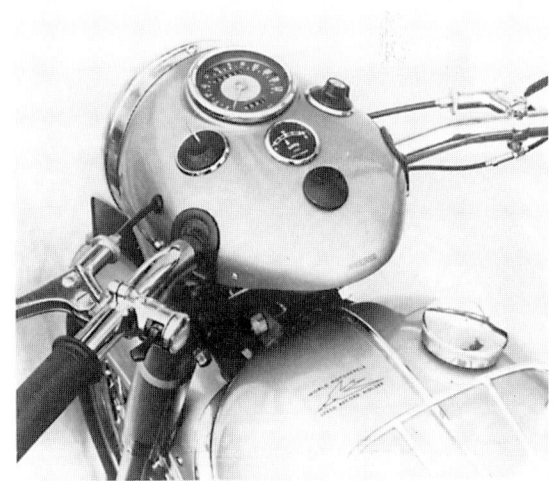

The famous nacelle carrying switches and instruments. World record transfer on tank with parcel grid

the housing was replaced with a plug in normal use.

A further version of the T120 appeared at the Earls Court Show fitted with high-performance parts, a fairing and rear sets ready for production racing and was called the Thruxton Bonneville. In fact it was only to remain in the lists for six months before being discontinued. As it was, any owner could build up the same machine using the listed extras provided he could obtain them, and at the time there was some argument as to the real availability of extras from any of the makers of machines whose products competed in production races. This naturally mainly concerned those makes which habitually finished first and this was a Triumph in many cases.

During 1964 Edward Turner officially retired, although he remained very much in touch with the industry and was to lay down the prototype design of the 350 cc twin described in a later chapter. With his departure the dynamic, single-minded determination to build motorcycles and sell them at a good profit began to slip away to be replaced by committee control, excess management and, eventually, design from afar. It was a gradual process and for some years all appeared well, as the company continued to trade profitably. Such problems as did occur tended to be put down to one piece of real bad luck. Turner's successor was Harry Sturgeon, a man of energy, and although he did not have a motorcycle background it seemed that he would continue both the technical leadership into new areas and maintain the commercial strategy which brought the company Queen's Awards to Industry in 1967 and 1968. Very sadly, he died after a short illness after three years with the company, when he would have begun to implement policies for the 1970s. His position was taken by Lionel Jofeh, who started up a new and expensive research and development centre at Umberslade Hall in Warwickshire. By this time the managers in both Triumph and BSA, who had a real solid background of motorcycling, were

1964 model Twenty-one with partial rear enclosure and points in timing case

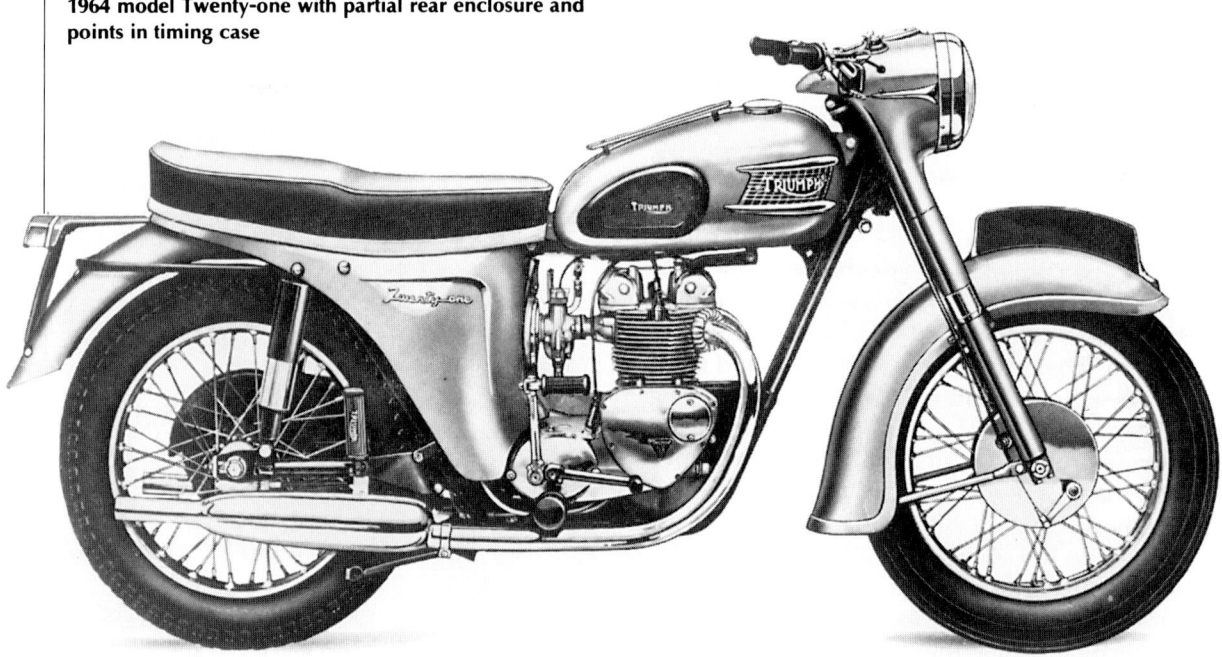

beginning to feel more than a little worried. They found themselves beginning to be hemmed in on many sides by quick-fire executives with expertise in accountancy, marketing and public relations but no knowledge of motorcycles and the people who bought them.

Two changes at the top in quick succession seldom help a company and for the group other problems began to appear. A series of financial deals to streamline the group cost them several million pounds in the end, and, after years of producing lightweights, the Japanese were to move into the traditional British market of large-capacity machines in the late 1960s. The 500 cc Kawasaki triple may not have handled very well, but the performance was electrifying, as it could outrun just about every 650 then available. It was followed by the first CB750 Honda in 1968 and, from then on, a steady stream of sophisticated machines came out of the East.

Triumph continued with their range of 360-degree twins, although the public was to gradually become less tolerant of the inherent vibration problems. Other makes began to enlarge their parallel twins and so achieved faster road-test speeds. Most buyers went for this, because anyone could hide behind the filler cap and watch the often optimistic speedometer. The enthusiast preferred less top end, better economy, good handling, comfort and the ease of travelling long distances without strain, but he did not buy many new machines.

Edward Turner would have known this and

Above **Press photo of Trophy issued by BSA on behalf of Triumph. Nice house as well**

Below **Single carburettor Trophy for 1965. Very similar to Bonneville but more tractable**

Above **Control layout of Trophy with Watsonian on test late 1965**

Left **A picture that captures the spirit of riding a Triumph in the 1960s**

produced an answer. Just as in 1937 it would have appealed to all types of riders and been a commercial success. Whether the climate of the times would have put up with someone such as Turner is possibly doubtful, but he would have just ignored the critics and committees and done what he felt to be best as always.

In the middle of 1965 the Thruxton Bonneville was dropped and in September the range for the next season announced. All the twins received a revised oil tank of 6 pints capacity with an improved mounting. From it was taken a metered supply to the rear chain, and this came from the return line. The regulating screw was in the neck of the filler and very accessible once the cap was removed.

Twelve-volt electrics were adopted by all the twins, with the zener diode mounted behind the left side panel away from the steering head position used on the Thunderbird. The rear enclosure disappeared, even in its abbreviated form, and so did the 17 in. wheels of the smaller tourers and the special tyre sizes on the Trophy, which changed to the Bonneville sizes in the interests of standardization.

On the 350 and 500 cc models the frame was modified to have a straight top tube braced by a tank tube in the normal manner and the ignition of the Tiger versions was controlled by a barrel lock mounted in the left side panel and switched with a car-type key. A red tell-tale light was fitted in the

Unit construction

headlamp shell and a cut-out button on the right handlebar. As the light remained on all the time the ignition was on it did cause some confusion. The rev-counter drive from the 650, with its right-angle gearbox, also became available as an option for the Tigers, the direct drive being dropped as it had made the cable rather vulnerable. The right-angle drive would, in fact, fit earlier models, but its use required a change of counter head as the cable speed was halved.

All the twins were given a new tank badge with the name of the company made more prominent, while they continued to fit kneegrips carrying the Triumph logo, which also appeared on the footrest and pedal rubbers.

The three 650 cc machines also had frame changes, as the steering-head angle was altered to improve the handling and the new headstock incorporated lugs for mounting a fairing and a recess for a steering lock. On the Thunderbird the nacelle had to be removed if the fairing lugs were to be used. The front brakes were changed to give a considerable increase in width by the addition of a spoke flange. This allowed the drum surface to extend to the edge of the hub and the flange improved the rigidity of the drum itself. The rear wheel was changed slightly to allow the speedometer drive to be taken from it, so the gearbox also was modified to delete the speedometer driving gear and its mating pinion.

The flywheel weight in the 650 cc engines was reduced to improve acceleration and the drive-side main bearing changed from a ball to a lipped roller, while the pushrod-tube oil seals were

Top **The T100C Tiger built for the USA and later sold on the home market. Designed for enduro use with energy transfer ignition**

Above **Trophy for 1967. A very fine motorcycle and one of the nicest Triumph twins**

Left **1966 Tiger 100 now without enclosure and fitted with more sporting mudguards**

improved. The kickstarter lever was lengthened by 1 in., and one reason for this was an increase in compression ratio on the Bonneville to 9:1. This engine was also fitted with racing tappets which had a much larger base radius to provide faster lift and so 'beef-up' the midrange torque. These tappets normally wore the cams more rapidly than usual, so an oil supply was provided through drillings from the pressure-release valve to the exhaust tappet block and so down onto the working faces. Like the Tiger models, both the Bonneville and the Trophy were fitted with a cut-out on the handlebars and had provision for the right-angle rev-counter gearbox driven from the end of the exhaust camshaft remote from the contact breakers.

Early in 1966 *Motor Cycling* tested the Bonneville and reported that the new frame was an improvement giving taut steering. However, they criticized the position of the bars as being too far behind the steering head and the hardness of the rear suspension. Other complaints concerned the position of the light switch, the dipswitch—which was too far from the grip—the bright ignition light and the unnecessary cut-out button. The tools were still crammed into a small space, so required careful packing, but most of the routine service tasks were easy enough to carry out. Vibration occurred to some extent between 3000 and 5000 rpm and one or two parts dropped off. So, despite the machine's speed and undoubted many good points, there were signs that practising motorcyclists were becoming less involved with its design.

Other tests of other machines in the range during the year confirmed that the handling was now really excellent on both large and small models, although just as consistently the testers reported vibration somewhere in the speed range and a complete reluctance of the clutch to free itself. This clutch problem sometimes made the gearchange noisy, but itself stood up to innumerable standing starts during performance testing.

In July the three touring models, the 350 cc 3TA, the 500 cc 5TA and the 650 cc Thunderbird, were dropped from the range, so the famous nacelle, first seen in 1948, was no longer a feature. November saw the launch of the 1967 range and in their place was a super sports 500 twin with two carburettors, the Daytona Tiger, evolved from the machine which had won the American classic that year. To distinguish it from its simpler companion it was coded T100T and the engine was built to a high-performance specification, being fitted with a new-type cylinder head with shallow combustion chamber, narrower valve angle, splayed inlet ports, 9:1 compression ratio and with Bonneville-type cams operating tappets with large-radius feet. It was fitted in a new frame which changed the head angle and braced the fork pivot while reducing the seat height slightly. It carried a new dualseat, which was slimmer at the front, had a small rise at the rear and was transversely ribbed.

The new 500 was fitted with the 8 in. Bonneville front brake and its frame was also used by the remaining two Tiger models. These and the two larger models all had changes to the gearbox splines and the mainshaft thread extended to allow the use of a self-locking nut to hold the clutch on in place of the old nut and lockwasher.

The 650 cc models were both fitted with a new oil pump with increased scavenging capacity, the new dualseat and a steering lock built into the top yoke. Some of the Bonneville parts were used in the Trophy to give it a Jekyll and Hyde character and it now also had a 9:1 compression ratio. All models had the lighting switch in the headlamp and a louder horn.

The accent of the range was very much on high performance and some began to feel that, while fitting the high-performance parts as standard might have won an added horse at the top end of the power scale, it was to the detriment of the machine's general performance. Much of this stemmed from the needs of the USA and, during the 1960s, variants were built to suit both East and West Coast requirements. This resulted in a substantial number of alternative parts as machines were built with or without lights and with high- or low-level exhausts, with or without silencers. Alternative handlebars, fuel tanks, competition levers and mudguards were all produced and many variations built up by ringing the changes with these. Power outputs also rose to over 50 bhp using 11:1 pistons, large inlet valves and big carburettors, all of which was far beyond Turner's original conception for a 360-degree twin.

Back in England *Motorcycle Sport* tested the single-carburettor Tiger 100 and reported that it still performed much as the original had in 1938, with high average speeds possible from the combination of power, handling and low weight. *Motor Cyclist Illustrated* had the Bonneville and a Saint and it was the latter they preferred for all-round use, although it was of course not on general sale. *Motor Cycle News* had the Daytona Tiger and achieved 111 mph with it, together with an overall fuel consumption of 64 mpg.

At least one 500 cc model to American specification reached the English market, for *Motor Cycle* ran a competition in the middle of the year for a T100C. This was built for enduro use with a single-carburettor engine producing 38 bhp at 7000 rpm with high-level exhausts, both swept round onto the left side of the machine. It had energy transfer ignition, no battery and quickly detachable lights. Later in the year the model with some changes became available in its own country fitted with 12-volt coil ignition and trials tyres of 3·50 and 4·00 in. section on 19 in. rims. It was priced at £315.

For 1968 the Daytona head was also fitted to the single-carburettor Tiger 100 and the 650s were fitted with an 8 in., twin leading-shoe front brake. All the twins had the electrics and the left side panel modified, as the panel itself was hinged to the frame and carried the tools in a

The 1967 Bonneville with two carburettors and splayed inlet port cylinder head

compartment on its inner face, which gave far more room than before. To assist in this the zener diode was given a new finned heat sink of nose-cone shape sited under the headlamp, while the ignition switch was fitted to the left headlamp stay and the light switch, changed for a toggle type, to the headlamp.

All engines now had the notched flywheel and location plug together with a detachable plate in the primary chaincase, whose removal allowed the ignition timing to be checked with a strobe light. The contact-breaker design was changed so that each pair of points could be independently set and timed.

The internals of the front forks were improved with a floating shuttle valve and all machines fitted with Amal concentric carburettors in place of the earlier Monobloc. The new front brake incorporated an air scoop with mesh cover and, by the end of the year, was fitted to the Daytona Tiger as well as the 650 cc machines.

So the Triumph twins ran to the end of the sixties with the accent firmly on high performance, even if more and more road tests began to remark on the intractable manner in which the power was produced and the vibration problems. The latter began to leave a trail of

Above **1968 model Bonneville with twin leading shoe brake, high bars and side reflectors**

Below **Drive side of 1968 Trophy, little different from the T120. Home market finish**

Unit construction

Left **Timing side of 1968 Tiger 90. Few engine changes from first 21 but very different styling**

Below left **The 1969 model Trophy with revised front brake linkage and exhaust balance pipe**

Below **1970 Bonneville in home market form. The last model before the Umberslade Hall frame**

shattered bulbs and broken brackets in its wake, but the only remedy was an attempt to rubber mount some items while engine speeds continued to rise.

Late in 1968 the Tiger 90 was dropped from the range but during the year a five-speed gearbox cluster became available for the 650 cc models. It was made and sold by Rod Quaife and intended for both road racing and fast road use.

The changes for 1969 were minor, as the real news was the introduction of the Trident, recorded in a later chapter. The twins received new tank badges and lost the covers from the rear spring units. An oil pressure warning switch replaced the tell-tale button and was wired to an indicator light, which replaced the ignition-on one. The Bonneville carburettor mounting was changed to combat vibration and this model was fitted with twin windtone horns and, for the first time, air cleaners. All models had modified silencers and were fitted with balance pipes between the exhausts near to the cylinder head and had front brake stop light switches fitted. The Tiger 100 was fitted with a twin leading-shoe brake of 7 in. diameter. Front brake operation on all models

followed group practice with BSA and had the two cam levers linked and a second arm on one for the cable to connect to. It was to prove rather spongy compared with the earlier and more direct arrangement.

In this form the four twins ran on into 1970 up to the tremendous group launch held in November. At this time the group was in serious financial trouble due to a number of major technical and managerial blunders, but held a massive trade and press release with 13 new or revised models on show. Among them were the 350 cc ohc twin, covered later, the Ariel 3, and a revised list of twins with much in common with the BSA range.

The 500 cc range was comprised of two machines, the T100R, which was a direct replacement for the Daytona Tiger, with minimal change, and the T100C, a street scrambler with one carburettor and twin upswept exhaust pipes on the left of the machine.

The 650 cc range comprised three models, and it was these that received the bulk of the changes. The Bonneville was recoded the T120R and the Trophy renamed as the TR6R, or Tiger 650. The third model was called the Trophy 650 TR6C and was a street scrambler similar to the 500 cc model but based on the Tiger 650.

The main change was to the frame, which was designed to contain the engine oil, but new forks, hubs, and many detail parts were also fitted. The

Daytona Tiger 100 of 1970 fitted with twin leading shoe front brake

Unit construction

new frame was based on a very large-diameter tube, which ran back from the headstock and at the seat nose turned to drop vertically behind the engine unit. This tube carried the oil and was sealed at its lowest point by a plate which located a gauze filter onto the outlet pipe and carried a drain plug. The filler cap was at the bend in the frame tube.

The remainder of the frame comprised duplex tubes and the new forks had exposed stanchions without gaiters and new internals. The wheels had new conical hubs, the front containing a new design of 8 in. twin leading-shoe brake operated by a single cable which pulled one cam lever and pushed the other. Adjustment was by serrated cam accessible via a hole in the hub, which was sealed with a plug. The rear hub contained a single leading shoe brake and had lost the quickly detachable facility.

The problems of Meriden really began to take hold at this point. The plant was in trouble due to the lack of finance and had been kept on a very short rein by the group for some while. Relations within the group had become strained as Umberslade Hall began to dictate design and the group management set general policy. It is possibly significant that Edward Turner retired from the BSA board the same year that Umberslade was set up. The outcome of the changes was that machine alterations began to take months to be incorporated, most of the gearbox parts were altered by minute amounts that were difficult to detect but unacceptable on assembly, and the Triumph development department became more of a Trident race shop.

When the new range was launched in November 1970 there were no tools available to build the new frames so a crash programme had to be undertaken that winter, while the works built 500 cc machines and 650 cc engine units. Crash programmes are always costly and, once the works had used up all the available 500 cc parts and had run out of space for storing engine units, they had to sit and wait for the tooling and new

Top **The five-speed gearbox produced by Rod Quaife for the 650 cc models**

Above **1970 Trophy model of 500 cc in trail bike form but with indicators**

production lines to be completed.

Then the engine could not be fitted to the frame unless the rocker boxes were removed and once this was done and the engine installed the boxes could not be refitted. After modification this and other problems were sorted out and machines began to reach the market, only to be ridiculed by trade, press and public. The seat was a good inch too high, so that coming to a halt became a decided hazard except for very above-average-height riders.

With major design problems to solve, severe financial cramp and so many new machines, the group troubles began to go from bad to worse and Triumph began to slide, with BSA, towards the end. However, unlike BSA, which just came to an untidy halt, Meriden and Triumph were on the point of becoming a nationwide news item. Late in 1971 a company doctor was appointed, this being a fashionable business policy at that time. Machine ranges were drastically pruned, the Ariel 3 dropped, the 350 Bandit not started, and Umberslade Hall closed. Machines continued to be built at Meriden with some engine production at Small Heath.

In August 1971 the two street scrambler models were dropped from the home-market range and production continued with three twins into 1972 with some substantial price rises. During that year a five-speed gearbox became available for the Bonneville and, in time, the four-speed unit was phased out. In August an enlarged version of the twin was introduced, originally bored to 75 mm to give 725 cc capacity, but quickly opened up a further millimetre to give 744 cc capacity.

This enlarged engine produced much more mid-range torque than the 650 cc twin and its appearance required new crankcases to accommodate the larger barrel. The head fixing was changed to a 10-stud layout, the primary chain to a triplex type, and the transmission 'beefed up'. It was fitted with a five-speed gearbox as standard and for 1973 a 10 in. diameter disc brake on the front wheel. At the same time a street scrambler version, the TR7RV, was introduced along with a trail 500 cc model. This last, known as the Adventurer but carrying logos of 'Trophy Trail' on its side covers, was reminiscent of the early TR5. However, the exhaust pipes led to a joint in front of the crankcase, only protected by a plate, and on to a nondescript black silencer. The arrangement lacked the style of the earlier machine.

Production continued, but by this time the future of Meriden had become a political matter involving the government at high level and

Top **1972 Bonneville engine with new valve covers and push-in exhaust pipes without stubs**

Middle **New style twin leading shoe front brake and modified fork end. Introduced for 1971**

Bottom **1973 Tiger 750 out on road test with Bob Currie aboard. Disc front brake**

Unit construction

Dennis Poore of Norton-Villiers. Early in 1973 the NVT group came into existence and, with a cash injection from the Department of Trade, it seemed that the British motorcycle industry would continue.

On August 15, 1973, Edward Turner died at his home at Dorking and with his death vanished one of the most dominant figures from the industry, whose work was to continue on as a legend.

A month later it was announced that Meriden was to be closed down and the work force promptly responded by locking the gates and staging a sit-in. They were totally disillusioned by the events of the previous years and intended to sit firmly, even if illegally, on the tools, parts, machines and equipment at Meriden and sit they did for some 18 months. For all practical purposes production of Triumph motorcycles ceased, although some spares were allowed out to maintain existing machines.

There were many discussions and many proposals, with the work force seeking to form a worker's co-operative. This, however, fell on stony ground as far as the then Conservative government was concerned.

So the workers dug in with their pickets and Triumph dealers and owners found their businesses and machines becoming more and more difficult to maintain.

Stalemate, but not the end.

Top left **Bonneville 750 engine in 1973 during a road test. Air lever mounted by carburettors**

Top middle **Police Saint in 1973. Based on the 750 cc twin with extra equipment added to suit police work. Used by police everywhere**

Top right **The Trophy Trail introduced for 1973 as the Adventurer. Lacks TR5 style**

Right **The Triumph factory in October 1973 at the start of the long, long sit-in**

STAYS AT MERIDEN WHERE THE LEGEND WAS MADE

7 | After Meriden

Early in 1975 NVT ran a 'Bike British' campaign to promote Trident and Commando machines. This was one of the posters used along with combined sales brochures to proclaim the end of hostilities

During the long sit-in at Meriden there were two general elections resulting in a change of government to Labour. As a result of this Tony Benn and Eric Heffer became involved to prevent NVT from taking legal action to retrieve their tools and drawings, which were needed at Small Heath to continue Trident production.

In the second half of 1974 Tridents began to flow from the Birmingham factory and some twins were released from Meriden. However, with the second general election in October the government achieved a working majority and negotiations between them, NVT, Small Heath and Meriden took a turn for the worse. As a result the blockade was reimposed in full strength, so stopping the flow of machines.

Further visits by government ministers finally came up with a solution and, in March 1975, a co-operative was formed and two years later it finally retrieved all rights to the company name from the collapsed NVT group.

Meriden Motorcycles Limited could trade the Triumph machine in the manner of the past, although their troubles were by no means over.

The machines began rolling out from Meriden in March 1975 and, at first, comprised 650 and 750 cc models. However, the smaller twin was dropped as soon as what was the balance of the 1974 production had gone, and in April the first of the co-operative's new 1975 machines was built. In June the last machine with a right gear pedal was produced and from then on the gear levers were fitted on the left of the machine, as had become virtually standard throughout the world.

Only two models were produced for 1976 and these were single- and twin-carburettor versions of the same machine. With two Amals it was called the T140V Bonneville and with one, the TR7RV Tiger, the side panels carrying the appropriate name. Both machines employed the 744 cc twin-cylinder engine with the five-speed gearbox built-in unit. The frame was a modified version of the earlier one carrying the engine oil

Some of the machines that left Meriden when the blockade was temporarily lifted in 1974

in the main spine and the forks were unchanged. The rear wheel gained a disc brake to match the front and was hydraulically operated from a right brake pedal. Handlebar switches were Lucas console type with a rather vague action and crude appearance, and the instruments were changed to types without the NVT logo.

1977 was the Silver Jubilee of Queen Elizabeth's reign and to commemorate this, and in anticipation of a demand for limited-edition ranges, Triumph built the Silver Jubilee Bonneville. The machine was based on the standard 750 twin with a very nice finish in red, white and blue on silver. The primary chaincase and timing cover were chrome plated and Red Arrow tyres and Girling gas rear units were fitted as standard. The tank, mudguards, wheel rims, chain guard and side covers were all very elegantly hand lined in red on white surrounding blue. The body of the tank was finished in silver as were the mudguards and the side covers. These each carried a white panel with a Union Jack, Silver Jubilee 1977 and Limited Edition on them.

One thousand of these machines were built for sale in the UK, each with an individual certificate of origin. A similar quantity went to the USA and a further 400 to other countries.

Few changes were introduced in 1978, although the headlamp became fitted with a halogen bulb and the T140E variant was introduced fitted with Mark 2 Amal concentric carburettors and revised engine breathing. A new cylinder head was introduced to assist running on leaner mixtures and had parallel inlet ports which allowed the use of a common choke lever to both carburettors. These moves all went to help the machine to comply with USA emission legislation. This type of work and the lengthy tests required were particularly difficult for the small factory to carry out, but essential to allow machines to be sold in the important USA market. It did not leave much effort available for other engineering work, but 1979 saw the introduction of electronic ignition as standard with the trigger housed in the former points location. The handlebar controls were cleaned up and better switches fitted.

With the troubles of the early 1970s now well behind them, and only one basic machine to build and sell, Triumph became successful once more and in the late 1970s outsold all their rivals in the 750 cc class in the UK. Whether this was the result of price, nostalgia or the desire for a simpler motorcycle, it was fact and kept Meriden turning out machines at a steady rate. This success culminated in the Bonneville winning the

Top left **1974 Bonneville, one of the few released that year before negotiations went sour**

Top right **Bonneville 750 out on test late in 1978. T140V model with five speeds**

Left **Daytona Tiger not registered until 1974/75 during factory blockade. Drum front brake**

Above **Tiger 750 handlebar layout, controls and instruments in 1976. Note wriggly NVT logo**

prestigious *Motor Cycle News* 'Machine of the Year' title in 1979.

During 1979 a new version was launched, the Bonneville Special. This had cast-alloy Lester wheels and a two-into-one exhaust system with the pipes joining low down at the bottom of the frame to feed the single silencer on the right. It was fitted with a stepped seat and smartly finished in black and gold.

Throughout the period the Triumph retained its light weight and good handling, which, with its mechanical simplicity, ensured a steady demand. Various magazines ran comparative tests against other makes of vertical twins, but nobody came up with any clear answer as to why the Triumph in general, and the Bonneville in particular, had such a loyal following.

As early as 1971 the 650 cc Benelli was being compared with the English machine and this gave a glimmer of the essential cachet of the Triumph for the Italian machine had, and needed, its five speed gearbox. The Triumph could manage with four and five were only fitted because it was expected.

Other comparisons were made with the Laverda, Yamaha and Kawasaki twins but these

Top left **1976 Tiger 750 drive side. Left gear pedal and discs on both wheels**

Bottom left **Silver Jubilee Bonneville with special finish in red, white and blue on silver. Limited edition**

Below **Rear wheel disc brake adopted in 1976, hydraulically operated by right side pedal**

all lacked the low weight and lean lines of the simple Triumph. The most interesting clash was not with a vertical twin but with the big Harley-Davidson vee for both had their own unique charisma and supporters.

So Triumph rolled into 1980 with its own special niche in the world of motorcycling, set by its own brand of style and simplicity.

For 1980 an electric starter was added tucked behind the engine in the old magneto position. A train of gears in a new timing case connected it to the crankshaft while further improvements include a new oil pump and modified exhaust system with more ground clearance.

Outwardly it seemed that the company had at last put its troubles behind it but sadly this was not so. Late in 1979 there were talks of a link with a Japanese trading house associated with Suzuki and then the strong pound inflated US prices so much that sales dropped off badly.

Harry Hooper, chairman of Armstrong Equipment, then came on the scene but while he had the money, he had no intention of taking on the Meriden debt which was up to 12 million pounds and rising another million every three months. He insisted on the government debt being waived and a cut back in the workforce and while the latter took place the former did not.

So the Armstrong bid was not accepted but still the factory persevered. As suggested by Hooper, they planned to move production into a smaller factory behind the main building to reduce a crippling rates bill and, at the Earls Court Show, had a new variant of the Bonneville. This was a Low Rider version called the Phoenix with modified frame, stepped seat, high bars, small tank and fat rear tyre. It was shown to evaluate public reaction with a view to future production.

Then in October 1980 came the startling news that most of the Meriden debts had been wiped off. Some conditions were imposed but none that could prove very arduous, and almost in celebration the factory prepared a new trail bike in two weeks for the Paris Show. It took the name

Top right **Lucas electronic ignition trigger fitted on exhaust camshaft end in place of contact points**

Bottom right **Bonneville Special introduced in 1979 with alloy wheels. Outside company headquarters at Meriden**

Below **Timing side of 1977 Bonneville 750, the year the cooperative retrieved their rights**

'Tiger Trail' and was basically a 750 Tiger with trials tyres, high swept siamezed exhaust system on the left finished in black, high bars, sprung front mudguard, small tank and short dualseat.

In April 1981 the firm revived the Thunderbird name for a reduced cost 650. This was achieved by shortening the stroke to 71.5 mm which meant a new crankshaft and shorter block but put the machine in a better insurance bracket for some. To cut costs a drum rear brake and points ignition were fitted and the engine covers painted matt black. A two-into-one exhaust went on the left.

That month the eight valve engine was shown in the TS8-1 which was styled by Ian Dyson with a fairing and twin headlamps. The engine was rubber mounted to a design from Bernard Hooper who had been responsible for the Commando isolastic system. The eight valve variation was based on a Weslake conversion that had been available for a long time but on the Triumph

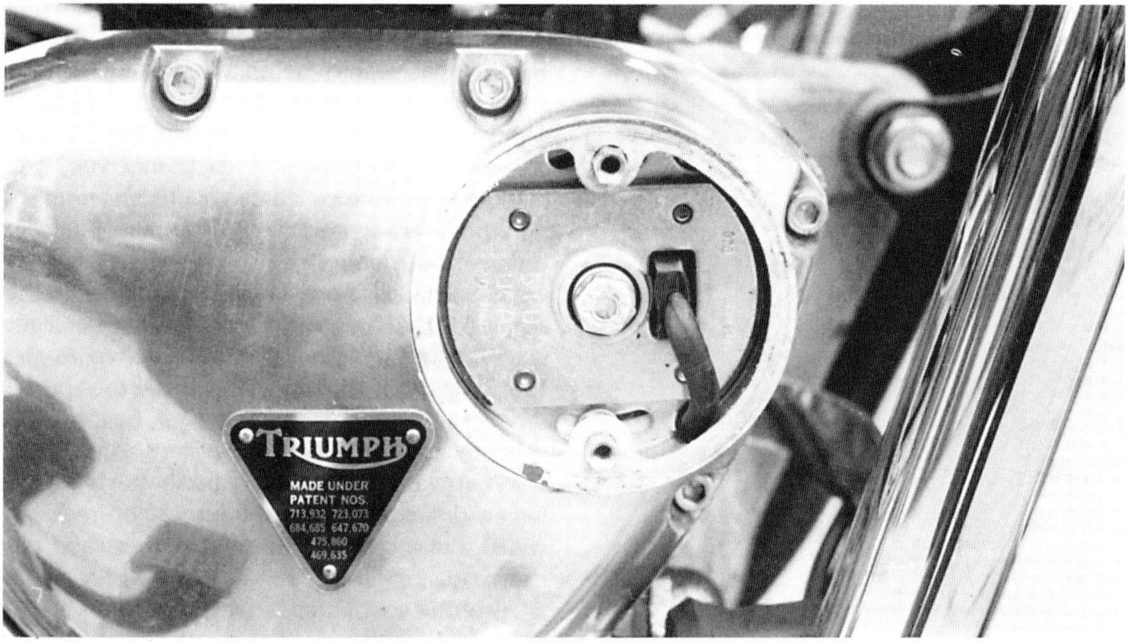
TRIUMPH
MADE UNDER
PATENT NOS.
713,932 723,073
684,685 647,670
475,860
469,635

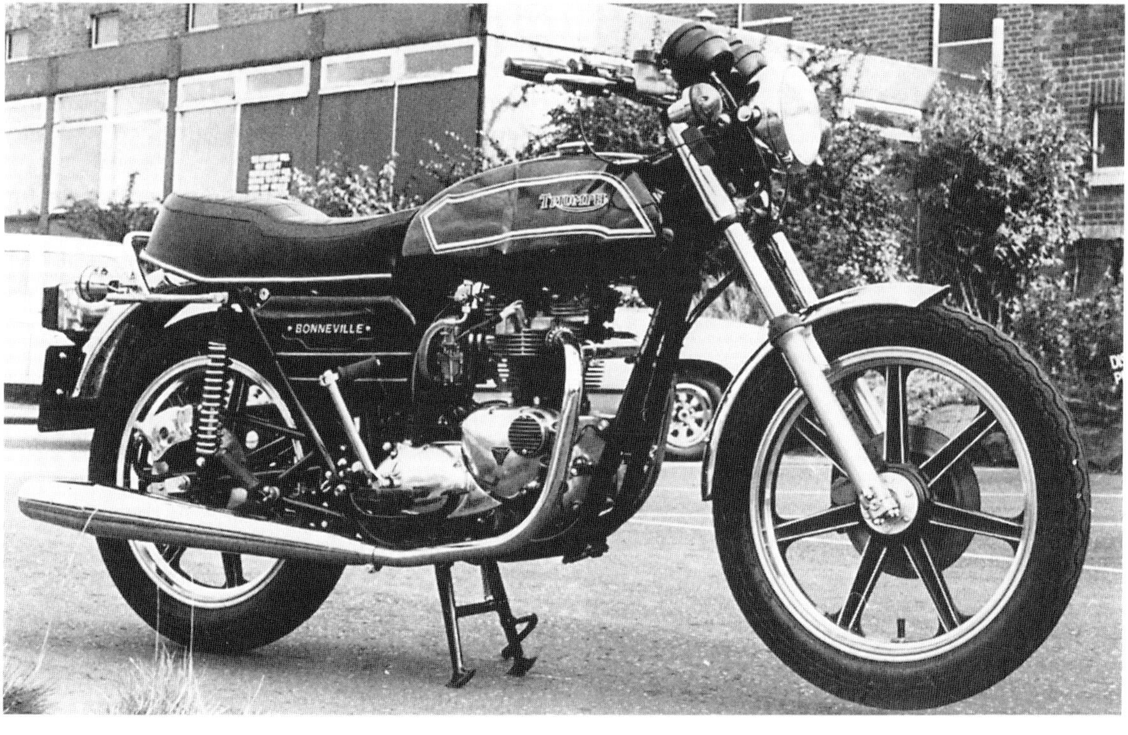
TRIUMPH
BONNEVILLE

Below **Happy indeed is the rider of the Special with the American style high-rise bars and two-into-one exhaust system**

Bottom **Electric start Bonneville introduced in 1980. Neat installation in old magneto position with drive in timing case. Works well**

was to run into a number of problems when it finally reached production.

Later that year came a limited edition of the Bonneville to celebrate the royal wedding of Charles and Diana. The finish was special with chrome plated tank and each machine was marked and came with a certificate.

A trail version of the TR65 appeared late in the year but neither size sold very well so both were dropped during late 1982. Earlier, in the spring of that year, the model with the eight valve engine had finally been launched as the TSS. In its production form it had lost the special styling and rubber mounting to become, in essence, an eight valve Bonneville.

What was new was the crankshaft which had larger diameter big end journals of reduced width that increased the shaft stiffness and cut down on vibration.

Also new in the range was a custom version of the Bonneville known as the TSX. It had Morris cast wheels, 16 inch rear tyre, high bars and megaphone style silencers. Otherwise the Bonneville and Thunderbird continued with each in UK and USA forms along with the Tiger Trail and Bonneville Executive Electro with its cockpit fairing, panniers and top box.

Times were however getting even harder for the workers at Meriden and there was talk of moving into a smaller factory. The snag as always was money and the costs of just owning Meriden for there were few customers for factories in 1982.

Somehow production continued and the firm was on show early in 1983. Of real interest was an all-new, water-cooled, twin overhead camshaft vertical twin built as a prototype and also shown as a complete machine. At the same time the TSX was listed with the eight valve engine and the TSS with the rubber mount frame. The Thunderbird came down even more in stroke to 66 mm so its capacity became 599 cc. It was also offered with twin carburettors as the Daytona 600.

This was the last throw for the exhausted company for soon after the show they simply ran out of money. By the autumn the workforce had decided to call in the liquidator and late in the year the plant, machines and factory contents were auctioned off. A little later the famous Triumph Engineering works were demolished.

Even then all was not lost for John Bloor bought the manufacturing rights and licensed Les Harris to produce the Bonneville. Les, who ran Racing Spares, had been making Triumph parts for a long time and set up a firm in Devon to build the machine. Research stayed with Bloor but the Bonneville finally reappeared in Devon during 1985.

The Bonneville as it reappeared in 1985 thanks to Les Harris

The new machine had Italian forks and brakes and German controls but predominantly was the same Bonnie as of old. With wire spoke wheels and traditional Triumph lines it may have looked old but was as up-to-the-minute as any owner would want.

Left **Executive Bonneville for 1980 as shown to press and public at TT that year**

Bottom left **Tiger Trail prepared very quickly for Paris Show late 1980. High level, black exhaust system**

Below **Prototype Phoenix shown at 1980 Earls Court to test public reaction to Low Rider theme**

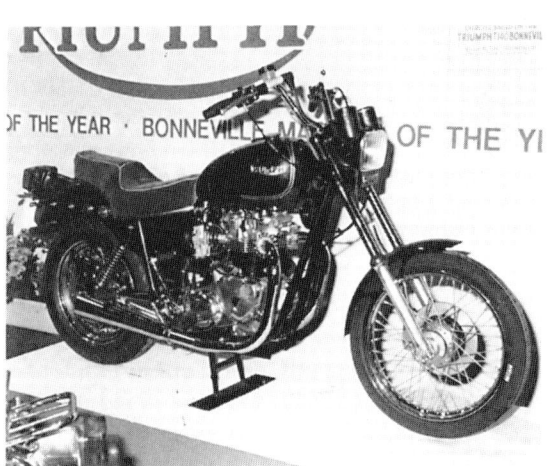

8 | The Trident

During the late 1960s there were a number of rumours that a larger-capacity machine was under development at Triumph and BSA to be produced by both companies. In time these hardened up and it became known that the machine was to have three cylinders and be of larger capacity than either of the existing 650 cc twins. It was, however, not until 1968 that details of the two newcomers were finally released to the press and public and initially all output went for export, so that it was 1969 before they were sold on the home market.

The two machines followed the same general specification with many common detail parts, but were different in the appearance of both engine and gearbox unit as well as the cycle parts and finishing touches.

The triple was designed at the Triumph works at Meriden and the chief architects were Bert Hopwood, Doug Hele and Jack Wicks. The engine followed Triumph practice more than BSA and was designed by adding a third cylinder to the existing twin. Valve gear followed the pattern set by Edward Turner, with two camshafts fore and aft of the cylinder block, driven by gears and operating pushrods enclosed in vertical tubes lying between the cylinders.

The three was based on a forged crankshaft which, after the initial operation, was reheated and twisted to give the 120-degree crank throws. Balance was by the integral webs, no flywheel being fitted. The big-end bearings were plain, as were the two inner mains, but the ends of the

Early Trident with easily recognised tail pipes. This is the view most people saw when the triple first reached the public highway

shaft ran in drive-side ball and timing-side roller bearings. The stroke of the crank was 70 mm which, with the 67 mm bore, gave a capacity of 740·4 cc.

The crankshaft was carried in a three-piece aluminium crankcase, split vertically into a centre section to which two outer parts bolted, with these seeming much like two halves of a pre-unit Triumph twin crankcase. Like the early pre-unit cases they carried the two camshafts in plain bearings with an intermediate gear, driven by the crankshaft gear, meshing with gears attached to the ends of the two camshafts.

The centre crankcase section was open at the top so that the crankshaft dropped into place with the two main bearing caps clamping it down into position. This section extended to the rear to include the gearbox shell, which was closed on the left side to carry the main and layshaft bearings. The finned underside of the case carried a finned sump plate which retained a gauze filter as on the twins.

The BSA and Triumph engines were not identical as the BSA had the cylinders sloping forward and the early Triumph had them mounted vertically, later models changing to the BSA layout. Thus the cases were also different, as were the timing-side and gearbox covers, these two items being designed to appear as a single flowing shape on the BSA and as two distinct covers on the Triumph.

The cylinder block was an aluminium-alloy casting with pressed-in steel liners forming deep spigots for the pistons to run in. These were of conventional design giving a 9:1 compression ratio and carried two compression and one scraper ring. The gudgeon pins ran direct in the forged, light-alloy connecting rods, which had steel-backed, white-metal-lined big-end shells. The big-end caps were retained by fitted bolts which located the caps and were clamped up with locknuts. The cylinder casting also carried the pressed-in, aluminium-alloy tappet guide blocks, one being housed between each cylinder at front and back of the block. The two on the right each contained a pair of tappets while that on the left had one only. Each tappet moved an aluminium pushrod fitted with hardened steel ends.

The cylinder head was a one-piece aluminium casting to which the two separate rocker boxes were bolted, one containing the three inlet rockers and the other the three exhausts. The head had the three separate inlet stubs bolted to it, but the exhaust stubs were screwed in and are generally never disturbed. The casting was very well finned with six wells formed in its top surface for the valves, which were each controlled by two coil springs held by a conventional collar and collet arrangement.

The rocker boxes were also well finned, with lids finished to match and fitted to the angled outer faces of the boxes. The vertical inner faces of these each carried a pair of inspection caps positioned to allow the fit of the pushrod cup onto the rocker end to be checked. The rockers

1969 Trident on test. Upright cylinders and a different frame distinguished between Triumph and BSA threes. They used common forks and hubs

had adjusters with locknuts at their outer ends and pivoted on fixed shafts lubricated by an external oil pipe branching from the scavenge pump feed to the oil cooler.

This cooler was mounted just below the steering head and was part of the original equipment. The lubrication was otherwise by a conventional dry-sump system with separate oil tank with filter which fed the gear pump located in the left crankcase and gear driven by spurs from the crankshaft. The oil was passed through a second filter located in the centre crankcase casting behind the engine and below the gearbox. From there it supplied the two centre main bearings, which connected to the other crankshaft bearings in turn. Originally the main bearing caps carried feed pipes to the tappets and cams, but this feature was discarded as those parts were lubricated by splash as were the pistons and timing gears. The removal of the oil pipes when they were found to be unnecessary enhanced crankshaft life. Oil drained into the crankcase from where it was scavenged by the second oil pump, which passed it through the oil cooler before it returned to the oil tank. This was vented to the primary chaincase, while the

return in the tank incorporated a drip-feed adjuster and supply pipe for lubricating the rear chain. The engine lubrication system also maintained the primary chaincase oil at its correct level.

A rev-counter drive housing was bolted to the top centre of the crankcase and the drive spindle was skew-gear driven from the exhaust camshaft. This also drove the contact breaker cam and advance and retard mechanism from its right-hand end, the plate carrying the three sets of points being mounted in the outer timing cover with a small circular cover plate providing access. Ignition was normally by battery and three separate coils mounted in a pack beneath the seat, but some machines use the Lucas capacitor system, which relies on the generator to provide the ignition power, so allowing the 12-

1970 Trident at a presentation, hence the indoor location. Group front brake

Trident engine in Rickman Metisse frame in 1972. Competition but only one front disc

volt battery to be dispensed with if desired but retaining the points to act as a trigger. Many triples have been converted to full electronic ignition, usually using the Boyer system, which dispenses with the mechanical advance and the points, these being replaced by an electromagnetic trigger which connects to an electronic box incorporating ignition advance circuits.

Three separate Amal concentric carburettors were used, fitted to a manifold which connected to the inlet ports with short rubber hoses. The carburettors were without throttle springs, each slide being positively connected to a throttle linkage mounted on the manifold and this in turn being coupled to the twistgrip and returned by a single spring. The air slides were originally controlled by a single handlebar lever, which was later moved to a position next to the carburettor. Two petrol taps supplied the three units, but neither had a reserve position, while all three carburettors were supplied by a common air cleaner.

The exhaust system was a three-into-four-into-two device as the pipe from the centre cylinder split and was connected into both of the outer cylinder pipes, which then swept back into individual silencers on each side of the machine. In their early form, these were instantly recognizable, for they terminated in a laid-back flat plate with three small outlet pipes with their ends cut off at an angle.

The engine produced 58 bhp at 7250 rpm in this form and the power was transmitted by a triplex chain from a sprocket mounted outboard of the oil-pump drive. To save space on that side of the engine and to avoid too much shaft overhang, the alternator was fitted to the opposite end of the crankshaft, in the timing case. The primary chain was tensioned by a blade fitted in the bottom of the chaincase and adjusted from the front. It drove a shock absorber unit which in turn was coupled to a Borg and Beck diaphragm clutch with single plate which lay within a casting fitted between the inner primary chaincase and the gearbox housing. The clutch was lifted by a ball and ramp device carried in the outer chaincase and drove a conventional four-speed, direct-top gearbox.

The gearbox contained the usual main and layshafts with the latter running on needle races and had the gear-selector forks moved by a circular camplate geared to a quadrant worked by the positive stop mechanism. As on the 650 cc twins, the quadrant pivot lay in the fore-and-aft direction in the inner cover. Alternative outer covers were fitted to suit the two makes of machine, but both supported the outer ends of the gear pedal and kickstart lever shafts. The kickstart quadrant operated the normal arrangement of mainshaft-mounted gear driving through a face ratchet. The final-drive sprocket was mounted inboard of the clutch in the normal English fashion and drove the rear wheel by chain on the machine's left.

The new engine and gearbox unit was mounted in a frame based on that used for the Bonneville with a single top tube braced by a second tube from the bottom of the headstock. The lower ends of saddle and down tubes were joined by duplex engine rails and the sub-frame was bolted on. The BSA had a frame with duplex down and saddle tubes.

The front forks of the new three were similar to those used on the twin at the time with gaiters protecting the sliders and brackets attached to the shrouds to support the headlamp. A friction-steering damper was fitted as standard. The fork ends were split to clamp on the front-wheel spindle, the wheel containing the Triumph 8 in. diameter twin leading-shoe brake with air scoop and linked cam arms. Like the twin unit, the cable was connected to the extended front cam lever and lay horizontal at the wheel. The front rim was a WM2 of 19 in. diameter shod with a 3·25 in.-section Dunlop K70 tyre. At the rear a 4·10 in. Dunlop K81 was fitted to a 19 in. WM3 rim, both rims being steel. The rear brake was a 7 in. diameter single leading-shoe type. Movement of the rear wheel was controlled by a pair of Girling spring units with pre-load adjustment and, unlike the BSA, the Triumph rear springs had covers fitted to them.

The oil tank was located behind the right-side panel and contained 6 pints of oil, while the petrol tank had a capacity of 4·25 gallons. The Triumph logo was carried on a small panel in front of the kneegrips and styled differently to the BSA. A ribbed dualseat was fitted with a suggestion of a hump at the rear and a grab rail fitted behind that and bolted to the rear mudguard. The first machines had high-rise bars to suit the US market, small chrome-plated headlamps and matched speedometer and rev-counter heads. The front and rear mudguards followed normal practice, the front supported by two short front stays with one at the rear.

Side reflectors were fitted, those at the front being fixed on the ends of the oil cooler, while those at the rear were fitted to the sides of the rear light housing. Controls followed the fashion of the time with steel, ball-ended clutch and brake levers, combined horn button and dip-switch on the left and air lever on the right handlebar. The ignition switch was located on the right-side headlamp support and the toggle light switch on the left one.

The finish was black with chrome-plated bright parts, only the petrol tank and mudguards being painted. The side panels were finished in black and carried 'Trident' motifs.

When first announced the Trident, or T150 as it was typed, was not available in England, but by early 1969 they were beginning to reach the home market and the price was given as £614 3s.

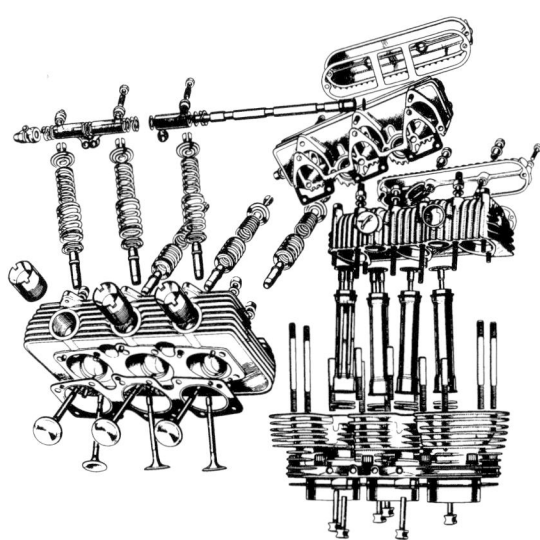

Line drawing of top half of Trident engine showing cylinder block, head, rocker boxes and complete valve gear. Very similar in concept and details to twin

5d. A road test of one appeared in *Motorcyclist Illustrated* at that time and reported very favourably on the machine's performance. Speed, acceleration, handling and brakes were all praised and complaints were limited to minor points, the main one being the effort needed to use the centre stand, although the point was made that the twin horns directed their notes to the rear of the machine so were less effective than they might have been.

One minor alteration had already been incorporated, the front brake forward cam lever having changed to the two-armed version used on the twins to allow the brake cable to lay parallel with the forks. The back plate was also changed to suit.

On the test machine the throttle linkage fouled the underside of the petrol tank, but once clearance was obtained, with a scientific half-brick, the full performance was available. This was of the order of 50, 80, 110 and 125 mph in the four gears. This performance was confirmed by other tests on both Triumph and BSA triples.

Unfortunately, the Trident appeared about the same time as the Honda CB750 four and the 500 cc Kawasaki triple of immense performance and less impressive handling. Both the Japanese machines had five-speed gearboxes, while the Honda had overhead cams, four cylinders, a disc front brake and electric starting, all of which were nearly unheard of in 1969 in what was basically a mass-produced motorcycle with volume sales. At that time only the rare exotica had such features and none had the established Honda name and reliability.

Despite this setback, the Triumph and BSA triples sold very well, boosted by some racing successes, and quickly earned themselves a good reputation with their owners.

For 1970 the triple received attention to a number of detail points but otherwise remained unchanged. The gearing between kickstarter and crankshaft was slightly lowered, so the task of turning the engine over became fractionally easier. The engine joint faces were broadened to improve oil sealing and the cylinder-base nut design was changed to allow a greater clamping force to be developed. The cylinder-base studs were also moved to new positions. The overall gearing was lowered a small amount by changing the rear-wheel sprocket for one with an extra tooth so that the power came in lower down the road speed range. Finally, the covers were removed from the rear damper units to leave the springs exposed and the finish changed to dark orange mudguards and petrol tank, the latter with white side panels. In this form it ran on for another year with a top-speed capability of 110 to 115 mph and a consumption that would rise to 30 mpg if it was cruised at 105 mph.

One further modification was introduced around that time to cure any tendency for the clutch to slip. This was dealt with by ensuring that its housing was ventilated and the later models had holes drilled in the casing to make sure it could breathe.

Late in 1970 Triumph launched a new version

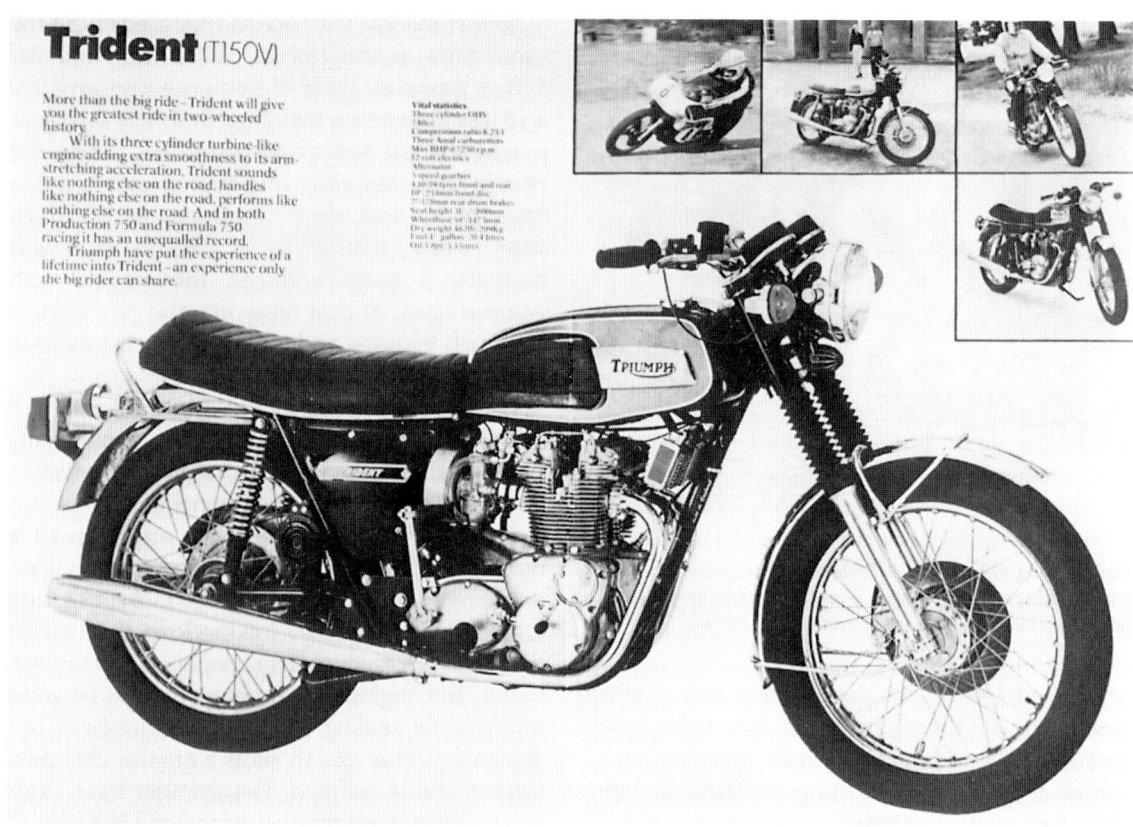

1973 Trident with five-speed gearbox and disc front brake

of the Trident along with many other new and revised models in the group ranges. The engine remained basically unchanged, although various minor modifications were incorporated.

More noticeable were the changes to the silencers, which took on a conventional slow-taper megaphone shape, so losing their distinctive ends with the three small outlet pipes. The frame remained as before, but the front forks and wheels were changed to the types used on the large-capacity twins. Thus the front forks lost the gaiters and assumed the popular slimline look while the front wheel gained the twin leading-shoe, conical-hub brake with the very short cam levers. The front tyre became the same section as that used by the rear wheel.

Further changes were mainly cosmetic, but did include the adoption of indicators. Both mudguards were changed in shape and mounting and their finish became chromium plating. The side-cover styling was changed and they no longer enclosed the air cleaners.

The circumstances that followed the lavish 1970 launch have already been covered and the Trident suffered as much as any other of the few models that remained in production. The BSA triple struggled into 1972 and final collapse, but the Trident carried on in a new colour of regal purple for tank and side panels. The gearing was lowered by fitting a gearbox sprocket with one tooth less and, with this specification, it was better geared than before so that it would run happily in the 30 mph-limit area in third gear, which also took it into three figures. Top speed was over 120 mph and acceleration was even better, especially in top gear between 40 and 70 mph, just where it was needed.

In the middle of 1972 the gearbox was changed to a five-speed unit and the complete new assembly would fit the earlier machines. Towards the end of the year the front brake was changed to a 10 in. diameter disc and, at Earls Court, a specially styled machine, the X75 Hurricane, was unveiled. This used the BSA version of the three-cylinder engine with a five-speed gearbox mounted in a Trident frame. The machine was styled by Craig Vetter from Illinois and caused something of a sensation at the time both for its lines and the UK price of £895 at a time when a CB750 cost £761. The styling theme was chopper and the forks were extended, which increased the wheelbase to 60 inches.

Most photographs taken were of the right side as all three exhaust pipes were taken that way to run together under the gearbox and terminate in three reverse megaphone-style silencers placed one on top of another. The small steel fuel tank was enclosed in a fibre-glass cover which flowed down and back from the rear of the tank into the side panels and the seat base. Front and rear wheels together with their mudguards were standard Triple, while high-rise bars were fitted along with a dualseat that complemented the style but was rather short for two. Colour was red with a pair of yellow strips running through the tank and side covers, the usual parts were chromed but the wheel rims were alloy. The drum front brake was fitted, not the new disc. It was of course designed for sidewalk cruising and to impress, but handled moderately well with a riding position that was comfortable at 70 mph. It had good brakes but a very large turning circle and was intended to be a limited-edition machine.

With the many financial problems that now beset the company the X75 Hurricane was soon dropped, leaving the five-speed Trident as the sole triple in the range. This had gained front-fork gaiters and some minor changes, but otherwise continued as before.

Then in autumn 1973 the factory blockade began and Trident production stopped for, although the engine units were built at Small Heath, the frame and final assembly work took place at Meriden. With no frames available NVT had to retool and it was not until the spring of 1974 that they were able to produce Tridents once again after a very costly and time-consuming exercise.

Production continued at Small Heath as the Meriden blockade came to its end and Triumph twins again became available. For early 1975 the Trident had the rear-wheel sprocket changed for one with three fewer teeth, so reverted to the 1970 top-gear ratio. The compression ratio was listed at 8·25:1, but otherwise the model continued just with a change of finish.

In the spring of that year a major change was made to the triple to produce its final form, the T160, which was based on the BSA version of the three with the cylinders sloping forward. Unlike the BSA it was matched to the five-speed

Craig Vetter styled X75 Hurricane version of Trident shown at 1972 Earls Court Show

gearbox, but with the timing and gearbox end covers styled into two separate items, not blended together as on the BSA. Thus the traditional Triumph timing cover was retained.

Internally the primary chain went up a size and down a strand to duplex and this resulted in changes to engine and clutch sprockets, although the reduction ratio was little affected. In addition, the gear pedal was transferred to the left side of the machine and this involved a number of detail modifications. The rev-counter drive was taken from the left end of the exhaust camshaft as on the twins and an electric starter was tucked in behind the cylinders. It was solenoid operated and of the pre-engaged drive type, which meshed with a gear on the back of the clutch.

The exhaust system was changed to look like a four-into-two arrangement with the centre cylinder feeding an alloy adaptor into which two pipes fitted. These swept down along with those from the outer cylinders into single upswept silencers on each side.

A rear disc brake, the same size as the front, was fitted and a neat panel added between the two instrument heads. It contained warning lights for turn, beam, neutral and ignition, together with the ignition key switch. Finally, the

Top left **Small Heath 1974 and the Trident line rolls once more in the old BSA works**

Top right **The T160 with discs, five speeds, left gear pedal, sloping cylinders and electric starter**

Above **Earls Court 1975 with the T160 highly polished for the two young ladies**

tank styling was changed to a scallop design.

Performance was of the 115 mph order, but fuel consumption had worsened to about 35 mpg. It was still quite a motorcycle, although by this time it was becoming a little old in comparison with the machines then coming onto the market.

The design team were aware of this and had built a prototype answer—a four-cylinder version that just had to be called the Quadrant. The crankcase was made by machining two triple cases and then welding them together before the final machining was done. The cylinder block, the head and the camboxes were all produced in the same way, but the crankshaft was built up and the camshafts were specially made and carried cams with mild timing. Most of the other parts were from the triple or the twin suitably modified where this was necessary. Two contact breakers were used and four carburettors. The exhaust system looked like that from the T160 except that the centre adaptor was missing and the rest of the machine was Trident. It pulled a top gear of about 4·2:1 and ran to nearly 125 mph on those very mild cams.

Only the one was made but other ideas included an overhead camshaft triple built around 1970–71 at Meriden. This was of 750 cc capacity with a single camshaft driven by a toothed belt under a cover on the right side of the engine. The belt drive was from what had been the exhaust camshaft gear, so occupied the position usually taken by the ignition points which were moved to the inlet camshaft gear. Conventional rockers opened the valves and, aside from the belt cover, the machine looked much like any other Trident for it used standard cycle parts.

The factory ran it and it went well but it, like an exercise with a 650 cc overhead camshaft twin, failed to be taken any further. Another NVT exercise was the fitting of a Trident engine in a Norton Commando frame using the Isolastic suspension. That machine was built in 1975–76 with the engine stretched out to 900 cc and with the raw edges of a prototype. Even the forks were hybrid, with Norton tops and Triumph sliders. While rough in places it went well and handled better. As with the ohc Trident, this machine, called the 'Trisolastic', together with an anti-pollution triple based on the T160, and a Thunderbird Three (built from Trident, BSA Rocket and Norton Commando parts), all passed into private hands in 1978 when Shenstone had a clear out.

Sadly, for the day of the triple was fast drawing to an end. In the backwash of a world excess of machines NVT found it hard to sell and combined with their earlier troubles and small size the combine ground to a halt.

At the end of 1975 the last Trident left Small Heath to bring to an end production of one of motorcycling's legends.

Quadrant, a four built from triple parts as a prototype exercise

9 The scooter twin

Tigress scooter built with Triumph and BSA badges and two engine types. Show picture hence model with model

After the Second World War Triumph concentrated their efforts on the twin-cylinder range and for a while only built machines of 500 cc or more. In 1953 they did introduce a small single, the Terrier, which grew up to be the Cub, but their main image was of large-capacity fast twins.

Other sections of the group produced utilitarian models, not Triumph, so it was with some surprise that it became known that they were to be involved in a joint exercise with BSA to build a scooter. BSA had done some work in the mid-1950s with the Beeza and Dandy models, although neither was very successful, the first never going into production, while the Dandy, a scooterette of 70 cc, was only built from 1956 to 1962.

It was with this rather inauspicious background that the group announced in 1957 that another prototype scooter, designed by Edward Turner, had been undergoing tests. The press statement of the time was made by the chairman, Jack Sangster, who stated that the scooter would go into production in the Triumph and Sunbeam ranges by the middle of 1958 and would offer not only excellent weather protection but a striking performance as well.

It was, however, not until October 1958 that a formal press presentation was made of the new models, although their existence had been an open secret for many months. Two versions were shown, both available either as the Triumph Tigress or the BSA-Sunbeam, one equipped with a 175 cc two-stroke engine based on Bantam engine dimensions, and the other fitted with a twin-cylinder four-stroke engine of 250 cc.

Aside from the two engine types, which were fitted to either make, the only differences between the two were the nameplates and the colours, the Triumph being shell blue and the BSA metallic green.

The twin-cylinder engine incorporated a number of unusual features and was built in unit with a four-speed gearbox. An electric starter could be supplied as an optional extra, but the kickstarter was still retained on all models. The rear wheel was carried by a single swinging arm on the left of the machine formed by the castings enclosing the final-drive chain and pivoted on the gearbox mainshaft axis.

The engine was of oversquare dimensions at 56 × 50·62 mm to give a capacity of 249 cc. It was based on a single light-alloy casting which formed the cylinder block, crankcase and gearbox shell. To this was fitted the cylinder head, end covers to the crankcase and a pressed-steel sump. The crankshaft was a one-piece forging in manganese-molybdenum steel incorporating a massive central bobweight between the cylinders and a sludge trap within the crankpin. It ran in a deep-groove ball race on the left side and a plain bush on the right and was assembled into the crankcase from the drive side. The connecting rods had conventional split big ends with shell bearings and supported full-skirted pistons carrying two compression rings and one scraper. The gudgeon pins ran in bushes in the small ends and were retained by circlips. Compression ratio was 6·5:1.

The cylinder head was cast in light alloy with the cast-iron valve inserts placed in the mould so that they were cast and locked into the cylinder head. The valve configuration was unusual, for the four valves lay in a line along the crankshaft axis across the engine. The two inner inlet valves were arranged vertically and operated by rockers which pivoted on a spindle lying parallel to the crankshaft. Thus the rocker arms were brought straight back to the pushrods situated at the rear of the engine. The two exhaust valves were, however, laid out at an angle to give short exhaust ports to the ends of the cylinder head as distinct from the inlets, which joined to a single port at its rear. The exhaust rockers were individually supported on spindles which ran across the head in the fore-and-aft direction. Thus the rocker ends also terminated at the pushrods at the rear of the engine. All three rocker spindles were supported by lugs standing up from the cylinder head and all four rockers carried screw adjusters and locknuts at the valve end. An oil gallery ran along the rear of the rocker box and was fed at both ends by two pipes connecting it to the crankcase. The valves were closed by dual springs held by collars and split cotters, ran in pressed-in guides and the whole assembly was enclosed by a rocker box cover carrying the oil filler cap in car style. The two sparking plugs fitted into the front of the cylinder head between each pair of valves.

The camshaft was positioned at the rear of the engine and operated the valves via flat-base tappets and pushrods. It ran in three bearings, one at its centre, to ensure stiffness at high speed and was driven by a pair of gears from the right-hand end of the crankshaft. The right-hand end of the camshaft drove a simple plunger oil pump by means of an eccentric on the shaft inboard of the driving gear, and a connecting piece. At its other end the camshaft drove the contact breaker cam and its automatic advance and retard mechanism by a tongue-and-slot arrangement which connected the two shafts. The cam opened two separate sets of points mounted on a single back plate that could be rotated to set the timing and the whole assembly was sealed by a small circular cover.

The alternator was mounted on the right-hand end of the crankshaft and its rotor incorporated both a cooling fan and the starter-gear ring. The starter itself was a Lucas pre-engaged type bolted to the crankcase right-side end cover and positioned in front of the engine. It was operated by a knob on the machine's front shield, connected to the starter motor by flexible cable. The electric switch was mounted on the starter and made contact once the starter gear had been moved into mesh.

The cooling fan was enclosed with a cowl which connected to a shroud fitted over the front of the engine. It was claimed that the use of forced-draught cooling allowed the fins on the cylinder block to be at a closer pitch than normal, which helped to reduce engine resonance and so gave a quieter machine.

The clutch was mounted on the left-hand end of the crankshaft and contained three bonded and three plain plates. Pressure was applied by three springs and the plates released by a simple lever arm operating a pushrod. The back of the clutch drum carried a gear which meshed with another on the gearbox mainshaft so the engine ran backwards and the primary drive was enclosed by two light-alloy castings, the inner acting as the left crankcase door while the outer also carried the contact-breaker assembly as well as the clutch release lever.

The gearbox followed conventional lines with the output sleeve gear concentric with the mainshaft and the layshaft positioned below it. The gears were selected by two forks moved by a sector-shaped camplate. This was shifted by a conventional positive-stop mechanism connected by a rod to a pedal protruding from the right floor panel. This was pressed forward to change down and back to change up. A second pedal on the right side of the floor panel but further to the rear next to the engine covers selected neutral if pressed down when the gearbox was in second gear.

The gearbox end cover, which supported the shafts, was an extension of the right-side crankcase door and itself carried a small cover to enclose the positive stop mechanism.

The kickstarter arrangements were a little unusual. As a scooter the machine required a forward-working pedal, as this was the convention on the great majority of scooters at that time. However, this moved its pivot position well away from the optimum at the gearbox to a point forward and below the crankshaft. A further difficulty lay in the need for the working shaft, which was concentric with the gearbox layshaft, to rotate in the opposite direction to the kickstarter pedal spindle. This was overcome by fitting small chain sprockets to both shafts and connecting the two by a short length of chain. By fitting the chain in the correct manner the direction of rotation of the shafts was reversed so that the pawl and ratchet rotated the layshaft bottom-gear pinion as required.

The final drive was by an enclosed duplex chain running inside a single swinging arm which carried the rear wheel. The arm was built up from three light-alloy castings and pivoted on the gearbox mainshaft axis. The two main castings turned on a bush fitted to a flanged boss bolted to the left side of the gearbox shell, while the

Halt during an ACU observed demonstration run. Initial riding was done by Geoff Duke and John Surtees, who then handed the machines over

third, an outrigger arm, was bolted to the case about half-way along its length and pivoted on a bush fitted outboard on the primary-drive cover. Thus the chain tension remained constant during wheel movement and was adjusted by means of a screw on the underside of the case which moved a slipper tensioner. An inspection cap in the outer case allowed the play in the top chain run to be checked.

The engine breathed through a single Zenith carburettor of the semi-automatic type with slide and needle. It also had a float that was concentric with the main jet and a starter slide rather than a strangler. The carburettor was fitted to an inlet pipe with a double crank in it which lowered its height to a point that ensured an adequate head of petrol even when climbing steep hills with a low fuel reserve.

The exhaust system was also a little unusual by motorcycle standards, the makers adopting the sensible principle that the appearance of the mechanical parts under the covers is of no importance on a scooter. Thus, an exhaust pipe ran back from each side of the cylinder head to a silencer box, which was shaped to fit in the tail of the bodywork. From the box a single tailpipe protruded from the rear of the machine.

This engine unit was carried in a duplex frame which was bolted and clipped to the steering head at the front. From there the two main tubes swept under the floor to rise vertically behind the engine to support an oval-shaped structure which followed the seat outline. The main tubes were cross-braced at several points and the seat frame was held square by a tube running back to the top suspension-mounting point, there being of course, only one unit to match the swinging arm. The seat hinged up to disclose the 1½-gallon petrol tank and the rear structure was extended to support the silencer box and a small rear mudguard.

The front forks were designed to allow the use of stub axles, a normal scooter feature, but were telescopic in movement. This was achieved by placing two telescopic assemblies together on the same, left, side of the front wheel. Thus the stub axle, brake assembly and wheel were all carried by an alloy casting with two deep vertical holes in it. These slid on two tubes attached to a lower fork crown, the rear one of which contained a fork spring anchored both to the crown and the lower end of the slider casting, while the front tube contained the fork's hydraulic damping unit. A pressed shroud fitted onto the two fork tubes and extended down over the slider casting.

The lower crown was fitted to a long steering-column tube which turned on cup-and-cone head races and had the handlebars keyed to it. The bars were welded to the pinch clamp above the top race and were held in place by the two nuts used for steering-head adjustment. The steering lock was also welded to the bars to the left of the clamp in the same area.

Both brakes were conventional single leading-shoe drum types of 5 in. diameter and 1 in. width. The wheels fitted on three studs protruding from each brake drum as in normal car practice so were interchangeable and, like cars, fitted with hub caps. The wheels were pressed steel and of 10 in. diameter fitted with 3·50 in.-section tyres. The rear brake was operated by a pedal mounted above the floor on the left of the machine, while a conventional lever and cable worked the front brake. Clutch and throttle were as motorcycle practice and the controls were completed by a combined dip switch and horn push mounted on the left handlebar. Two switches were fitted either side of the speedometer on the machine's apron to control ignition, with both normal and emergency positions, and the lights. In addition to the starter knob in the centre of the apron, the cold-start control was fitted on the left side.

The bodywork was built up from pressed-steel parts bolted together to form the front shield, apron, mudguard, floor and rear body shell. All these parts were easily removed for major servicing but remained in place for routine maintenance.

The electrics were straightforward with the normal complement of head, pilot, rear, stop and speedometer lights, horn, ignition warning light and generation and ignition circuits. The 6-volt battery was carried under a cover on the rear of the apron on the left side. Where an electric starter was fitted a 12-volt system was obtained by the addition of a second battery fitted on the right side of the apron.

A whole range of accessories was made available for the machines, including a windscreen, spare wheel and its carrier. The usual scooter shopping-bag hook was fitted to the rear of the apron as standard. When announced the machine weighed 240 lb and was listed as the model TW2 with kickstarter at £187 2s. 6d, and as the model TW2S with electric starter at £200 17s. 0d.

The model launch was held at Grosvenor House in London and was attended by numerous celebrities. Some prophecies of the future sales of the models were made, but these proved somewhat optimistic, for the venture into the scooter world was none too successful.

In the middle of 1959 *Motor Cycle* road tested a Triumph Tigress and gave it a good write-up. Starting was immediate whether the engine was hot or cold, acceleration brisk and cruising at 55 mph the normal gait. Handling, comfort and braking were also praised, although the rear brake had lost much of its efficiency after 1000 miles, which was not so good on a vehicle sold mainly to riders who would use the rear brake more than the front. The centre stand grounded on left-hand corners on occasion and other criticisms concerned the need to free the clutch first thing in the morning, an only partly effective neutral selector and a small fuel tank, although consumption was around the 80 mpg mark. The dualseat was judged to become rather hard after some three hours' riding, and became warm as a result of engine heat, especially in traffic.

As a result of tax changes, the prices had fallen slightly to £194 4s. 2d and the test machine was fitted with the windscreen at £4 19s. 6d, the rear carrier at £3 15s. 6d, the spare wheel at £5 9s. 0d and the spare wheel cover at £2 2s. 0d.

The various versions of the scooter continued on for some years with virtually no changes, although for 1961 the Triumph was made available in primrose or grey as well as the usual shell-blue sheen either as single-colour finishes or combined with ivory-coloured weathershield panels. The BSA was also offered in a further choice of colours and the prices remained at £180 18s. 9d for the model TW2 and £194 4s. 2d when the electric starter was fitted. Accessories also included a front carrier, pannier frames and bags, and wheel discs.

Press release used by Motor Cycle News **in October 1958. Machine is the electric start model, hence twin battery boxes, and is fitted with many of the optional extras**

The scooter twin

The scooter had become involved with some sporting activities by this time, as in 1960 a Tigress ridden by Don Leadbetter, David Hurst and Roy Banks broke Australian records for one, 12 and 24 hours in the 250 cc and 350 cc categories. The run was made at Caversham airstrip near Perth in poor conditions of rain, wind and sleet, and in the 24 hours the machine covered 1135·4 miles at an average speed of 47·3 mph.

Meanwhile, in England, Bunny Ward used the twin-cylinder engine to power a Greeves trials frame in scrambles. While no world-beater, it proved a successful operation, with the engine running without fan or cooling shroud. The power occurred where needed and it proved a reliable machine running in local events.

In the middle of 1961 prices rose by about £3 due to tax changes and remained there until a budget change in 1962 took them back to their original point.

A minor change was introduced to the exhaust system when the two pipes were siamezed, with the pipe from the right being carried across the front of the engine to join the left, which swept down from the port. The single pipe continued down to fit into a silencer extension.

For 1963 the scooters received only detailed improvements and their prices again rose, but only by a few pounds, so the TW2S reached £198.

This made little difference, for the day of the scooter had passed by and sales were dropping. The public demand moved on to other fields and it was to be another decade and a half before scooter sales began to pick up again.

Thus the venture of Triumph into the world of two tiny wheels went sour and in October 1964 the scooters were dropped from the range and the interesting 250 cc twin was no more.

Some scooter. Lambretta cycle parts with Triumph 500 cc pre-unit engine ridden by Keith Lee

10 The OHC twin

The last major press and trade launch of the Triumph/BSA group was held in November 1970 and among the many models shown was a completely new machine fitted with a 350 cc twin-cylinder engine. The basic design work was carried out by Edward Turner, who, although he had retired from Meriden in 1964, still maintained his interest in motorcycles and he worked on the 350 twin as a freelance. It was to be his last project, and as the founder of the vertical-twin success story with his 1938 Speed Twin, it was perhaps fitting that his final, albeit less successful, design should also have two cylinders.

The machine was to have been sold under two brand names, the Triumph Bandit and the BSA Fury, essentially the same with cosmetic variations. Both were also to have been built in street scrambler guise for the American market.

The engine was a completely new unit whose cylinders inclined forward slightly. In Turner's prototype the twin overhead camshafts were driven by a train of gears, but Umberslade Hall redesigned the engine for production and substituted chain-drive camshafts. It was based on dimensions of 63 × 56 mm with a 180-degree crankshaft, so had the uneven firing intervals and rocking couple out of balance forces normal with that engine layout.

The crankshaft was forged with an integral central flywheel and was machined all over to ensure consistency of balancing. The machining included slots in the flywheel periphery which located on a removable peg for ignition timing.

The crankshaft ran in two main bearings with the drive on the right a ball race and the timing a roller. The big ends were conventional shells of the same size as used in the triple and the connecting rods were aluminium-alloy forgings with steel caps located by dowels, a typical group design. They carried conventional three-ring pistons held by gudgeon pins working directly in the rods and retained by circlips. The compression ratio was 9·5:1.

The crankshaft was supported in a vertically split crankcase, the two halves being gravity die-

Exploded drawing of twin cylinder 350 cc engine and gearbox unit with gear and chain driven twin overhead camshafts. Unit construction and 180 degree crank but no balance shaft

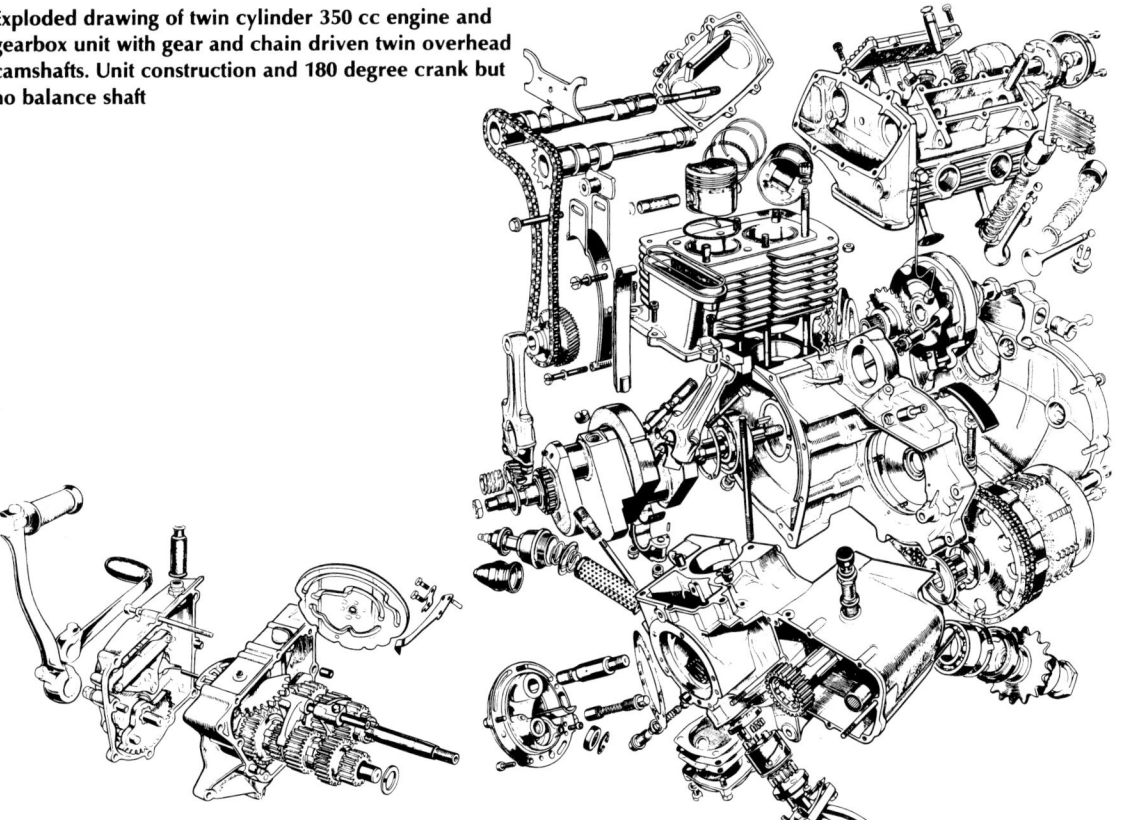

cast in aluminium. The inside gave considerable clearance to the crankshaft and flywheel and was free from ribs, so would have had minimal oil drag effect at high engine speeds.

The cylinder block was another gravity die casting in aluminium with the two alloy-iron cylinder liners pressed in. The cylinder head was made by the same process and in the same material as the block and was unusual in that the use of loose sand cores had been avoided except for the ports. The head casting contained the camshaft supports and was well finned, with air passages provided beneath the camshaft housings through the vertical fins rising directly from the combustion chambers. Although the cooling arrangements appeared adequate, little attempt was made to join the fins to prevent them from ringing, which would have reduced mechanical noise. This aspect was dealt with partially by a few rubber inserts.

The two cam boxes were open at the top, with the bearings for the camshafts in the end walls of the resulting trough.

The valves were set at an included angle of 60 degrees, which gave a shallow, compact combustion chamber. They worked against cast-in seats and ran in valve guides which were pressed in and located by circlips. Dual valve springs were fitted and retained by conventional collar and cotters, while the valves were opened by inverted bucket tappets under each cam. Valve clearances were set by shims inserted between the tappets and the valve heads, the shims being available in two-thou steps. Access for measurement of the valve clearance was by four screwed plugs in the sides of the cam boxes whose removal allowed the insertion of a feeler gauge.

The camshafts were formed in one with both cams and drive sprockets and ran directly in the cylinder head. As the shafts were assembled through one of the bearings, this limited the cam lift to some extent, although it would have been an easy problem to overcome.

The camshafts were driven by a chain on the left of the engine from a half-speed gear meshed to the crankshaft. The chain was enclosed in a chamber that rose from the crankcase on the left side of the cylinder block but to its rear so that it lay below the inlet camshaft. At cylinder-head level the chamber ran forward to encompass the exhaust camshaft. The chain ran straight down from the inlet camshaft, having travelled across from the exhaust before returning round a long curved tensioner that passed it from half-speed sprocket to exhaust camshaft and in the process changed its direction of movement from vertical to horizontal. The tensioner was rubber faced and thus acted as a jockey sprocket as well as being adjustable to set the chain tension. Fixed rubber-faced guides helped to control the other two chain runs.

The styling of the camshaft chain tunnel was not very smooth as distinct joints occurred at both cylinder base and head joint level, while the camshaft sprocket cover was retained by nine bolts and styled with two circular pads and five horizontal ribs. The two camshaft wells in the cylinder head were enclosed by flat covers with fins which ran across the engine and can hardly have assisted the air flow.

Dry-sump lubrication was employed with a double-gear pump skew driven from the left end of the crankshaft. A full-flow oil filter with replaceable paper element was located in the front of the crankcase on the left and covered by a cap which housed the oil-pressure warning switch.

Oil passed from the pump through a large junction block to the hollow timing-side mainshaft sealed by a lipseal in the timing cover and from there it was fed to the big ends via the removable sludge traps in the crankshaft. The timing cover also contained a small jet which sprayed oil onto the pump drive gears and the camshaft-drive reduction gears. From the main feed a bypass was taken to a point behind the left end of the cylinder block and connected to the rear of the camshaft-drive sprocket housing in

Prototype 350 cc twin with different form of camshaft drive. Stock cycle parts in the main

the cylinder head by a very small-bore pipe, external to the engine. This was intended to feed the camshaft bearings and, via them, the cams by means of cross-holes on the cam-base circle connected to the hollow camshafts.

The oil drained from the inlet cam box down through two holes which passed through the casting above the combustion chambers to reach the exhaust cam box. This was lower than the inlet by virtue of the inclined engine installation angle and from it the oil drained down the camshaft chain tunnel. It finally reached the sump, from where it was scavenged by the pump. An upward extension of the oil pump shaft was used to provide the rev-counter drive take-off point.

Engine breathing followed the design of the triple and was through the drive-side main bearing into the primary drive case and from there via a settling chamber to the air filter box. This satisfied the then current emission requirements and the breathing was a minimal problem anyway as the engine layout automatically gave nearly constant under-piston volume.

The mixture was provided by two Amal Concentric carburettors, which were joined by short rubber hoses to separate parallel inlet-port adapters screwed into the cylinder head. The exhaust ports were also parallel and connected to two separate exhaust pipes and silencers. On the road machines each pipe curved down and back to a point just behind and below the footrests. To them were clamped tubular megaphone-style silencers of the same pattern as was adopted at that time for both Triumph and BSA 650 cc twins. The silencers were supported by a plate suspended from the pillion footrest.

On the street scrambler models the two exhaust pipes were both carried round to the right side of the machine at high level. They connected to two megaphone-style silencers joined into one unit, with the left cylinder pipe above that from the right cylinder. The whole system was finished in matt black and carried two chromium-plated heat guards, one bolted to each system.

Although the contact breakers could easily have been driven from the half-speed timing gear, Triumph chose to mount them at the right-hand end of the exhaust camshaft, from where they controlled the coil ignition system.

An electric starter was announced as being available as an optional extra and when fitted was positioned behind the cylinders on top of the gearbox. The starter end cap contained an epicyclic gear reduction train and was con-

Left side of prototype 350 cc twin with Edward Turner on the right. Mechanical disc brake

nected to the crankshaft by chain. The overall reduction ratio was 14:1 and the crankshaft sprocket contained a one-way roller clutch and was mounted on a needle bearing. This sprocket lay outboard of the primary drive and just inboard of a Lucas alternator positioned at the extreme right-hand end of the crankshaft. This was a standard design mounted on three studs screwed into the crankcase wall, so overhanging the right main bearing by some distance.

The primary drive was by a duplex chain which lay between the right main bearing and the starter sprocket. It was slipper tensioned and drove a conventional multiplate clutch incorporating a shock absorber of the rubber and vanes type, the assembly being adapted from the BSA Victor component. It carried a centre adjuster screw accessible through a screwed plug in the cast-aluminium outer chaincase and was lifted by a triple ball-and-ramp mechanism, which was then being used on most of the group's machines.

The gearbox was a five-speed device built in unit with the engine and of typical English design with the output sprocket mounted on a sleeve gear, concentric with the mainshaft and positioned behind the clutch. The layshaft lay behind the mainshaft and the selectors slid on a rod positioned above the shafts and were controlled by a circular cam plate which pivoted on a pin fixed to the top of the gearbox casting. This was rotated by a quadrant moved by the positive stop mechanism, which was controlled with a pedal on the left side. Pivoted at a point just below the gear pedal was the kickstart lever, also on the left, with a folding pedal. The gearbox design was in essence a Triumph unit with an added fifth gear, but could have been more suited to the overall machine layout had it employed a crossover drive with the gearbox sprocket fitted to the layshaft. The final drive chain was positioned on the right side.

The power output of the engine was claimed to be 34 bhp at 9000 rpm with the maximum torque claimed to be 20 lb ft at 7000 rpm. The engine unit was fitted into a frame with well-splayed duplex down tubes which swept under the engine and up to the rear-unit top mounting points. A second pair of tubes ran from the top of the headstock over the inlet cam box to angle down to join the first pair just above the swinging fork pivot. A further pair of tubes ran forward horizontally from the rear-unit top mounting to the upper frame tubes and thus lay just below the line of the seat and tank. These tubes were extended rearwards by a smaller loop, which ran back to support the rear mudguard and tail light assembly and had the seat grab rail fitted to it.

The swinging fork was controlled by a pair of suspension units with exposed springs and the front forks were the new slim-line type with internal springs and two-way damping. Front fork movement was $6\frac{3}{4}$ in., good for the time.

The two hubs were the new BSA/Triumph conical type, cast in aluminium alloy as used for much of the range that year. The front hub contained an 8 in. two leading-shoe brake, which was operated by two very short cam levers pulled together by the cable action. The cast aluminium-alloy back plate carried a large air scoop and had small slots in it to let the air out, while the brake was adjusted with snail cams which were accessible through a hole in the brake cone. The rear hub was similar but housed a 7 in. single leading-shoe brake with floating cam action which allowed the shoes to move to their most effective position without hindrance. The brake, its operating pedal and the rod that connected them were all mounted on the right side of the machine.

The wheels were conventional and both the road and street scrambler machines were pictured as having the same roadster tyres. Both mudguards were sporting in style and the front one was rubber mounted to the fork legs.

The electrics of the machines were up-to-date with indicators, side reflectors, headlight flasher and a four-position ignition switch which allowed the machine to be parked with the ignition off and the parking lights on. Both speedometer and rev-counter were rubber mounted and warning lights were provided for oil pressure, headlight high beam and the indicators.

The seat and tank designs were different, the BSA being fitted with a smooth-finish dualseat while the Triumph had the ribbed top. Both seats were nearly flat with a slight upturn at the rear.

The Triumph tank was finished in a different style to the BSA in a light colour with two dark panels, lined in white, on each side with the Triumph logo between them. The side covers were in the same light colour for the major upper section and carried the model name, 'Bandit 350', in a line box or 'Bandit SS', according to type.

The new machines weighed 345 lb dry and were initially promoted at £380 with the optional electric starter available for a further £21.

Those shown at the launch differed in quite a number of ways from the original prototype. This used a different form of camshaft drive with the contact breaker on the left end of the inlet camshaft. It had different cylinders and many other parts.

This engine unit had been installed in a modified standard frame and the front forks had external springs. The front brake was experimental with a single disc and the rear was a full-width drum. Most other parts were from the standard range, modified as necessary to complete the machine.

Several of the final version of the machine had been seen about in the Birmingham area during 1970 prior to the launch as the prototypes went through their testing. As the year ended, more people had an opportunity to ride them and found that they were quick but mechanically noisy. The cycle parts were very good as would be expected when forks and wheels were from much larger machines.

At that time, late in 1970, the group was in serious financial trouble, and partly as the result of this the new 350 cc machine was tooled up for production before a number of development problems had been overcome. As a result of the ensuing delays and the subsequent company collapse, the Bandit never reached the market.

By August 1971 the street scramblers had been dropped as part of a streamlining operation carried out to try to save the day and at the same time the price was raised to £458 for the model with the electric starter.

Sadly this was to no avail and by the end of the year the final twin was no longer listed.

The pre-production prototypes lived on and some of these machines eventually finished up in the hands of BSA dealers when the firm finally closed. One of these was briefly tested by *Motor Cycle News* in 1973. It proved to be highly geared with the fifth speed acting as an overdrive ratio, while the engine was smooth but transmitted some vibration through the footrests. The handling was described as taut, although the bars were felt to be too wide and angled. The ride was not so good.

A tantalizing test, for many felt the machine had tremendous potential it had never had a real chance to show.

Triumph Bandit in its final form as shown to the public. In this publicity picture the lady is Carol Cleveland, a TV actress

11 | Competition

Ernie Lyons on the prototype Triumph racer in the 1946 Senior Manx Grand Prix. The picture gives some idea of the dreadful weather conditions that day. Note the Tiger 100 front mudguard fitted the evening before the race

It could well be argued that the Triumph twin was the most successfully versatile engine ever produced as it won events in every branch of motorcycle sport imaginable. Other makes may have dominated a particular field, but the Triumph performed in all and usually with success. The engine could be, and was, used in all manner of events with suitable modifications and the record stretches back to 1938, when the Turner twin first became available.

Road, track, grass, sand or salt surfaces were all the same to it and owners all over the world have sought and found success with it. Engines have had their heads turned round, been laid down, blown, doubled and tripled. Just about every tuning trick known must have been tried at one time or another and usually the engine has responded.

This is not, and cannot be, a total record of Triumph sporting success, which would run to many volumes, but is a résumé of some of the highlights over the years in the various branches of the sport that Triumph competed in.

Road racing

The events that occurred at Brooklands before the Second World War have already been covered, as has the background to the manufacture of the Grand Prix model. As recorded, the factory had little to please them in the TT races of the subsequent years although were much more successful in the Clubman's events, with Allan Jefferies taking second place in 1947 and 1949.

They repeated this placing for the next two years with A. Hill second in 1950 and Ivan Wicksteed, the one who had set the Brooklands record in 1938, taking this position in 1951. In both these years they nearly won, for Wicksteed led both races to their last laps, retiring in 1950 with a split tank and easing off too much the following year.

Finally in 1952 Bernard Hargreaves won the race on a Triumph at 82.45 mph, but following that success the weight of the Gold Star became too much and they only managed places.

Meanwhile, the Grand Prix had had its brief moment of glory with David Whitworth finishing third in the 1947 Dutch TT while local riders won the national race at the same meeting using Tiger 100s. Whitworth went on to fourth place in Belgium that year and in 1948 was fourth in Holland. In England the new machines were beginning to make their presence felt and Bob Foster won the important Blandford race. He won again in 1949 to set the pattern for a good number of Triumph wins around the world.

One was the Port Elizabeth 200, the premier race of South Africa, and Triumphs took the first three places. There were many more and during this period riders at home and abroad were tuning standard engines and fitting them into special frames. Two of the better known in England were Alan Dudley-Ward and Harry Bostock, who had considerable success with their machines fitted with swinging-fork suspension. Harry used his on the road at one time and I can still recall a lift he gave me one evening.

Once the featherbed Manx became available it became much harder for the private owners to succeed with their modified road machines, although many continued, especially in the sidecar class.

Across the Atlantic the Triumph began to make its mark at Daytona. This was well before the current road circuit was built, for at that time a unique 4.2-mile course was used comprising two miles of beach and two miles of narrow, tarmac road. These parallel stretches were joined by artificial banked turns and the course was ridden anticlockwise. Riders thus rode on the sand up to the north turn and on the road down to the south turn.

In 1950 two races were held, the 200-mile expert and the 100-mile amateur, and it was the latter which Rod Coates won on his Grand Prix. The following year Triumph were second in the 100-mile race and took third and fourth places in the experts event, while, during the race week, Bobby Turner broke records using a Thunderbird in the 40 cubic inch class. In class A using alcohol fuel and a 13:1 compression ratio he recorded a one-way speed of 136 mph and on the sand set a two-way figure of 129.24 mph. With a class C engine he achieved 118.40 mph.

While the Triumph twin was winning events worldwide it was having less success at home in road racing. However, as the 1950s moved to a close so production machine races began to be run in greater numbers and this trend was to grow and grow. It proved just the type of event to suit the Triumph and one of the first indications came in 1958 when Mike Hailwood and Dan Shorey won the Thruxton 500-mile event on a Tiger 110.

During the 1960s the Triumph was the frontrunner in production racing. Although challenged by many other makes it was by far the most popular large machine and the most successful.

The make also went back to Daytona in 1962, the year the speedway road circuit was first used, and broke the Harley monopoly to win the 200-mile race by a length from a Matchless. It was the first English machine victory since the BSA win of 1954.

In 1966 both Triumph and BSA sent factory machines to Daytona and, although BSA struck trouble, Buddy Elmore won on a Triumph on the 3·81-mile circuit adopted from 1964 onwards.

They returned in 1967 in even greater strength with six machines of each make and once again it was a disaster for BSA with all six machines retiring, but once again all the Triumphs finished and they took first and second places, Gary Nixon winning.

That same year saw the first production TT and Triumph recruited John Hartle, who took the lead soon after the Le Mans-style start and was never headed. Earlier in the year the make had repeated their 1966 win in the 500-mile race and later took second spot in the arduous 24-hour Barcelona event. The year closed with Gary Nixon winning the number-one plate in the USA from the Harley riders.

In 1968 Triumph missed out in the large-capacity production TT, but Ray Knight made up for this by winning the 500 cc class. The same size machine, ridden by Peter Butler and Dave Nixon, won the 500-mile race and in America Gary Nixon retained his number-one plate by a slender margin.

1969 brought the first three places in the 500-mile event and Malcolm Uphill won the production TT at 99·99 mph. He also became

Top **Allan Jefferies before the 1947 Senior Clubman's TT, in which he finished second**

Above **Dan Shorey and Mike Hailwood after winning the 1958 Thruxton 500 on a Tiger 110**

the first man to lap the TT circuit at more than 100 mph on a production machine and set a new lap record of 100·37 mph for the class. Works tester Percy Tait on a 500 cc twin scored a memorable second position to the MV of Agostini at the Belgium classic and a 650 won the 12-hour race at Jarama.

After 1969 the twin was displaced by the triple in the factory racing programme and the first major race was at Daytona, for which six machines were prepared, three with BSA and three with Triumph on the tank. The cylinders were inclined slightly forward as normal on the BSA, but the timing cover was cut off to increase clearance and the Triumph-type gearbox end cover fitted. Although this gave the engine the appearance of the Triumph, the timing cover had the characteristic BSA lines. The engines were very well worked on and power was up by 25 per cent on the standard unit. Much of this work was on the cams, valve gear and cylinder head, while breathing was through three $1\frac{3}{16}$ in. GP Amals. All three exhaust pipes joined together under the gearbox to feed a long plain megaphone that terminated above and behind the rear-wheel spindle. A capacitor ignition system triggered by points was fitted, with the electronic box mounted behind the steering head and containing the zener diode and capacitor. The condensers were attached to the top of the box while two coils were flexibly mounted on the timing side of the engine with the third on the drive side. A Quaife-type five-speed gearbox was fitted and the whole unit was installed in a new fully duplexed frame of triangular loop design. The

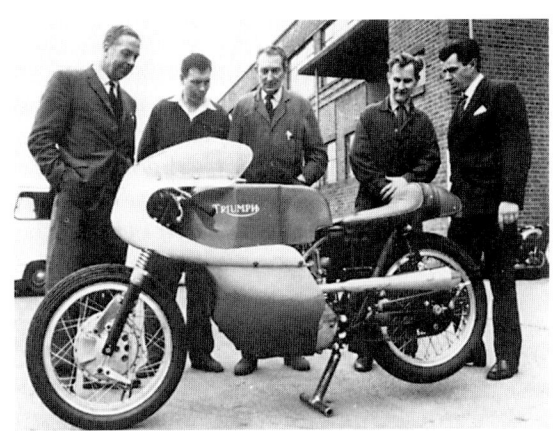

Below **One of the successful twins run at Daytona in 1966 and 1967. They won in both years, Buddy Elmore first, then Gary Nixon, and were second also in 1967**

Bottom **Owen Greenwood sidecar with its 650 cc engine. With 500 cc unit fitted was sixth in 1959 sidecar TT. Very successful on home circuits**

front brake was a double-sided, twin leading-shoe drum of 250 mm diameter and the rear a 9 in. disc with hydraulically operated pads.

The fuel tank was of 5 gallons capacity and it and the seat were made in fibre-glass. The oil tank fitted beneath the seat and carried 10 pints. Two variants of the fairing were produced and tried out during practice when the big triples showed they meant business, with Gene Romero qualifying fastest round the two-and-a-half-mile speedbowl at 157·34 mph. He was timed through the speed trap on the main straight at 165·44 mph. Although qualification was on the speedbowl the actual race included an infield section and, at first, things looked good for the group. Gary Nixon on one of the Triumphs and Mike Hailwood on a BSA went straight to the front and circulated in company, with the Triumph apparently the faster machine. It did not last for long, however, as after 38 miles Mike was forced out with flames coming from the exhaust, and gradually the BSA and Triumph efforts faded. It was a gruelling race, with only 16 of the original 98 starters still running at the end, and was won by Dick Mann riding a Honda CB750 with Gene Romero second on a Triumph.

Three months later, in June, the position improved when Gary Nixon won a 100-mile event at Laconia on a Triumph. In the same month in the Isle of Man Malcolm Uphill again won the production TT, this time on a Trident. The 24-hour Bol d'Or also fell to the three that year.

1971 was to be the great year for the racing triple. The machines were further improved by modifications to the contact breakers to stop the ignition timing from wandering and with other changes the power output was up to 84 bhp at 8500 rpm. New frames were built by Rob North with a modified head angle, the oil cooler was moved into the nose of the fairing, hence the slot in it to feed air through on the 1971 machines, and the drum front brakes were replaced by twin discs. The weight stayed at 370 lb dry, but the

handling was better and the machine was very durable.

The season kicked off at Daytona and BSA/Triumph were there in force with triples for Mike Hailwood, Jim Rice, Dick Mann, Don Emde, Paul Smart and Gene Romero, among others. For this meeting the engines were on 12:1 compression ratio and the gearbox contained special ratios suitable for Daytona. The standard clutch was used but the Renold chain was of racing quality. The Triumphs had engines with vertical cylinders and all models had shortened forks with two-way damping in special wide-centre yokes made to accommodate the disc brakes. All three discs were 10 in. diameter and both wheels had light-alloy symmetrical hubs laced to 19 in. WM3 alloy rims. Dunlop racing tyres were fitted, the final-drive sprocket was in light alloy and the spindle in titanium. Both tanks were in alloy, the oil tank under the seat containing 11 pints and the petrol tank 5 gallons.

The triples dominated the meeting with Smart taking pole position on the Triumph in practice. He took the lead on lap 5, but then Hailwood went past to head the field until lap 14, when a valve dropped in. At that point the triples occupied positions 1 to 5 and Smart continued to draw ahead until lap 41, when he stopped for a change of plugs but had to pull out with a holed piston. This left Mann on a BSA comfortably in a lead he held to the end, with Romero second on a Triumph and Emde third on a BSA after a race-long duel.

Most of the triples returned to England and commenced to dominate Formula 750, production and endurance racing, setting lap records at many major British circuits during the year. Most stayed with the original name on the tank, but that used by Ray Pickrell started as a BSA, being the one used by Hailwood at Daytona, but was later raced in the Triumph

Top left **John Hartle (1) and Malcolm Uphill (21) at Ballaugh Bridge in the 1968 Production TT**

Bottom left **Dave Croxford taking the flag on a Trident**

Below **Percy Tait on the 1971 version of the fabulous racing Trident**

MINTEX
8
49
12
4

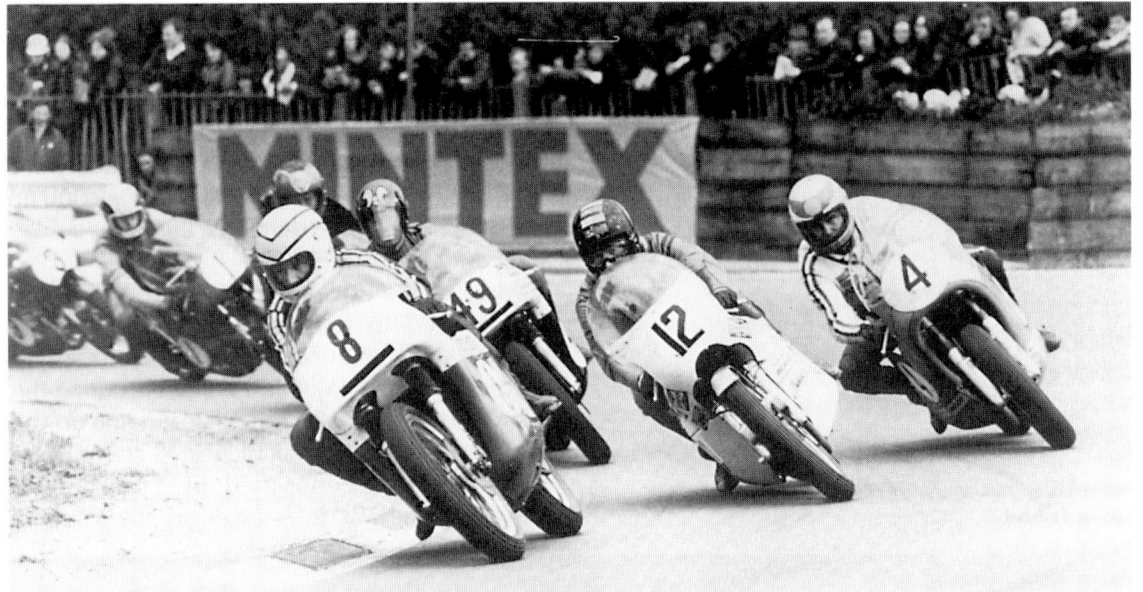

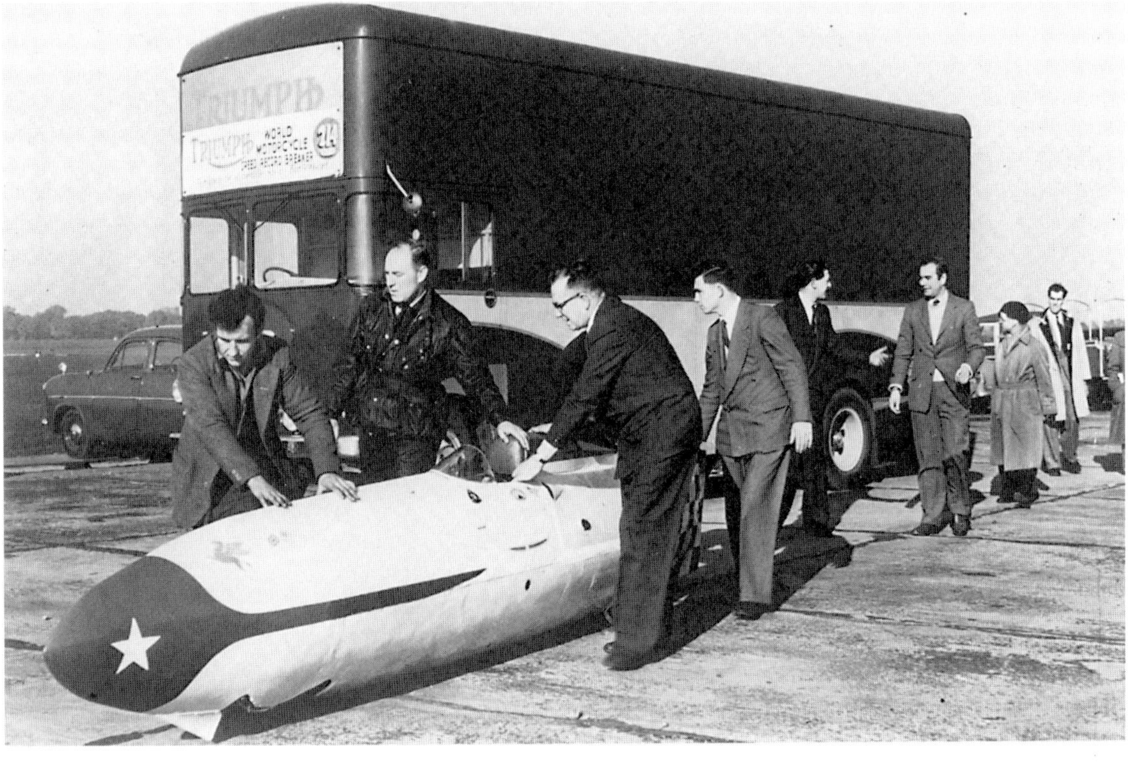
TRIUMPH
TRIUMPH
WORLD
MOTORCYCLE
SPEED RECORD BREAKER

Top left **1972 at Mallory Park. Ray Pickrell (8), John Cooper (49), Peter Butler (12), and Dave Croxford (4)**

Bottom left **Streamliner used by Johnny Allen in 1956 that ran at 214 mph. FIM refused to sanction**

Below **World record holder at 224 mph, ridden by Bill Johnson and powered by 650 cc Triumph**

colours. The 500-mile race that year was won by a three and the production TT went to Pickrell riding a Trident known as 'Slippery Sam'. There are two stories as to how this name arose, one concerning Tait who was always nipping out from Meriden on one errand or another and who became known as 'Sam, the transport man', this name later referring to his machine. The second evolved from the 1970 Bol d'Or when the machine drenched its riders in oil. It had originally been built for the 1970 TT, in which it finished fourth. It was to achieve fame by going on to win the production TT four more times to make it five in a row. 1971 also saw the introduction of the Formula 750 event at the TT, and Jefferies won this on a Triumph.

Later that year Tait and Pickrell rode one of the triples in the 24-hour Bol d'Or held on the 2·8-mile Bugatti circuit at Le Mans. The original entry was for a BSA, but the machine used was a Daytona Triumph. Because this was not notified to the organizers until after the race, it went into the records as a BSA and stayed that way. In the event the rain was pouring down when the flag fell and the triple at first refused to start and then ran on two cylinders for a lap before it cleared. Despite this handicap, the riders had fought their way up into the lead by the sixth hour, still in heavy rain. They lost the lead three hours later and were also delayed with a broken rear chain, but, around the 17-hour mark, the leading Guzzi broke a rocker and while it was being repaired the triple made up the five laps it was behind and re-took the lead. The sun had by then dried out the circuit and the triple held its lead to the end, covering a total of 616 laps at an average speed of 70·48 mph.

At the end of 1971 the factory were forced out of racing by their financial problems, but Slippery Sam was still in the Isle of Man in 1972 thanks to mechanic Les Williams. Ray Pickrell rode it in the production and formula 750 races and won both. In 1973 Jefferies won on it again, and the following year it was the turn of Mick Grant. Finally, in the 10-lap race of 1975, Slippery Sam pulled it off a fifth time with Alex George and Dave Croxford doing the riding. By this time it belonged to Les Williams and, like many of the racing threes, it is still preserved.

During the early 1970s the Triumph began to drop from favour in production racing but, within a few years, turned up again in yet another field—vintage racing. This became very popular from the middle 1970s and the twin proved very suitable for many riders, being cheap and easy to build with a vast store of tuning parts and knowledge to hand. They were used in quantity with every success.

Speed Records

Maximum speed in a straight line has been a target for riders since the dawn of the industry and, from the middle 1950s, most attempts were made at Bonneville Salt Flats in Utah. The world motorcycle speed record was set at 185 mph in 1955 in New Zealand, but from then on the vast expanse of the salt lake made it the only viable location for high-speed runs.

Later that year an indication of things to come was given by Texan Johnny Allen, who ran a long, low, fully streamlined machine through the kilometre at 193 mph. The power unit was a 650 cc Triumph twin running on alcohol and geared to run at 7000 rpm at 220 mph. Wheelspin and a less than perfect surface pulled the figures down, the mile being covered at just under 192 mph. As the record was timed by the American authorities it ranked as a US record, but the FIM refused to sanction it as a world record.

The following year NSU pushed the recognized record a little higher to 211 mph, but Allen ran again and at first had a Tiger 100 engine installed. With only 500 cc he pushed his US record to just over 198 mph and then fitted the 650 cc power unit. With this in place he was timed over the flying mile at a recorded 214.5 mph. This was to lead to a really big row, for he had been given assurance that the timing equipment was FIM approved. Then the FIM rejected the records on spurious technical grounds concerning the timing equipment and, despite two years of legal action by Triumph, the record was never accepted.

Two years later the machine was run again with Jesse Thomas on it and once again it broke the NSU record, but that time they did not bother to claim the world figure as it was the US one they were really interested in.

In 1962 another Triumph rider, Bill Johnson, raised the US record with another fully streamlined machine powered by a 650 cc twin running on alcohol. The new figure was 230 mph over the flying mile and by way of practice he set the pump fuel record to 205 mph. A week later he ran the alcohol engine machine under FIM supervision and recorded 224·57 mph and finally a Triumph record was accepted and they officially held the world record. For this attempt the engine was fitted with race cams and valve springs, 12:1 pistons and was ported and balanced—thus it was standard Triumph with stock, off-the-shelf, racing parts fitted.

Four years later, in 1966, the US record was pushed to the new level of 245 mph by Bob Leppan. Again this was not an FIM recognized figure, but by this time nobody was interested in their politics and the world saw Bob as the fastest man on two wheels. His machine was called the Gyronaut X-1, for originally it was to have had dual gyroscopes fitted along with a 4·7-litre V8 Ford engine. In fact he used two 650 cc Triumph engines running on alcohol. These were installed in tandem fashion and connected by chain. Compression ratios were 10·5:1 and claimed power was 110 bhp at 7300 rpm. Four years later it returned in an attempt to retrieve the record that Harley Davidson had pushed up to 265 mph, but, at high speed, it crashed due to a failure of the rear suspension fork arm. As a result Leppan nearly lost his left arm, but fortunately recovered.

Since then the motorcycle record has gone to three-wheeled jet engine devices at near sonic speeds, but Triumph twins still run on Bonneville Salt Flats each speed week.

Sprinting

Massive acceleration, whether against the clock, as in the original form of sprints, or against another rider, as in drag racing, is another field of Triumph success.

Sprinting regulations give riders more freedom than in any other form of motorcycle competition and so machines appear in all shapes, sizes and forms. One, two or even three engines may be used with supercharging and very special fuels to move the broad slick tyres over a quarter of a mile.

The sport had its origins in the very early days of motorcycling, but had a limited revival in England after the war. It was much more popular in America in the 1950s and the Triumph twin was quickly pressed into service, for it was fast, cheap and available with all the needed extra

Above **Twin engine sprinter. Two 650 cc engines plus supercharger. Ridden by Dave Clee in 1973**

Left **Side by side twin engine sprinter with superchargers. Note size of fuel taps and pipes**

parts. Within a few years twin-engined machines and blowers became common along with times that few in Europe chose to believe. It was simply the pressure of competition and it was not until well into the 1960s that this began to have a real impact in England.

Once this occurred times quickly dropped and the sport expanded into its two styles of sprints and drags with the occasional special records meeting, when both standing and flying start speeds would be set.

Sprinting machines show more variety and ingenuity than most others and the Triumph engine proved to be one of the most popular. They were used in every way and every form and responded by setting many records over the years. The most popular engine was the pre-unit 650 cc, but both a 350 cc twin and even a 250 cc Tigress engine were not only sprinted but supercharged as well.

International Six-Day Trials

Triumphs have been ridden in most ISDTs, but it was not until 1948 that the event led to a new model. This was based on the machine used by captain Allan Jefferies, who led his team to take the major trophy, known as the 'Trophy' to distinguish it from the less important 'Vase'.

141

Great Britain won that as well in 1948 with the help of Jim Alves on another Trophy, and the two Triumph riders, along with two more, won the manufacturer's team prize. It was hardly surprising that the new Triumph model was called the Trophy. It was one of the best all-round machines built and, like the Grand Prix, had its origins in the generator engine.

1948 was the start of a winning sequence for Great Britain, who retained the Trophy, and Triumph, who took the maker's team prize for the following three years. The first and last of these were held in Italy and the middle two in Wales. Jim Alves rode in the Trophy team from 1949 on up to 1955, using 500 or 650 cc machines, and Britain was again the Trophy winner in 1953.

This was Triumph's best period in the ISDT, but the machines continued to appear in the event for many years, either as complete Triumphs or as one of the specials in the next chapter, the Cheney being especially good in this field. In 1964 Triumph again won the manufacturer's team award with gold medal rides by Roy Peplow, John Giles, Ken Heanes and Ray Sayer. Machines were respectively Tiger 90 two TR6s and a Tiger 100.

From then on smaller two-strokes tended to dominate the event, although Britain came a close second in 1973—and four of the six team members were on Triumph twins.

Moto-cross and Enduros

Both these forms of racing take place over rough terrain at speed, the first over several laps of a circuit, the second over much longer distances. Triumphs, or machines with Triumph twin engines, have been used for this type of event for many years by riders all over the world.

Moto-cross or scrambles races soon found the twins in favour for they were light, easy to tune and available. The larger twins also made their mark in sidecar events for the same reasons.

The enduro-type event was more popular in the USA and often run over hundreds of miles

Top **Triumph ridden by A. F. Gaymer in the 1948 ISDT. Journalist Arthur Bourne at right**

Above **The manufacturers team for 1954. P. F. Hammond, Jim Alves and J. Giles on their 650 cc Trophy models (left to right)**

and more than one day. The Triumph Trophy was soon at home in these and was to prove very successful over the years. In many of these races to finish at all was often an achievement as perhaps only 50 out of 400 starters would receive the chequered flag. The Triumph was tough enough to succeed in this field and, because they were so plentiful, were popular with private owners. After all, if you did blow an engine or gearbox, another could be found with ease.

The scale of the American enduro events was something Europeans found hard to accept. For

Top **Don Rickman winning a** *moto-cross des nations* **on the Triumph powered Metisse**

Middle **John Giles in 1963 on a 350 cc twin riding in the Hoad Trial**

Bottom **Enduro riding in 1964. Very hard work indeed with a sidecar attached**

example, the 1956 Big Bear Run was contested by 626 starters of whom 92 finished the one lap of 151 miles. Triumph filled the first four places! The following year 174 of the 719 entries rode Triumphs, and 650 cc Trophy models took the first 12 places. And so it was all over America, and many, other countries.

Trials

The slow speed balance or the flat-in-second section were all the same to Jim Alves just after the Second World War. He rode a factory 350 cc twin at a time when the four-stroke single of 350 cc minimum was considered to be the only suitable engine for trials riding. He won many important trials.

In this period the Trophy played its part, the works ones tuned for low-speed running with very low compression ratios, but it was not every rider's choice. Alves could cope with the twin but the average club rider found a single from AJS or Norton more to his taste.

Johnny Giles took over from Alves in the 1950s, but in fact both men were more suited to ISDT events, being naturals at the longer distances, although quite capable of winning national trials.

Others

Grass track, sand races, hillclimbs, slant racing, stunts, wall of death, car jumps, rallies—solo or sidecar—mention a branch of motorcycling and the Triumph twin has run in it and done its share of winning. It is unlikely that any other make has been so successful over such a period of time in so many diverse and different fields.

12 | Specials

Top **Very smart Triton at a 1973 rally. Supercharging is unusual and whole execution very well carried out. Lovely detail work**

Above **Dave Degans on the Dresda Metisse in 1966, a product of his own and partner Dick Boone's company. A very successful combination on track and in business**

Specials powered by Triumph engines have been built in a greater variety than with any other engine and the resulting machines used for all manner of purposes. The practice began in the immediate postwar period and has never stopped. Practitioners range in their work from the simple use of a Triumph engine to propel a handy frame to the full-time manufacture of machines registered and approved for production racing.

Some of the better-known machines are described below, but these are only a few of the many that the twin has powered over the years.

Triton

The Triumph engine with its ease of maintenance and plentiful supply of tuning parts allied to the legendary Norton Featherbed frame was one of the earliest combinations that was built. It was an easy job to fit the engine in and at one time was so popular that proprietary engine plates were available. There are enough about for an owners' club to exist.

Early models used the racing frame, for that was all that was available and a factor was the frequent use of Norton engines in 500 cc car racing at that time. This resulted in numerous Manx Nortons being available less engine and gearbox and, although other engines were used, the Triumph was the most popular.

Once the road Featherbed models appeared the Triton became even more popular using either the Norton or the Triumph gearbox. Owners were able to add their own individual touches so that they finished up with a machine that was fast, steered, and was fitted out to the specification they sought.

Some riders went even further and supercharged the engine, but this was not usual, it was more common to custom finish the machine with chrome and polish in the café racer style.

Rickman

The Rickman brothers, Derek and Don, were consistent winners of scrambles in the 1950s and in 1958 decided to replace their Gold Star BSAs with something faster. The result was christened 'Metisse', French for mongrel, and was the combination of a Tiger 100 power unit in a Gold Star frame. The BSA gearbox was retained but Norton forks were fitted.

The machines were very successful and in 1962 the brothers expanded their motorcycle business to include the building of their own frames. These were fitted with the BSA gearbox and wheels, the Norton front fork and the Triumph engine. The assembly rapidly proved itself in competition and so the brothers soon became motorcycle manufacturers, although much of their business was still in frame kits and accessories.

They changed to Matchless engines for three years, but in 1965 were back with Triumph using a Tiger 100A unit. At the end of 1966 the first street machine appeared powered by a Bonneville engine and fitted with a Lockheed disc brake on the front wheel.

Below **The Rickman eight valve head developed for the Triumph engine by Weslake. A bolt-on kit which also enlarged the capacity to 700 cc**

Bottom **Triumph fitted with many of the Paul Dunstall custom parts. Tank, seat unit, fairing and swept-back pipes are all special**

The business expanded and, in the late 1960s, an association with Weslake led to an eight-valve conversion for the 650 cc Triumph which also pushed the capacity up to 700 cc. It was a bolt-on kit but just failed to really catch on, for it met with the larger new superbikes which had performance built in. The Rickmans went back to their forte, the chassis, and began producing them for more and more engines.

Eventually the supply of Triumph engines dried up, but you can still buy a Rickman frame.

Dunstall

Paul Dunstall is more usually associated with Nortons but has also produced custom parts for Triumphs. He specialized in accessories and could supply new machines with his parts fitted. Most items were for the café racer style with swept-back exhaust pipes being very popular. Rear sets, tanks, racing seats and clip-ons were among the many items available, and at a later stage he marketed a 750 cc conversion kit for the Bonneville. This used the 76 mm bore that the factory used later on and a complete machine was capable of 125 mph.

Dresda

Dave Degans founded Dresda Autos in 1959 to market Tritons and, with partner Dick Boone, soon found that they had a steady flow of customers for whom to build individual machines. Degans was already a successful road racer and continued to ride his own machines, particularly in long-distance events.

The firm produced both tuning and custom parts so that as well as the Triton a number of Dresda-Triumph machines were built using the complete Triumph as the basis. A later development, in 1966, was the Dresda-Metisse, a combination of Dresda-tuned Triumph and Rickman frame built for short-circuit racing. At 290 lb it was light enough to have exceptional acceleration.

In 1970 the Dresda-Triumph won the arduous 24-hour race at Barcelona ridden by Degans and Ian Goddard and, by that time, the engine was installed in a lighter and more compact frame of Degans' own design. The firm continued to race its machines and used the knowledge gained to improve those they sold. Triumph engines had to give way to others when supply became difficult, but not before Dresda had established itself as one of the leading Triton builders.

1965 style Dresda Bonneville.

Cheney

Eric Cheney is best known for the moto-cross and six-day specials he has built, many of them using Triumph twin engines. He used other engines as well, but it was the 500 cc twin that powered the machines used by Britain in the 1970 ISDT in Spain.

The engines for this were tuned to give good power, while remaining tractable at low speed, and capacitor ignition ensured easy starting. The cycle parts were finished in the normal Cheney manner—immaculate.

Chuck

Bill Chuck produced a range of accessories for Triumph machines in the 1960s and also worked on the engines, so they went fast as well as looking good.

The range included petrol tanks, seats, exhaust systems and clip-ons for external wear together with camshafts, rockers, valve springs and high-compression pistons on the inside. The results could be applied to any of the faster twins and resulted in some quick machines.

From these came some useful club racing machines, which were competitive at that level and both fast and reliable enough to run in the Manx GP.

Monard

The Monard was the product of the extremely fertile imaginations of business and racing partners Geoff Monty and Alan Dudley-Ward. Alan had extensive racing and tuning experience of the Triumph, while Geoff had produced a number of very successful lightweight specials in the 1950s.

The Monard first appeared in 1964 ridden by Bill Ivy and two machines were built. One used the 500 cc pre-unit engine and the other the similar 650 cc one, both driving through racing Norton gearboxes. Frames followed the lines of Geoff's earlier specials with a single large-diameter top tube which curved down behind the gearbox. Twin down tubes bolted to the front of the engine and the rear sub-frame was bolted to the same mounting as the plates that supported the swinging fork and the back of the gearbox. Front forks were Norton or, on the 500, short leading-link Renolds.

In the end the intended small production batch of Monards did not get built, but a special 500 cc engine did. This used a short-stroke crankshaft of 62·5 mm and a 650 cc iron barrel of 71 mm bore. The result was an extremely fast and vice-free engine in a chassis with an all-up weight of 250 lb. The forks reverted to Norton telescopics and the machine handled very well.

It failed to make the impact it deserved due to outside circumstances, but on its day was a winner.

Alves

Back in 1953 Jim Alves built a few frames for scrambling which were designed primarily to take the Triumph twin engine. The frame comprised two main loops with the headstock braced by a top tube. Swinging-arm rear suspension was used and controlled by Feridax-McCandless units. Front fork and wheel were Triumph.

The frame weighed 29 lb with the rear fork and the complete machine was finished in a very businesslike manner.

Magnum

This machine was conceived by Anthony Hilder and Roger Northcote-Smith, who had a background of consulting design work in the racing-car field. Their ideas on motorcycle design took an astonished world by storm in 1971, when the Deeprose-Magnum was first seen.

The frame was built up from magnesium-alloy castings and tubing. The main spine ran straight back from the steering head to form the petrol tank, the seat, support the rear suspension units and could also act as the rear number plate in road use. Two pairs of tubes ran down to support the swinging fork, which was again magnesium. For cost reasons it was triangulated in tubes rather than cast. The controlling suspension units were hydraulically linked.

The engine was a unit-construction Triumph opened up to 750 cc and worked on. Front brake was disc in a drum hub and the whole machine was extremely light.

When the machine was run the rear suspension had been changed to a more orthodox fork and the oil was carried in a tank slung in front of the crankcase. Weight in this form and ready to race was 258 lb.

Wasp

The Wasp comes from Winchester and is a scrambles machine in solo or sidecar form. The men behind it in 1965 were George Shawyer and Mike Guildford, who combined to produce a very neat 500 cc scrambler using their own frame, the Triumph engine and Norton front forks.

The machine was successful and in later years the company moved into the sidecar class to produce machines using a variety of engines. These won many moto-cross sidecar events at international level, but the use of Triumph engines fell over the years as others became more powerful or easier to obtain.

However, without the Triumph it is unlikely they would have begun in the first place.

Tribsa

Although this combination was much less popular than the Triton, a good number of Triumph engines have been fitted into BSA frames over the years. Norton forks were popular, especially for scrambles, and the gearbox could be from BSA, Norton or Triumph. Most of the machines were built for competition, but a few found their way onto the road.

Italjet Grifon 650

This machine was built in prototype form in 1971 as a design exercise and used the Triumph Bonneville engine as a basis. Frame, forks, wheels and styling were all Italian with the frame down tube line being matched by the exhaust pipes.

Slimline forks were fitted and carried a front wheel with alloy rim laced onto a drum of impressive size containing a single leading-shoe brake on each side. The rear wheel also had an alloy rim and a single drum brake and its movements were controlled by damper units with exposed springs. The seat, petrol tank and side panels were all styled to produce a new line, while the front mudguard was of a very short racing pattern attached to the fork legs only.

The machine was the design of Leo Tartarini, who did freelance work for Ital, but it failed to go into production.

Choppers

Mention choppers to the traditional motorcyclist and he sees red, but the best of them are well engineered and superbly finished. They represent an art form of their own and can be the result of many hours of painstaking labour. Sadly not all are prepared to the same high standard as the best, but good or bad, most built in Britain use a Triumph as a basis. The twin lends itself to the sometimes outrageous styling executed on it and it sits neatly in the variety of machines it has been tailored to. Not mainstream, but still a motor-cycle.

Above **Pretty Italjet Grifon 650 with Italian chassis and cycle parts**
Top **The motorcycle as an artform. The best choppers were well engineered as is this low rider**

The Home Specials

Tricati, Trimax, Trigusta, Tridot, Trinelli, Trihonda and Greenmph were all the result of mating the Triumph twin engine unit with, respectively, Ducati, NSU Max, MV175, Dot, Benelli, Honda and Greeves frames. The first and last of these were quite popular at one time, while the Dot exercise was with the Dot factory's blessing, but the others were specials built by riders seeking something a little out of the ordinary.

Machines were built for use on the road, for competition and, sometimes, because the parts were there and a machine was needed. Most were well built and some were quite superb in their workmanship and design.

Engines were usually the unit construction 500 as it fitted in well in so many frames, but all the other sizes, including the scooter engine, were used at some time. In some cases the brakes had to be improved, but this was seldom a problem as the resulting machines were usually quite light.

The Trio was one of the more unusual machines for it had the engine, a 500 cc pre-unit job, laid horizontally in a special frame built for scrambles by Swede Bjorn Hansson. To obtain good cooling all the fins were shaved from head and barrel and a new set welded back on in the correct orientation.

Three Wheels

For most riders this signified a sidecar outfit, but for Terry Smith and Howard Stapleton in 1968 it meant a machine for the chair class with two Mini wheels at the front for steering. The driver knelt between them with the 650 cc Triumph engine behind him which drove the single normal-size rear wheel. The passenger sat astride this and hung out on the appropriate side for the corners.

The machine built by Colin Saunders fell into the chopper class and as far back as the gearbox it was normal chopper with racked forks, special seat and Triumph powered as usual. Behind the gearbox the machine became more special with two large rear wheels attached to an Austin rear axle modified to accept chain final drive. The engine was a 1955 Tiger 110 with twin Del'Orto carburettors and the machine was built in 1972. Similar styles were seen in the USA but not often in Britain.

Bore Kits

Long before Triumph got round to stretching their 650 to a larger size small firms were producing conversion kits. A few tried boring out the eight-stud barrel but this left insufficient metal between the studs and the bore, so all the better conversions were based on the nine-stud.

Many kits were available in the late 1960s and a few firms went on to make better cylinder heads, one such being the Weslake Company.

Racing Specials

Many Triumph-engined machines have been raced over the years, but some deserve a special mention because they were more than just an engine in a frame. One such was the original LEF, the initials standing for Lewis, Ellis and Foster; Triumph agents at Watford whose 250 cc twin was based on a 3T and built in 1947. The machine had a special three-piece crankshaft made by its constructors, modified Tiger 100 rods, and eccentric small-end bushes to allow various compression ratios to be tried. The cylinder head was converted to accept two carburettors and special camshafts designed and made.

The machine ran well in 1948 at circuits such as Ansty, Dunholme and Eppynt and was further improved for 1949 with a swinging-fork frame, a racing magneto and alloy wheel rims. In this form it ran in the TT that year but retired after six and a half laps when the primary chain broke. The following year it returned but again retired, this time with engine trouble, on the fourth lap. The LEF made a reappearance in 1980 in vintage racing, after a long sleep.

Alan Dudley-Ward kept to a more conventional engine built up from a pre-war Tiger 100 and GP rods and barrels. An alloy head with single carburettor was obtained from a stationary charging plant. The frame was part Velocette and the forks were girders with aeroelastics used as the spring medium. A twin leading-shoe front brake was constructed. Later changes were to move the oil tank in front of the crankcase and run the exhaust pipes over the gearbox in a cross-over pattern. He won the Grand Prix of Finland more than once in the early 1950s.

Owen Greenwood is best known for his Mini tricar, but before he raced that he was very successful with a Triumph sidecar outfit. His machine was the first British outfit to finish in the 1959 sidecar TT and was exceedingly well prepared. A good many other people raced Triumph sidecars at that time but few were as fast as Greenwood. The outfit was conventional, not a kneeler, and could be fitted with either a 500 or a 650 cc engine.

Another sidecar racer in the mid-1960s was Ian Johnson. He decided that a 180-degree twin would pull better so converted his Tiger 110 engine to that layout. The crankshaft was relatively easy to modify, being the built-up type, but the camshafts were less so. Each had to be cut between the cams and then rewelded with one lobe advanced 90 degrees on. Ignition was less of a problem, with a Honda contact breaker giving the required firing intervals.

With its two-into-one exhaust system the exhaust note was very flat and it usually sounded as if it was only firing on one cylinder. It went well enough to prompt others to carry out the same change, one of these being Ian Fillery.

More unusual was the 180-degree twin built by Rob Collett for sprinting. The engine began as a 500 cc Triumph twin and finished up as a 180-degree two-stroke twin with double exhaust valves and two superchargers. This unusual device used the blowers to force the charge into slots cut in the base of the cylinder block, the two being needed to obtain the required boost pressure and to suit the mechanical layout of the ports. The camshafts were retimed so both valves opened together and their lift reduced to avoid them hitting. Rather more tricky was rearranging the timing gears so that the camshafts ran at crankshaft speed.

Above **Double twin for the road. Neat installation to fit engines in so closely and connect everything up. Reversed head on rear engine**

Left **Rob Collett sprinter. 180 degree two-stroke twin with duplex exhaust valves and twin superchargers. Inlets at base of barrel, four exhaust pipes**

Double Twins

For some owners two Triumphs had to be better than one and the practice began in the American sprint world with engines in tandem. The transverse layout was also used and one such four was built by Frank Marton in the early 1960s. His machine was used for sidecar racing and had one engine in the usual position and the second alongside it but slightly to the rear so the two could be coupled by chain. As this meant that it was also turned round it had the cylinder head reversed and the camshafts swapped over, an easy modification on the Triumph engine.

Bill Plummer adopted a rather different approach to build a super Triton four. His machine had a 60-degree vee-four engine produced by machining the twin crankcases and then welding them together. The result just went into the Norton frame and had the two crankshafts joined by chain. The rear cylinder head was reversed to help the carburettor installation and the necessary camshaft changes made. The firing intervals were normal four cylinder so a car distributor in the magneto position of the front half served the coil ignition system. Built in Napier, New Zealand, the machine was brought to England by scrambler Arthur Harris after a short trial ride, but he never used it.

Appendix

Specifications

Model	6/1	3TU	TRW	GP
Year from	1933	1946	1948	1948
Year to	1935			1950
Bore (mm)	70	57	63	63
Stroke (mm)	84	68·6	80	80
Capacity (cc)	646	350·1	499	499
Inlet valve dia. (in)			1·14	
Exhaust valve dia. (in)			1·14	
Inlet valve inclination °	45	Vertical	2 from vertical	45
Exhaust valve inclination °	45	Vertical	2 from vertical	45
Compression ratio (to 1)	6·2		6·0	8.3
Compression ratio option high	6·6			8·8 & 12·5
Con rod centres			6·5	
Spark plug (Champion)			L5 or L11S	LA15
Spark plug (NGK)			B7HS	B10HN
Gudgeon pin dia. (in)			·625	
Valve timing:				
inlet opens BTDC			16	
inlet closes ABDC			56	
exhaust opens BBDC			56	
exhaust closes ATDC			16	
Valve clearance (time) (in)			Nil	
Valve clearance (cold) inlet (in)			0·002	
Valve clearance (cold) exhaust (in)			0·004	
Ignition timing °			21	
Ignition timing piston (in)			0.125	0.437
Points gap (in)	·012		0·012	0·012
Valve seat angle °			45	45
Valve lift—inlet (in)			0·30	
Valve lift—exhaust (in)			0·30	
Valve spring free length (in)			1·812	
Drive main ID (in)			1·125	
Drive main OD (in)			2·812	
Drive main width (in)			0·812	
Timing main ID (in)			1·375	
Timing main width (in)			1·125	
Big end rod dia. (in)	1·750			
Big end rod width (in)	1·25			
Big end pin dia. (in)	1·750		1·500	

Model	6/1	3TU	TRW	GP
Year from	1933	1946	1948	1948
Year to	1935			1950
Oil pressure (psi)	60			
Primary drive (in)	double helical gear		$\frac{1}{2} \times \frac{5}{16}$	$\frac{1}{2} \times \frac{5}{16}$
Rear chain (in)	chain		$\frac{5}{8} \times \frac{3}{8}$	$\frac{5}{8} \times \frac{3}{8}$
Sprockets: engine (T)	1·7:1			24 **1**
Sprockets: clutch (T)				43
Sprockets: gearbox (T)	18			18
Sprockets: rear wheel (T)	49 **1 2**			46
Box ratio: top	1·0		1·0	1·0
Box ratio: 3rd	1·23		1·42	1·10
Box ratio: 2nd	1·84		2·21	1·44
Box ratio: 1st	2·50		2·91	1·73
O/A ratio: top	4·63 **1 2**		5·8	4·58
O/A ratio: 3rd	5·7		8·25	5·04
O/A ratio: 2nd	8·5		12·8	6·58
O/A ratio: 1st	11·6		16·85	7·93
Front tyre (in)	26 × 3·5	4·00 × 15	3·25 × 19	3·00 × 20
Rear tyre (in)	26 × 3·5	4·00 × 15	4·00 × 19	3·50 × 19
Rim front		pressed steel disc		Alloy
Rim rear				
Brake front dia. (in)	8		7	8
Brake front width (in)	1			1·375
Brake rear dia. (in)	8		7	8
Brake rear width (in)	1			1·375
Front suspension	Girder		Telescopic	Telescopic
Rear suspension	Rigid		Rigid	Sprung hub
Petrol tank (Imp. gal)	3·25		3·0	4·25
Petrol tank (US gal)	3·9		3·6	5·1
Petrol (litre)	14·7		13·6	19·3
	2 4·9 available – 52T			**1** 22 & 23 available
	1 5·3 for sidecar – 56T			
Oil tank (Imp. pint)	4 + 2 = 6		4	8
Oil tank (US pint)	7·2		4·8	9·6
Oil tank (litre)	3·40		2·27	4·54
Ignition system	Magneto	Coil	Magneto **1**	Magneto
Gen. type	Dynamo	Dynamo	Alternator	None
Output (watt)			35	
Battery (volt)	6		6	
Wheelbase (in)			53	55
Ground clear. (in)			6·25	6
Seat height (in)	28		31	29·5
Width (bars) (in)			28.5	28
Length (in)			80	84
Dry weight (lb)			340 **2**	314
Power: bhp	25		18 **3**	40
@ rpm	4500		5000	7200
Torque (ft lb)			22	
@ rpm			3000	

3 1953 — 16·8
2 1953 — 320 lb
1 1953 — coil

Triumph Twins & Triples

Appendix

Model	5T	T100	5T	T100
Year from	**1937**	**1938**	**1946**	**1946**
Year to	**1939**	**1939**	**1954**	**1954**
Bore (mm)	63	63	63	63
Stroke (mm)	80	80	80	80
Capacity (cc)	498·76	498·76	498·76	498·76
Inlet valve dia. (in)	1·31	1·31	1·31	1·31
Exhaust valve dia. (in)	1·31	1·31	1·31	1·31
Inlet valve inclination °	45	45	45	45
Exhaust valve inclination °	45	45	45	45
Compression ratio (to 1)	7·2	8·0	7·0 **1**	7·6 **1**
Compression ratio option high				8·25, 9·5, 12 **1**
Spark plug (Champion)			L85	L11S **4**
Spark plug (NGK)			B7HS	B8HS **5**
Valve timing:				
inlet opens BTDC			26·5	26·5
inlet closes ABDC			69·5	69·5
exhaust opens BBDC			61	61·5
exhaust closes ATDC			25	35·5
Valve clearance (time)			Nil	Nil
Valve clearance (cold) inlet (in)			0·001 **3 2**	0·001 **3 2**
Valve clearance (cold) exhaust (in)			0·001 **3 2**	0·001 **3 2**
Ignition timing °			37	37
Ignition timing piston (in)			0·375	0·375
Points gap (in)	0·012	0·012	0·012 **4**	0·012
Drive main ID (in)	1·25		1·125	1·125
Drive main OD (in)	2·75		2·812	2·812
			4 1953 on 0·015	**5** Alloy head— B8ES
			3 or 0·002/ 0·004	**4** Alloy head— N3
			2 or 0·010	**3** or 0·002/ 0·004
			1 1950 on	**2** or 0·010
				1 1950 on
Drive main width (in)	0·687		0·812	0·812
Timing main ID (in)	1·25		1·0	1·0
Timing main OD (in)	2·75		2·5	2·5
Timing main width (in)	0·687		0·75	0·75
Big end rod dia. (in)	1·437		1·437/1·4375	1·437/1·4375
Big end rod width (in)	1·0			
Big end rod side play (in)			0·0305/0·030	0·0305/0·030
Big end pin dia. (in)	1·437	1·437	1·437	1·437
Crank end float (in)			0·004/0·013	0·004/0·013
Cam bush dia. (in)	0·875 drive/ 0·812 left	0·875 drive/ 0·812 left	0·874/0·8745	0·874/0·8745
Idler wheel bush (in)			0·4995/0·5005	0·4995/0·5005
Tappet guide dia. (in)			0·3120/0·3125	0·3120/0·3125
Small end bush dia. (in)			0·812/0·8125	0·812/0·8125
Small end bush width (in)	1·0	1·0	1·0	1·0
Oil pressure (psi)	50 psi (new)	50 psi (new)	50 psi (new)	50 psi (new)
Primary drive (in)	$\frac{1}{2} \times \frac{5}{16}$	$\frac{1}{2} \times \frac{5}{16}$	$\frac{1}{2} \times \frac{5}{16}$	$\frac{1}{2} \times \frac{5}{16}$

Triumph Twins & Triples

Model	5T	T100	5T	T100
Year from	**1937**	**1938**	**1946**	**1946**
Year to	**1939**	**1939**	**1954**	**1954**
No. of pitches	70 solo, 69 s/car		78	78 **2**
Rear chain size (in)	$\frac{5}{8} \times \frac{3}{8}$	$\frac{5}{8} \times \frac{3}{8}$	$\frac{5}{8} \times \frac{3}{8}$	$\frac{5}{8} \times \frac{3}{8}$
No. of pitches	100		93	93
Sprockets: engine (T)	22 solo 19 s/car		22	22
Sprockets: clutch (T)	43		43	43
Sprockets: gearbox (T)	18		18	18
Sprockets: rear wheel (T)	46		46	46
Box ratios: top	1·0	1·0	1·0	1·0
Box ratios: 3rd	1·2		1·2	1·2
Box ratios: 2nd	1·73		1·73	1·73
Box ratios: 1st	2·54		2·54	2·54
O/A ratios: top	solo 5·0 s/car 5·79		5	5
O/A ratios: 3rd	solo 6·00 s/car 6·95		6	6
O/A ratios: 2nd	solo 8·65 s/car 10·0		8·65	8·65
O/A ratios: 1st	solo 12·7 s/car 14·7		12·7	12·7
Front tyre (in)	3·00 × 20	3·00 × 20	3·25 × 19	3·25 × 19
Rear tyre (in)	3·50 × 19	3·50 × 19	3·50 × 19	3·50 × 19
Rim—front			WM2 × 19	WM2 × 19
Rim—rear			WM2 × 19	WM2 × 19
Brake—front dia. (in)	7		7	7 **1**
Brake—front width (in)			1·12	1·12
Brake—rear dia. (in)	7		7 **1**	7
Brake—rear width (in)			1·12	1·12
			1 8 with sprung hub	**1** 1954—8 in
Front suspension	Girder			
Rear—type	Rigid	Rigid	Rigid **1**	Rigid **1 2**
Petrol Tank (Imp. gal)	3·5	4	4	4
Petrol tank (US gal)	4·2	4·8	4·8	4·8
Petrol tank (litre)	15·9	18·1	18·1	18·1
Oil tank (Imp. pint)	5 **1**	8	6	6
Oil tank (US pint)	6	9·6	7·2	7·2
Oil tank (litre)	2·8	4·5	3·4	3·4
Box capacity (Imp. pint)			1	1
Box capacity (US pint)			1·2	1·2
Box capacity (litre)			0·57	0·57
Chain case (Imp. pint)			0·33	0·33
Chain case (US pint)			0·4	0·4
Chain case (cc)			190	190
Front forks/leg (Imp. pint)			0·17	0·17
	1 For 1940—6		**1** Sprung hub option	**2** 1954—S/A **1** Sprung hub option

Appendix

Model	5T	T100	5T	T100
Year from	1937	1938	1946	1946
Year to	1939	1939	1954	1954
Front forks/leg (US pint)			0·2	0·2
Front forks/leg (cc)			100	100
Oil grade			SAE20/50	SAE20/50
Box oil grade			SAE50	SAE50
Case oil grade			SAE20	SAE20
Fork oil grade			SAE20	SAE20
Ignition system	Magneto	Magneto	Magneto **7**	Magneto
Gen. type	Dynamo	Dynamo	Dynamo **3**	Dynamo
Output (watt)	35	35	35 **2**	35 **1**
Battery (volt)	6	6	6	6
Earth	Neg	Neg	Neg **8**	Neg **7**
Wheelbase (in)	54	54	54 **4**	54 **5**
Ground clear. (in)	5	5	5 **5**	5 **6**
Seat height (in)	27·75		28 **6**	28 **3**
Width (bars) (in)	30		28·5	28·5
Length (in)	84	84	84	84
Dry weight (lb)	353		365	365 **4**
Wet weight (lb)	365	365	381 (with sprung hub)	
Power: bhp	26	34	28 **1**	30 **2**
@ rpm	6000	7000	6000 **1**	6500
			8 1952—Pos	
			7 1953—Coil	**7** 1952—Pos
			6 1950 on 29·5	**6** 1950 on 6
			5 1950 on 6	**5** 1950 on 55
			4 1950 on 55	**4** 1950 on 355
			3 1953—Alt	**3** 1950 on 31
			2 1949 on 60 watt	**2** 1950 on 32
			1 1950 on 27/6300	**1** 1949 on 60 watt

Model	T100c	5T	T100
Year from	1953	1955	1955
Year to		1958	1959
Bore (mm)	63	63	63
Stroke (mm)	80	80	80
Capacity (cc)	499	499	499
Compression ratio (to 1)	8·0	7·0	8·0 **1**
Compression ratio opt. high	9·0		
Spark plug (Champion)	NA12 or NA14	L85	N3
Spark plug (NGK)	B9EN	B7HS	B7ES
Valve timing:	**1**		
Inlet opens BTDC	34	26·5	26·5
Inlet closes ABDC	55	69·5	69·5
exhaust opens BBDC	55	61·5	61·5
exhaust closes ATDC	34	35·5	35·5
Valve clearance (cold) inlet (in)	0·002	0·010	0·010

Model	T100c	5T	T100
Year from	**1953**	**1955**	**1955**
Year to		**1958**	**1959**
Valve clearance (cold) exhaust (in)	0·004	0·010	0·010
Ignition timing °	42		37
Ignition timing piston (in)	0·469		0·375
Points gap (in)	0·012	0·015	0·012
Primary drive (in)	$\frac{1}{2} \times \frac{5}{16}$	$\frac{1}{2} \times \frac{5}{16}$	$\frac{1}{2} \times \frac{5}{16}$
No. of pitches	78	70	70
Rear chain size (in)	$\frac{5}{8} \times \frac{3}{8}$	$\frac{5}{8} \times \frac{3}{8}$	$\frac{5}{8} \times \frac{3}{8}$
No. of pitches	93	100	100
Sprockets: engine (T)	22	22	22
Sprockets: clutch (T)	43	43	43
Sprockets: gearbox (T)	18	18	18
Sprockets: rear wheel (T)	46	46	46
	1 Valves ·02 in from seats		**1** 1957—9·0
Box ratios: top	1·0 **1**	1·0	1·0
Box ratios: 3rd	1·19	1·19	1·19
Box ratios: 2nd	1·69	1·69	1·69
Box ratios: 1st	2·44	2·44	2·44
O/A ratios: Top	5·0	5·0 **1**	5·0 **1**
O/A ratios: 3rd	5·95	5·95	5·95
O/A ratios: 2nd	8·45	8·45	8·45
O/A ratios: 1st	12·20	12·20	12·20
	1 Close ratio option	**1** S/car 5·8, 6·9, 9·8, 14·2	**1** S/car 5·8, 6·9, 9·8, 14·2
Front tyre (in)	3·25 × 19	3·25 × 19	3·25 × 19
Rear tyre (in)	3·50 × 19	3·50 × 19	3·50 × 19
Pressure solo (psi)		18/19	17/19
Rim—front	WM2	WM2	WM2
Rim—rear	WM2	WM2	WM2
Brake—front dia. (in)	7	7	8
Brake—rear dia. (in)	7 **1**	7	7
	1 8 with sprung hub		
Front suspension	Telescopic	Telescopic	Telescopic
Rear—type	Rigid **1**	S/A	S/A
Petrol tank (Imp. gal)	4	4	4
Petrol tank (US gal)	4·8	4·8	4·8
Petrol tank (litre)	18·1	18·1	18·1
Oil tank (Imp. pint)	8	6	6
Oil tank (US pint)	9·6	7·2	7·2
Oil tank (litre)	4·5	3·4	3·4
Box capacity (Imp. pint)	1	1	1
Box capacity (US pint)	1·2	1·2	1·2
Box capacity (litre)	·57	·57	·57
Chaincase (Imp. pint)	·33	·25	·25
Chaincase (US pint)	·4	·3	·3
	1 Sprung hub option		

Appendix

Model	**T100c**	**5T**	**T100**
Year from	**1953**	**1955**	**1955**
Year to		**1958**	**1959**
Chaincase (cc)	190	142	142
Front forks/leg (Imp. pint)	·17	·17	·17
Front forks/leg (US pint)	·2	·2	·2
Front forks/leg (cc)	100	100	100
Oil grade	SAE20/50	SAE20/50	SAE20/50
Box oil grade	SAE50	SAE50	SAE50
Case oil grade	SAE20	SAE20	SAE20
Fork oil grade	SAE20	SAE20	SAE20
Ignition system	Magneto	Coil	Magneto
Gen. type	Dynamo	Alternator	Dynamo
Output (watt)	60	60	60
Battery (volt)	6	6	6
Earth	Pos.	Pos.	Pos.
Wheelbase (in)	55	55·75	55·75
Ground clear. (in)	6	5	5
Seat height (in)	31	30·5	30·5
Dry weight (lb)	362 **1**	380 **1**	375 **1**
Power: bhp	40	27	32
@ rpm	7000	6300	6500
	1 In road trim	**1** 1957—395	**1** 1957—385

Model	**3T**	**TR5**	**TR5**	**TR6**
Year from	**1946**	**1948**	**1955**	**1955**
Year to	**1951**	**1954**	**1958**	**1962**
Bore (mm)	55	63	63	71
Stroke (mm)	73·4	80	80	82
Capacity (cc)	349	499	499	649
Compression ratio (to 1)	7·0 **1**	6·0	8·0	8·5 **1**
Compression opt. low			6·0	
Spark plug (Champion)	L85	N3	N3	N3
Spark plug (NGK)	B7HS	B7ES	B7ES	B7ES
Gudgeon pin dia. (in)	0·6845			
Valve timing:			**1**	
inlet opens BTDC	22	26·5	27	
inlet closes ABDC	66	69·5	48	
exhaust opens BBDC	63	61·5	48	
exhaust closes ATDC	25	35·5	27	
Valve clearance (time) (in)	Nil			
Valve clearance (cold) inlet (in)	0·001	0·002	0·002	
Valve clearance (cold) exhaust (in)	0·001	0·004	0·004	
	1 1951—6·3		**1** Soft cam option	**2** 1961—8·5
				1 1957—8·0

Model	3T	TR5	TR5	TR6
Year from	**1946**	**1948**	**1955**	**1955**
Year to	**1951**	**1954**	**1958**	**1962**
Ignition timing °	37	37	42	
Ignition timing piston (in)	0·344	0·375	0·469	
Points gap (in)	0·012	0·012	0·012	
Drive main ID (in)	1·0			
Drive main OD (in)	2.5			
Drive main width (in)	·75			
Timing main ID (in)	1·250			
Big end rod dia. (in)	1·374/1·3745			
Big end rod side play (in)	0·0085/0·009			
Big end pin dia. (in)	1·373/1·3735			
Crank end float (in)	0·0075/0·0155			
Cam bush dia. (in)	0·874/0·8745			
Idler wheel bush (in)	0·4995/0·5005			
Tappet guide dia. (in)	0·3120/0·3125			
Small end bush dia. (in)	0·6848/0·6853			
Primary drive (in)	$\frac{1}{2} \times \frac{5}{16}$	$\frac{1}{2} \times \frac{5}{16}$	$\frac{1}{2} \times \frac{5}{16}$	$\frac{1}{2} \times \frac{5}{16}$
No. of pitches	74	76	70	70
Rear chain size (in)	$\frac{5}{8} \times \frac{3}{8}$	$\frac{5}{8} \times \frac{3}{8}$	$\frac{5}{8} \times \frac{3}{8}$	$\frac{5}{8} \times \frac{3}{8}$
No. of pitches	90	90	100	101
Sprockets: engine (T)	19	21	21	24
Sprockets: clutch (T)	43	43	43	43
Sprockets: gearbox (T)	18	18	18	18
Sprockets: rear wheel (T)	46	46	46	46
Box ratios: top	1·0 **2**	1·0	1·0	1·0
Box ratios: 3rd	1·2	1·45	1·19	1·19
Box ratios: 2nd	1·73	2·29	1·69	1·69
Box ratios: 1st	2·54	3·07	2·44	2·45
O/A ratios: top	5·8 **1**	5·24 **1**	5·24 **1**	5·24 **1**
O/A ratios: 3rd	6·95	7·60	6·24	5·45
O/A ratios: 2nd	10	12·02	8·85	7·75
O/A ratios: 1st	14·7	16·08	12·8	11·2
Front tyre (in)	3·25 × 19	3·00 × 20	3·00 × 20 **1**	3·00 × 20 **2**
Rear tyre (in)	3·25 × 19	4·00 × 19	4·00 × 18	4·00 × 18 **3**
Pressure solo (psi)	16/18		21/16	
Rim—front		WM1		
Rim—rear		WM3		
Brake—front dia. (in)	7	7	7	8 **1**
Brake—rear dia. (in)	7 **1**	7	7	7
Front suspension	Telescopic	Telescopic	Telescopic	Telescopic
Front movement (in)	6·25			

1 8 with sprung wheel

1 1958— 3·25 × 19

3 1962— 4·00 × 19
2 1958— 3·25 × 19
1 1955/6—7 in

Appendix

Model	3T	TR5	TR5	TR6
Year from	**1946**	**1948**	**1955**	**1955**
Year to	**1951**	**1954**	**1958**	**1962**
Rear—type	Rigid **1**	Rigid	S/A	S/A
Petrol tank (Imp. gal)	3	2·5	3	3
Petrol tank (US gal)	3·6	3	3·6	3·6
Petrol tank (litre)	13·6	11·3	13·6	13·6
Oil tank (Imp. pint)	6	6	6	6
Oil tank (US pint)	7·2	7·2	7·2	7·2
Oil tank (litre)	3·4	3·4	3·4	3·4
Box capacity (Imp. pint)	1	1	1	1
Box capacity (US pint)	1·2	1·2	1·2	1·2
Box capacity (litre)	·57	·57	·57	·57
Chaincase (Imp. pint)	·33	·33	·25	·25
Chaincase (US pint)	·4	·4	·3	·3
Chaincase (cc)	190	190	142	142
Front forks/leg (Imp. pint)		·17	·17	·17
Front forks/leg (US pint)		·2	·2	·2
Front forks/leg (cc)		100	100	100
Oil grade	SAE20/50	SAE20/50	SAE20/50	SAE20/50
Box oil grade	SAE50	SAE50	SAE50	SAE50
Case oil grade	SAE20	SAE20	SAE20	SAE20
Fork oil grade	SAE20	SAE20	SAE20	SAE20
	1 Sprung wheel option			
Ignition system	Magneto	Magneto	Magneto	Magneto
Gen. type	Dynamo	Dynamo	Dynamo	Dynamo **3**
Output (watt)	35 **1**	60	60	60
Battery (volt)	6	6	6	6
Earth	Neg.	Neg. **2**	Pos.	Pos.
Wheelbase (in)	52.2 **2**	53	55·75	55·75
Ground clear. (in)	6	6·5	5	5
Seat height (in)	28·5	31	30·5	30·5
Width (bars) (in)	28·5	29		
Length (in)	82·5	80		
Dry weight (lb)	335	304 **1**	365 **1**	370 **5 4 2**
Power bhp	19 **3**	25	33	42 **1**
@ rpm	6500 **3**	6000	6500	6500
				5 1962—383
				4 1961—393
		3 1951—17 @ 6000		**3** 1961—alternator
		2 1950 on 53·25	**2** 1952—Pos.	**2** 1957—380
		1 1949 on 60 watt	**1** 1950 on 295	**1** 1957—375	**1** 1957—40

Model	6T	6T	6T
Year from	**1949**	**1955**	**1962**
Year to	**1954**	**1962**	**1966**
Bore (mm)	71	71	71
Stroke (mm)	82	82	82
Capacity (cc)	649	649	649

Model	6T	6T	6T
Year from	**1949**	**1955**	**1962**
Year to	**1954**	**1962**	**1966**
Inlet valve inclination °	45	45	
Exhaust valve inclination °	45	45	
Compression ratio (to 1)	7·0	7·0 **1**	7·5
Compression ratio opt. high	8·5		
Con rod centres	6·50		
Spark plug (Champion)	L85	L85	N4
Spark plug (NGK)	B7HS	B7HS **3**	B7ES
Gudgeon pin dia. (in)	0·687		
Valve timing:			
inlet opens BTDC	26·5	26·5	25
inlet closes ABDC	69·5	69·5	52
exhaust opens BBDC	61·5	61·5	60
exhaust closes ATDC	35·5	35·5	17
Valve clearance (time) (in)	0·020	0·020	0·020
Valve clearance (cold) inlet (in)	0·002 **2**	0·002 **2**	0·002
Valve clearance (cold) exhaust (in)	0·004 **2**	0·004 **2**	0·004
Ignition timing °	39	39	35
Ignition timing piston (in)	0·375	0·375	0·375
Points gap	0·012 **1**	0·015	0·015
Valve seat angle °	45		
Valve lift—inlet (in)	0·294		
Valve lift—exhaust (in)	0·294		
Big end rod dia. (in)	1·437		
Oil pressure (psi)	60		
Primary drive (in)	½ × 5⁄16	½ × 5⁄16	⅜ Duplex
No. of pitches	80	70	84
Rear chain (in)	⅝ × ⅜	⅝ × ⅜	⅝ × ⅜
No. of pitches	93	101	103
		3 1961—B7ES	
	2 or 0·001 or 0·010	**2** or 0·010	
	1 1953 on 0·015	**1** 1961—7·5	
Sprockets: engine (T)	24 **1**	24	29
Sprockets: clutch (T)	43	43	58
Sprockets: gearbox (T)	18	18	20 **2**
Sprockets: rear wheel (T)	46	46	46
Box ratios: top	1·0	1·0	1·0
Box ratios: 3rd	1·19	1·19	1·19
Box ratios: 2nd	1·70	1·70	1·69
Box ratios: 1st	2·45	2·45	2·48
O/A ratios: top	4·57	4·57 **2 1**	4·6 **1**
O/A ratios: 3rd	5·46	5·46	5·47
O/A ratios: 2nd	7·75	7·75	7·77
O/A ratios: 1st	11·20	11·20	11·43
	1 21 for sidecar	**2** 1961—4·67	**2** sidecar—18
		1 sidecar 5·2	**1** sidecar—5·1
Front tyre (in)	3·25 × 19	3·25 × 19 **1**	3·25 × 18
Rear tyre (in)	3·50 × 19	3·50 × 19 **1**	3·50 × 18
Pressure solo (psi)		18/19	

Appendix

Model	6T	6T	6T
Year from	**1949**	**1955**	**1962**
Year to	**1954**	**1962**	**1966**
Rim—front	WM2	WM2	WM2
Rim—rear	WM2	WM2	WM2
Brake—front dia. (in)	7	7 **2**	8
Brake—front width (in)	1·12		
Brake—rear dia. (in)	8 **1**	7	7
Brake—rear width (in)	1·12		
		2 1961—8	
	1 7 with rigid frame	**1** 1960—18	
Front suspension	Telescopic	Telescopic	Telescopic
Rear—type	Rigid **1**	S/A	
Petrol tank (Imp. gal)	4	4	4
Petrol tank (US gal)	4·8	4·8	4·8
Petrol tank (litre)	18·1	18·1	18·1
Oil tank (Imp. pint)	6	6	5 **1**
Oil tank (US pint)	7·2	7·2	6
Oil tank (litre)	3·4	3·4	2·8
Box capacity (Imp. pint)	1	1	0·875
Box capacity (US pint)	1·2	1·2	1·05
Box capacity (litre)	0·57	0·57	0·50
Chaincase (Imp. pint)	0·33	0·25	0·625
Chaincase (US pint)	0·4	0·3	0·75
Chaincase (cc)	190	142	354
Front forks/leg (Imp. pint)	0·17	0·17	0·33
Front forks/leg (US pint)	0·2	0·2	0·4
Front forks/leg (cc)	100	100	190
	1 Sprung hub option		**1** 1966—6
Oil grade	SAE20/50	SAE20/50	SAE20/50
Box oil grade	SAE50	SAE50	SAE50
Case oil grade	SAE20	SAE20	10W/30
Fork oil grade	SAE20	SAE20	10W/30
Ignition system	Magneto **4**	Coil	Coil
Gen. type	Dynamo **4**	Alternator	Alternator
Output (watt)	60		
Battery (volt)	6	6	6 **1**
Earth	Neg. **5**	Pos.	Pos.
Wheelbase (in)	55	55·75	55
Ground clear. (in)	6	5	5
Seat height (in)	31·5 **3 2**	30·5	30
Width (bars) (in)			27·5
Dry weight (lb)	385 **1**	385 **2 1**	369
Wet weight (lb)	397		
Power: bhp	34	34	34 **2**
@ rpm	6300	6300	6300 **2**
	5 1952—Pos.		
	4 1953—coil & alternator		
	3 With saddle 29·5		
	2 Twin seat fitted	**2** 1961—371	**2** 1964—37/6700
	1 With sprung hub	**1** 1957—395	**1** 1964 on 12 volt

162

Model	3TA	T90
Year from	**1957**	**1962**
Year to	**1966**	**1968**
Bore (mm)	58·25	58·25
Stroke (mm)	65·5	65·5
Capacity (cc)	349	349
Inlet valve dia. (in)	1·25	
Exhaust valve dia. (in)	1·25	
Inlet valve inclination °	45	
Exhaust valve inclination °	45	
Valve stem dia. (in)	·312	
Compression ratio (to 1)	7·5	9·0
Spark plug (Champion)	N3	N4
Spark plug (NGK)	B7ES	B7ES
Gudgeon pin dia. (in)	0·562/0·5617	
Valve timing:		
inlet opens BTDC	26·5	34
inlet closes ABDC	69·5	55
exhaust opens BBDC	61·5	48
exhaust closes ATDC	35·5	27
Valve clearance (time) (in)	0·020	0·020
Valve clearance (cold) inlet (in)	0·010	0·002
Valve clearance (cold) exhaust (in)	0·010	0·004
Ignition timing °	30	40
Drive main fitted ID (in)	1·437	
Timing main ID (in)	1·439	
Big end rod sideplay (in)	0·008/0·012	
Big end pin dia. (in)	1·437/1·4375	
Drive main shaft dia. (in)	1·438/1·4375	
Timing main shaft dia. (in)	1·438/1·4375	
Crank end float (in)	Nil	
Small end bush dia. (in)	0·562/0·5625	
Primary drive (in)	⅜ Duplex	⅜ Duplex
No. of pitches	78	78
Rear chain size (in)	⅝ × ⅜	⅝ × ⅜
No. of pitches	100	103
Sprockets: engine (T)	26	26
Sprockets: clutch (T)	58	58
Sprockets: gearbox (T)	18	17
Sprockets: rear wheel (T)	43	46
Box ratios: top	1·0	1·0
Box ratios: 3rd	1·17	1·18
Box ratios: 2nd	1·74	1·62
Box ratios: 1st	2·41	2·42
O/A ratios: top	5·31	6·04
O/A ratios: 3rd	6·30	7·15
O/A ratios: 2nd	9·32	9·8
O/A ratios: 1st	13·0	14·67

Model	3TA	T90
Year from	**1957**	**1962**
Year to	**1966**	**1968**
Front tyre (in)	3·25 × 17 **2**	3·25 × 18
Rear tyre (in)	3·25 × 17 **2 1**	3·50 × 18
Pressure solo (psi)	20/22	24/24
	2 1966—18	
	1 1963—3·50	
Rim—front		WM2
Rim—rear		WM2
Brake—front dia. (in)	7	7
Brake—rear dia. (in)	7	7
Front suspension	Telescopic	Telescopic
Rear—movement (in)	2.5	
Petrol tank (Imp. gal)	3·5 **1**	3·0
Petrol tank (US gal)	4·2	3·6
Petrol tank (litre)	15·9	13·6
Oil tank (Imp. pint)	5 **2**	5 **1**
Oil tank (US pint)	6	6
Oil tank (litre)	2·8	2·8
Box capacity (Imp. pint)	0·67	0·67
Box capacity (US pint)	0·8	0·8
Box capacity (litre)	0·38	0·38
Chaincase (Imp. pint)	0·5	0·5
Chaincase (US pint)	0·6	0·6
Chaincase (cc)	284	284
Front forks leg (Imp. pint)	0·25 **3**	0·25 **2**
Front forks leg (US pint)	0·3	0·3
Front forks leg (cc)	142	142
	3 1964—0·33	
	2 1966—6	**2** 1964—0·33
	1 1963—3	**1** 1966—6
Oil grade	SAE20/50	SAE20/50
Box oil grade	SAE50	SAE50
Case oil grade	SAE20	SAE20
Fork oil grade	SAE20	SAE20
Ignition system	Coil	Coil
Gen. type	Alternator	Alternator
Output (watt)		60
Battery (volt)	6 **2**	6 **1**
Earth	Pos.	Pos.
Wheelbase (in)	52·75	53·5
Ground clear. (in)	5	7·5
Seat height (in)	28·5 **1**	30
Width (bars) (in)	27	26·5
Length (in)	81	82·25
Dry weight (lb)	340	336
Power: bhp	18·5	27
@ rpm	6500	7500
	2 1966—12	
	1 1963—29·25	**1** 1966—12

Appendix

Model	5TA	T100T	T100A	T100 SS
Year from	**1958**	**1966**	**1959**	**1961**
Year to	**1966**	**1970**	**1961**	**1970**
Bore (mm)	69	69	69	69
Stroke (mm)	65·5	65·5	65·5	65·5
Capacity (cc)	490	490	490	490
Inlet valve inclination °	45	39	45	45 **1**
Exhaust valve inclination °	45	39	45	45 **1**
Valve stem dia. (in)	0·312		0·312	
Compression ratio (to 1)	7·0	9·0	9·0	9·0
Spark plug (Champion)	N3 **1**	N4	N3 **2**	N4
Spark plug (NGK)	B7ES	B8ES	B7ES	B8ES
Gudgeon pin dia. (in)	0·562/0·5617		0·562/0·5617	
Valve timing:				
inlet opens BTDC	26·5	40	27 **1**	34
inlet closes ABDC	69·5	52	48	55
exhaust opens BBDC	61·5	61	48	48
exhaust closes ATDC	35·5	31	27	27
Valve clearance (time) (in)	0·020	0·020	0·020	0·020
Valve clearance (cold) inlet (in)	0·010	0·002	0·002	0·002
Valve clearance (cold) exhaust (in)	0·010	0·004	0·004	0·004
Ignition timing °	30	37	37	37
Points gap (in)	0·015	0·015	0·015	0·015
Drive main ID (mm)				30
Drive main OD (mm)				72
Drive main width (mm)				19
Timing main ID (in)	1·439		1·439	1·439
Big end rod side play (in)	0·008/0·012		0·008/0·012	
			2 1961—N4	
	1 1963—N4		**1** 1961—34/ 55/55/34	**1** 1968—39 °
Big end pin dia. (in)	1·438/1·4375		1·438/1·4375	
Drive main shaft dia. (in)	1·438/1·4375		1·438/1·4375	
Timing main dia. (in)	1·438/1·4375		1·438/1·4375	
Crank end float (in)	Nil		Nil	
Small end bush dia. (in)	0·562/0·5625		0·562/0·5625	
Primary drive (in)	⅜ Duplex	⅜ Duplex	⅜ Duplex	⅜ Duplex
No. of pitches	78	78	78	78
Rear chain size (in)	⅝ × ⅜	⅝ × ⅜	⅝ × ⅜	⅝ × ⅜
No. of pitches	101 **2**	102	101 **2**	101 **3**
Sprockets: engine (T)	26	26	26	26
Sprockets: clutch (T)	58	58	58	58
Sprockets: gearbox (T)	20 **1**	18	20 **1**	18
Sprockets: rear wheel (T)	43	46	43	43 **1**
Box ratios: top	1·0	1·0	1·0	1·0
Box ratios: 3rd	1·17	1·22	1·17	1·17
Box ratios: 2nd	1·74	1·61	1·74	1·74 **2**
Box ratios: 1st	2·41	2·47	2·41	2·41
				3 1963—103
	2 1961—102		**2** 1961—102	**2** 1963—1·62
	1 1961—19T		**1** 1961—19T	**1** 1963—46

Model	5TA	T100T	T100A	T100 SS
Year from	**1958**	**1966**	**1959**	**1961**
Year to	**1966**	**1970**	**1961**	**1970**
O/A ratios: top	4·8	5·7	4·8	5·33
O/A ratios: 3rd	5·62	6·95	5·62	6·34
O/A ratios: 2nd	8·35	9·18	8·35	9·37
O/A ratios: 1st	11·56	14·09	11·56	12·96
Front tyre (in)	3·25 × 17 **1**	3·25 × 18	3·25 × 17	3·25 × 19 **1**
Rear tyre (in)	3·50 × 17 **1**	3·50 × 18	3·50 × 17	3·50 × 18
Pressure solo (psi)	20/20	24/25	20/20	24/24
Brake—front dia. (in)	7	8	7	7
Brake—rear dia. (in)	7	7	7	7
Front suspension	Telescopic	Telescopic	Telescopic	Telescopic
Rear movement (in)	2·5		2·5	
	1 1966—18			**1** 1963—18
Petrol tank (Imp. gal)	3·5 **1**	3	3·5	3·5 **1**
Petrol tank (US gal)	4·2	3·6	4·2	4·2
Petrol tank (litre)	15·9	13·6	15·9	15·9
Oil tank (Imp. pint)	5 **2**	6	5	5 **2**
Oil tank (US pint)	6	7·2	6	6
Oil tank (litre)	2·8	3·4	2·8	2·8
Box capacity (Imp. pint)	0·67	0·67	0·67	0·67
Box capacity (US pint)	0·8	0·8	0·8	0·8
Box capacity (litre)	0·38	0·38	0·38	0·38
Chaincase (Imp. pint)	0·5	0·5	0·5	0·5
Chaincase (US pint)	0·6	0·6	0·6	0·6
Chaincase (cc)	284	284	284	284
Front forks/leg (Imp. pint)	0·25 **3**	0·33	0·25	0·25 **3**
Front forks/leg (US pint)	0·3	0·4	0·3	0·3
Front forks/leg (cc)	142	190	142	142
Oil grade	SAE20/50	SAE20/50	SAE20/50	SAE20/50
Box oil grade	SAE50	SAE50	SAE50	SAE50
Case oil grade	SAE20	SAE20	SAE20	SAE20
Fork oil grade	SAE20	SAE20	SAE20	SAE20
	3 1964—0·33			**3** 1964—0·33
	2 1966—6			**2** 1966—6
	1 1963—3			**1** 1963—3
Ignition system	Coil	Coil	Energy transfer **2**	Coil
Gen. type	Alternator	Alternator	Alternator	Alternator
Battery (volt)	6 **2**	12	6	6 **1**
Earth	Pos.	Pos.	Pos.	Pos.
Wheelbase (in)	52·75	53·5	52·75	53·5
Ground clear. (in)	5	7·5	5	7·5
Seat height (in)	28·5 **1**	30	28·5	30
Width (bars) (in)	27		26	26·5
Length (in)	81		81	83·25
Dry weight (lb)	341	337	350	336
Power: bhp	27	39	32 **1**	34
@ rpm	6500	7400	7000	7000
	2 1966—12		**2** 1961—Coil	**1** 1966—12
	1 1963—29·25		**1** 1961—34	

Appendix

Model	T100R	T100C	TR5T
Year from	**1970**	**1970**	**1972**
Year to	**1973**	**1971**	**1973**
Bore (mm)	69	69	69
Stroke (mm)	65·5	65·5	65·5
Capacity (cc)	490	490	490
Compression ratio (to 1)	9·0	9·0	9·0
Con rod centres	5·312		
Spark plug (Champion)	N3	N3	N4
Spark plug (NGK)	B8ES	B8ES	B7ES
Gudgeon pin dia. (in)	0·6885		
Valve timing:			
inlet opens BTDC	40	40	34
inlet closes ABDC	52	52	55
exhaust opens BBDC	61	61	48
exhaust closes ATDC	31	31	27
Valve clearance (time) (in)	0·020	0·020	0·020
Valve clearance (cold) inlet (in)	0·002	0·002	0·002
Valve clearance (cold) exhaust (in)	0·004	0·004	0·004
Ignition timing °	38	38	38
Points gap (in)	0·015	0·015	0·015
Drive main ID (mm)	30		
Drive main OD (mm)	72		
Drive main width (mm)	19		
Timing main ID (mm)	35		
Timing main OD (mm)	72		
Timing main width (mm)	17		
Oil pressure (psi)	60		
Primary drive (in)	$\frac{3}{8}$ Duplex	$\frac{3}{8}$ Duplex	$\frac{3}{8}$ Duplex
No. of pitches	78	78	78
Rear chain size (in)	$\frac{5}{8} \times \frac{3}{8}$	$\frac{5}{8} \times \frac{3}{8}$	$\frac{5}{8} \times \frac{3}{8}$
No. of pitches	102	102	110
Sprockets: engine (T)	26	26	26
Sprockets: clutch (T)	58	58	58
Sprockets: gearbox (T)	18	18	18
Sprockets: rear wheel (T)	46	46	53
Box ratios: top	1·0	1·0	1·0
Box ratios: 3rd	1·22	1·22	1·22
Box ratios: 2nd	1·61	1·61	1·76
Box ratios: 1st	2·47	2·47	2·84
O/A ratios: top	5·70	5·70	6·57
O/A ratios: 3rd	6·97	6·97	8·04
O/A ratios: 2nd	9·16	9·16	11·60
O/A ratios: 1st	14·10	14·10	18·70
Front tyre (in)	3·25 × 19	3·25 × 19	3·00 × 21
Rear tyre (in)	4·00 × 18	4·00 × 18	4·00 × 18
Pressure solo (psi)	24/25	24/25	25/25
Rim—front	WM2	WM2	WM2
Rim—rear	WM3	WM3	WM3
Brake—front dia. (in)	8 **1**	8	6

1 1973—disc on a few machines

Model	**T100R**	**T100C**	**TR5T**		
Year from	**1970**	**1970**	**1972**		
Year to	**1973**	**1971**	**1973**		
Brake—front width (in)			0·875		
Brake—rear dia. (in)	7	7	7		
Brake—rear width (in)			1·125		
Petrol tank (Imp. gal)	3 **1**	3	2		
Petrol tank (US gal)	3·6	3·6	2·4		
Petrol tank (litre)	13·6	13·6	9·1		
Oil tank (Imp. pint)	5·8	5·8	4		
Oil tank (US pint)	7·0	7·0	4·8		
Oil tank (litre)	3·3	3·3	2·3		
Box capacity (Imp. pint)	0·67	0·67	0·67		
Box capacity (US pint)	0·8	0·8	0·8		
Box capacity (litre)	0·38	0·38	0·38		
Chaincase (Imp. pint)	0·5	0·5	0·5		
Chaincase (US pint)	0·6	0·6	0·6		
Chaincase (cc)	284	284	284		
Front forks/leg (Imp. pint)	0·33	0·33	0·33		
Front forks/leg (US pint)	0·4	0·4	0·4		
Front forks/leg (cc)	190	190	190		
Oil grade	SAE20/50	SAE20/50	SAE20/50		
Box oil grade	SAE50	SAE50	SAE50		
Case oil grade	SAE20/50	SAE20/50	SAE20/50		
Fork oil grade	SAE10/30	SAE10/30	SAE10/30		
Ignition system	Coil	Coil	Coil		
Gen. type	Alternator	Alternator	Alternator		
Battery (volt)	12	12	12		
Earth	Pos. **1** Optional 2	Pos.	Pos.		
Wheelbase (in)	53·5 **1**	53·5	54		
Ground clear. (in)	7·4	7·4	7·5		
Seat height (in)	30	30	32		
Width (bars) (in)	27 **3**	27	32		
Length (in)	83·25 **2**	83·25	85		
Fork angle °			63		
Dry weight (lb)	356	356	322		

3 1973—29
2 1973—84
1 1973—55

Model	**T110**	**T120**	**T120**	**T120R**
Year from	**1953**	**1958**	**1962**	**1970**
Year to	**1961**	**1962**	**1970**	**1973**
Bore (mm)	71	71	71	71
Stroke (mm)	82	82	82	82
Capacity (cc)	649	649	649	649
Compression ratio (to 1)	8·0 **1**	8·5	8·5 **1**	9·0
Compression ratio opt. high	8·5			
Spark plug (Champion)	N3	N3 **1**	N4 **3**	N3
Spark plug (NGK)	B7ES	B8ES	B8ES	B8ES

Triumph Twins & Triples

Appendix

Model	T110	T120	T120	T120R
Year from	1953	1958	1962	1970
Year to	1961	1962	1970	1973
Valve timing:				
inlet opens BTDC	27	34	34	34
inlet closes ABDC	48	55	55	55
exhaust opens BBDC	48	48	48	55
exhaust closes ATDC	27	27	27	34
Valve clearance (time) (in)	0·020	0·020	0·020	0·020
Valve clearance (cold) inlet (in)	0·002	0·002	0·002	0·002
Valve clearance (cold) exhaust (in)	0·004	0·004	0·004	0·004
Ignition timing °	35	39	39	38
Ignition timing piston (in)	0·359	0·437	0·435 **2**	0·415
Points gap (in)	0·012	0·012	0·015	0·015
			3 1968—N3	
			2 1970—0·415	
	1 1955/56 only—8·5	**1** 1962—N4	**1** 1966—9·0	
Primary drive (in)	½ × 5⁄16	½ × 5⁄16	⅜ Duplex	⅜ Duplex
No. of pitches	70	70	84	84
Rear chain size (in)	⅝ × ⅜	⅝ × ⅜	⅝ × ⅜	⅝ × ⅜
No. of pitches	101	98 **4**	103 **2**	106
Sprockets: engine (T)	24 **1**	24 **1 2**	29	29
Sprockets: clutch (T)	43	43	58	58
Sprockets: gearbox (T)	18	18	19 **1**	19
Sprockets: rear wheel (T)	46	46 **3**	46	47
Box ratios: top	1·0	1·0	1·0	1·0
Box ratios: 3rd	1·19	1·19	1·19	1·24
Box ratios: 2nd	1·69	1·69	1·69	1·69
Box ratios: 1st	2·44	2·44	2·44	2·44
		4 1959—101		
		3 1960 on—43		
		2 1961/62—21	**2** 1968 on—104	
	1 S/car 21T	**1** 1960—22	**1** S/car 17	
O/A ratios: top	4·57	4·57	4·84	4·95
O/A ratios: 3rd	5·45	5·45	5·76	6·15
O/A ratios: 2nd	7·75	7·75	8·17	8·36
O/A ratios: 1st	11·20	11·20	11·81	12·08
Front tyre (in)	3·25 × 19	3·25 × 19	3·25 × 18 **1**	3·25 × 19
Rear tyre (in)	3·50 × 19	3·50 × 19 **1**	3·50 × 18	4·00 × 18
Pressure solo (psi)	18/19			
Brake—front dia. (in)	8	8	8	8 **1**
Brake—rear dia. (in)	7	7	7	7
Brake—rear width (in)	1·12			
		1 1961 on 4·00 × 18	**1** 1967 on 3·00 × 19	**1** 1973— 10 in disc
Front suspension	Telescopic	Telescopic	Telescopic	Telescopic
Rear—type	S/A	S/A	S/A	S/A
Rear movement (in)		2·2	2·5	2·2
Petrol tank (Imp. gal)	4	4 **2 1**	4	4
Petrol tank (US gal)	4·8	4·8	4·8	4·8
Petrol tank (litre)	18·1	18·1	18·1	18·1

Model	T110	T120	T120	T120R
Year from	**1953**	**1958**	**1962**	**1970**
Year to	**1961**	**1962**	**1970**	**1973**
Oil tank (Imp. pint)	6	6	5 **1**	4
Oil tank (US pint)	7·2	7·2	6·0	4·8
Oil tank (litre)	3·4	3·4	2·8	2·3
Box capacity (Imp. pint)	1	1	0·875	0·875
Box capacity (US pint)	1·2	1·2	1·05	1·05
Box capacity (litre)	0·57	0·57	0·50	0·50
Chaincase (Imp. pint)	0·25	0·25	0·625	0·25
Chaincase (US pint)	0·3	0·3	0·75	0·3
Chaincase (cc)	142	142	354	142
Front forks/leg (Imp. pint)	0·17 **1**	0·25 **3**	0·33 **2**	0·33
Front forks/leg (US pint)	0·2	0·3	0·4	0·4
Front forks/leg (cc)	100	142	190	190
Oil grade	SAE20/50	SAE20/50	SAE20/50	SAE20/50
Box oil grade	SAE50	SAE50	SAE50	SAE50
Case oil grade	SAE20	SAE20	SAE10W/30	SAE10W/30
Fork oil grade	SAE20	SAE20	SAE10W/30	SAE10W/30
		3 1958/59 only—0·17		
		2 1962—3 gal	**2** 1962/63 only—0·25	
	1 1958—0·25	**1** 3 gal option	**1** 1966—6	
Ignition system	Magneto	Magneto	Coil	Coil
Gen. type	Dynamo **1**	Dynamo **1**	Alternator	Alternator
Output (watt)	60	60		
Battery (volt)	6	6	6 **1**	12
Earth	Pos.	Pos.	Pos.	Pos.
Wheelbase (in)	55·75	55·75 **2**	55	56
Ground clear. (in)	5	5	5	7
Seat height (in)	30·5	30·5	30·5	31 **1**
Width (bars) (in)		28·5	27	33
Length (in)			84	87·5
Fork angle °		64·5 **5 4**	65 **3**	62
Dry weight (lb)	395 **3**	404 **3**	363	387
Wet weight (lb)	420			
Power: bhp	42 **2**	46	46 **2**	50
@ rpm	6500	6500	6500 **2**	7000
		5 1961/62—65°		
		4 1960—67°		
	3 1957—390	**3** 1962—390	**3** 1966 on—62°	
	2 1957—40	**2** 1961—56·5	**2** 1964—47/6700	
	1 1960 on— alternator	**1** 1960 on— alternator	**1** 1966—12	**1** 1973—29

Appendix

Model	TR6 SS	TR6R	TR6C	TR7RV
Year from	1962	1970	1970	1973 & 1975
Year to	1970	1973	1971	1980 on
Bore (mm)	71	71	71	76 **1**
Stroke (mm)	82	82	82	82
Capacity (cc)	649	649	649	744 **2**
Compression ratio (to 1)	8·5 **1**	9·0	9·0	7·9
Spark plug (Champion)	N4	N4	N4	N3
Spark plug (NGK)	B7ES	B8ES	B8ES	B7ES
	1 1967—9·0			**2** few at 725
				1 few at 75
Valve timing:				
inlet opens BTDC	34	34	34	19″ at TDC
inlet closes ABDC	55	55	55	
exhaust opens BBDC	48	55	55	
exhaust closes ATDC	27	34	34	·13″ at TDC
Valve clearance (time) (in)	0·020	0·020	0·020	Nil
Valve clearance (cold) inlet (in)	0·002	0·002	0·002	0·008
Valve clearance (cold) exhaust (in)	0·004	0·004	0·004	0·006
Ignition timing °	39	38	38	38
Points gap (in)	0·015	0·015	0·015	0·015
Primary drive (in)	⅜ Duplex	⅜ Duplex	⅜ Duplex	⅜ Triplex
No. of pitches	84	84	84	84
Rear chain size (in)	⅝ × ⅜	⅝ × ⅜	⅝ × ⅜	⅝ × ⅜
Sprockets: engine (T)	29	29	29	29
Sprockets: clutch (T)	58	58	58	58
Sprockets: gearbox (T)	19 **1**	19	18	20
Sprockets: rear wheel (T)	46	47	47	47
Box ratios: top	1·0	1·0	1·0	5 1·0
Box ratios: 4th				4 1·19
Box ratios: 3rd	·1·19	1·24	1·24	1·40
Box ratios: 2nd	1·69	1·69	1·69	1·84
Box ratios: 1st	2·44	2·44	2·44	2·60
O/A ratios: top	4·84	4·95	5·22	5 4·70
O/A ratios: 4th				4 5·59
O/A ratios: 3rd	5·76	6·15	6·47	6·58
O/A ratios: 2nd	8·17	8·36	8·83	8·63
O/A ratios: 1st	11·81	12·08	12·74	12·25 **1**
	1 S/car 17			**1** 1979—12·14
Front tyre (in)	3·25 × 19 **1**	3·25 × 19	3·25 × 19	3·25 × 19 **2**
Rear tyre (in)	4·00 × 18 **2**	4·00 × 18	4·00 × 18	4·00 × 18
Brake—front dia. (in)	8	8	8	10 in disc
Brake—rear dia. (in)	7	7	7	7 **1**
	2 1966—3·50			**2** 1979—4·00
	1 1966—68			**1** 1976 on—
	18			10 in disc
Front suspension	Telescopic			
Petrol tank (Imp. gal)	4	4	4	4
Petrol tank (US gal)	4·8	4·8	4·8	4·8
Petrol tank (litre)	18·1	18·1	18·1	18·1
Oil tank (Imp. pint)	5 **1**	4	4	4
Oil tank (US pint)	6	4·8	4·8	4·8

Triumph Twins & Triples

Model	TR6 SS	TR6R	TR6C	TR7RV
Year from	**1962**	**1970**	**1970**	**1973 & 1975**
Year to	**1970**	**1973**	**1971**	**1980 on**
Oil tank (litre)	2·8	2·3	2·3	2·3
Box capacity (Imp. pint)	0·875	0·875	0·875	0·875
Box capacity (US pint)	1·05	1·05	1·05	1·05
Box capacity (litre)	0·50	0·50	0·50	0·50
Chaincase (Imp. pint)	0·625	0·25	0·25	0·625
Chaincase (US pint)	0·75	0·3	0·3	0·75
Chaincase (cc)	354	142	142	354
Front forks/leg (Imp. pint)	0·33	0·33	0·33	0·33
Front forks/leg (US pint)	0·4	0·4	0·4	0·4
Front forks/leg (cc)	190	190	190	190
Oil grade	SAE20W/50	SAE20W/50	SAE20W/50	SAE20W/50
Box oil grade	SAE50	SAE50	SAE50	SAE50
Case oil grade	SAE10W/30	SAE10W/30	SAE10W/30	SAE10W/30
Fork oil grade	SAE10W/30	SAE10W/30	SAE10W/30	SAE10W/30
Ignition system	**1** 1966—6 Coil	Coil	Coil	
Gen. type	Alternator	Alternator	Alternator	
Battery (volt)	6 **1**	12	12	12
Earth	Pos.	Pos.	Pos.	Pos.
Wheelbase (in)	55·5	56		56
Ground clear. (in)	7·12	7		7
Seat height (in)	30·5	31		31
Width (bars) (in)	27	33 **1**		29 **1**
Length (in)	84·5	87·5		87·5
Dry weight (lb)	363	387		413 **2**
Power: bhp	40			
@ rpm	6500			
				2 1979—395
	1 1966—12	**1** 1973—29		**1** 1979—27 in

Model	T120V	T140V	X75	TR65
Year from	**1972**	**1973 & 1975**	**1973**	**1981**
Year to	**1975**	**1980**		**1983**
Bore (mm)	71	76 **1**	67	76
Stroke (mm)	82	82	70	71·5
Capacity (cc)	649	744 **2**	740	649
Compression ratio (to 1)	9·0	7·9	9·0	8·9
Con rod centres		6·0		
Spark plug (Champion)	N3	N3	N3	
Spark plug (NGK)	B8ES	B8ES	B8ES	
		2 very early 725		
		1 very early 75		
Valve timing:				
inlet opens BTDC	34	0·19 in at TDC		
inlet closes ABDC	55			
exhaust opens BBDC	55			
exhaust closes ATDC	34	0·13 in at TDC		
Valve clearance (time) (in)	0·020	Nil		

171

Appendix

Model	T120V	T140V	X75	TR65
Year from	**1972**	**1973 & 1975**	**1973**	**1981**
Year to	**1975**	**1980**		**1983**
Valve clearance (cold) inlet (in)	0·002	0·008		
Valve clearance (cold) exhaust (in)	0·004	0·006		
Ignition timing °	38	38	38	
Points gap (in)	0·015	0·015	0·015	
Primary drive (in)	⅜ Duplex	⅜ Triplex	⅜ Triplex	⅜ Duplex
No. of pitches	84	84	84	
Rear chain size (in)	⅝ × ⅜	⅝ × ⅜	⅝ × ⅜	
No. of pitches	107	106		
Sprockets: engine (T)	29	29	28	29
Sprockets: clutch (T)	58	58	50	58
Sprockets: gearbox (T)	19	20	19	19
Sprockets: rear wheel (T)	47	47	53	47
Box ratios: top	1·0	1·0	1·0	1·0
Box ratios: 4th	1·19	1·19	1·19	1·19
Box ratios: 3rd	1·40	1·40	1·40	1·40
Box ratios: 2nd	1·84	1·84	1·84	1·84
Box ratios: 1st	2·60	2·60	2·60	2·60
O/A ratios: top	4·90	4·70	4·98	4·90
O/A ratios: 4th	5·89	5·59	5·93	5·89
O/A ratios: 3rd	6·92	6·58	6·98	6·92
O/A ratios: 2nd	9·09	8·63	9·15	9·09
O/A ratios: 1st	12·80	12·25 **1** **1** 1979—12·14	12·87	12·80
Front tyre (in)	3·25 × 19	3·25 × 19 **2**	3·25 × 19	3·25 × 19
Rear tyre (in)	4·00 × 18	4·00 × 18	4·25 × 18	4·00 × 18
Rim—front			Alloy	
Rim—rear			Alloy	
Brake—front dia. (in)	8 **1**	10 disc	8	10 disc
Brake—rear dia. (in)	7	7 **1** **2** 1979 on— 4·00	7	7
	1 1973—10 in disc	**1** 1976 on— 10 in disc		
Front trail (in)		4·87		
Petrol tank (Imp. gal)	4	4	2·2	4
Petrol tank (US gal)	4·8	4·8	2·6	2·3
Petrol tank (litre)	18·1	18·1	9·8	10·4 or 18·1
Oil tank (Imp. pint)	4	4	5	4
Oil tank (US pint)	4·8	4·8	6	4·8
Oil tank (litre)	2·3	2·3	2·8	2·3
Box capacity (Imp. pint)	0·875	0·875	2	
Box capacity (US pint)	1·05	1·05	2·4	
Box capacity (litre)	0·50	0·50	1·36	
Chaincase (Imp. pint)	0·625	0·625	0·5	
Chaincase (US pint)	0·75	0·75	0·6	
Chaincase (cc)	354	354	284	
Front forks/leg (Imp. pint)	0·33	0·33	0·33	
Front forks/leg (US pint)	0·4	0·4	0·4	
Front forks/leg (cc)	190	190	190	

Model	T120V	T140V	X75	TR65
Year from	**1972**	**1973 & 1975**	**1973**	**1981**
Year to	**1975**	**1980**		**1983**
Oil grade	SAE20W/50	SAE20W/50	SAE20/50	
Box oil grade	SAE50	SAE50	EP90	
Case oil grade	SAE10W/30	SAE10W/30	SAE20/50	
Fork oil grade	SAE10W/30	SAE10W/30	TQF	
Ignition system	Coil	Coil	Coil	Coil
Gen. type	Alternator	Alternator	Alternator	Alternator
Battery (volt)	12	12	12	12
Earth	Pos.	Pos.	Pos.	
Wheelbase (in)	56	56	60	56
Ground clear. (in)	7	7		
Seat height (in)	31	31	31	31
Width (bars) (in)	29	29 **1**		27
Length (in)	87·5	87·5		87·5
Dry weight (lb)	387	413 **2**	444	395
Power: bhp/rpm	7000	7000		38/6500

2 1979—395
1 1979—27

Model	Scooter	Bandit
Year from	**1958**	**1971**
Year to	**1964**	
Bore (mm)	56	63
Stroke (mm)	50·62	56
Capacity (cc)	249	349
Inlet valve dia. (in)	1	1·25
Exhaust valve dia. (in)	1	1·09
Inlet valve inclination °	Nil	60 included
Exhaust valve inclination°	Approx. 45	
Valve stem dia. (in)	$\frac{9}{32}$	$\frac{5}{16}$
Compression ratio (to 1)	6·5	9·5
Con rod centres	3·875	4·724
Spark plug (Champion)	L85	N3
Spark plug (NGK)	B6HS	B8ES
Gudgeon pin dia. (in)		0·625
Valve timing:		
inlet opens BTDC	10	
inlet closes ABDC	50	
exhaust opens BBDC	50	
exhaust closes ATDC	10	
Valve clearance (cold) inlet (in)	0·005	0·006
Valve clearance (cold) exhaust (in)	0·005	0·008
Ignition timing °	5 full retard	30
Ignition timing piston (in)		0·180

Model	Scooter	Bandit
Year from	**1958**	**1971**
Year to	**1964**	
Points gap (in)	0·015	0·015
Oil pressure (psi)		70–80
Primary drive	gear	$\frac{3}{8}$ Duplex
No. of pitches	–	72
Rear chain size (in)	$\frac{3}{8}$ Duplex	$\frac{5}{8} \times \frac{1}{4}$
No. of pitches		112
Gear engine	49	23
Gear clutch	98	52
Sprockets: gearbox (T)	2:1 ratio	17
Sprockets: rear wheel (T)		48
Box ratios: top	1·0	1·0
Box ratios: 4th		1·156
Box ratios: 3rd	1·3	1·413
Box ratios: 2nd	2·025	1·872
Box ratios: 1st	3·0	2·70
O/A ratios: top	4·0	6·38
O/A ratios: 4th		7·38
O/A ratios: 3rd	5·2	9·02
O/A ratios: 2nd	8·1	11·95
O/A ratios: 1st	12·0	17·24
Front tyre (in)	3·50 × 10	3·25 × 18
Rear tyre (in)	3·50 × 10	3·50 × 18
Pressure solo (psi)	17/24	22/23
Pressure dual	17/30	
Rim—front	Pressed steel wheels	WM2
Rim—rear		WM2

Appendix

Model	Scooter	Bandit
Year from	**1958**	**1971**
Year to	**1964**	
Brake—front dia. (in)	5	8
Brake—front width (in)	1	
Brake—rear dia. (in)	5	7
Brake—rear width (in)	1	1·12
Front suspension	Telescopic	
Front spring rate (psi)		22
Front movement (in)	4·375	6·75
Front trail (in)	3·75	4·29
Rear—type	S/A	S/A
Rear—movement	2·59	2·5
Petrol tank (Imp. gal)	1·5	2·25
Petrol tank (US gal)	1·8	2·5
Petrol tank (litre)	6·8	10
Oil tank (Imp. pint)	2·5	5
Oil tank (US pint)	3·0	6
Oil tank (litre)	1·42	2·8
Box capacity (Imp. pint)		1
Box capacity (US pint)		1·2
Box capacity (litre)		0·56
Chaincase (Imp. pint)		0·25
Chaincase (US pint)		0·33
Chaincase (cc)		140

Model	Scooter	Bandit
Year from	**1958**	**1971**
Year to	**1964**	
Front forks/leg (Imp. pint)		0·33
Front forks/leg (US pint)		0·40
Front forks/leg (cc)		190
Oil grade		SAE20/50
Box oil grade		EP90
Fork oil grade		SAE10W/30
Ignition system	Coil	Coil
Gen. type	Alternator	Alternator
Output (watt)		110
Battery (volt)	6 or 12	12
Earth	Pos.	
Wheelbase (in)	48	58·5
Ground clear. (in)	5	7
Seat height (in)	28	30
Width (bars) (in)	24	27
Length (in)	72	79·5
Dry weight (lb)	244	345
Power: bhp	10	34
@ rpm		9000
Torque (lb ft)		20
@ rpm		7000

Model	**Trident T150**	**T150**	**T150V**	**T160**
Year from	**1968**	**1970**	**1972**	**1975**
Year to	**1970**	**1972**	**1975**	
Bore (mm)	67	67	67	67
Stroke (mm)	70	70	70	70
Capacity (cc)	740	740	740	740
Inlet valve dia. (in)	1·53	1·53		
Exhaust valve dia. (in)	1·31	1·31		
Valve stem dia. (in)	0·3095	0·3095		
Compression ratio (to 1)	9·5 **1**	9·5 **1**	9·0	9·5
Con rod centres	5·750	5·750		
Spark plug (Champion)	N3	N3	N3	N3
Spark plug (NGK)	B8ES	B8ES	B8ES	B8ES
Gudgeon pin dia. (in)	0·6884	0·6884		
Valve timing:				
inlet opens BTDC	50	50	0·152 at TDC	0·152 at TDC
inlet closes ABDC	64	64		
exhaust opens BBDC	67	67		
exhaust closes ATDC	47	47	0·146 at TDC	0·146 at TDC
Valve clearance (time) (in)	0·020	0·020	Nil	Nil
Valve clearance (cold) inlet (in)	0·006	0·006	0·006	0·006
Valve clearance (cold) exhaust (in)	0·008	0·008	0·008	0·008
	1 1968 only 9·0	**1** 1971 on 9·0		

Model	Trident T150	T150	T150V	T160
Year from	**1968**	**1970**	**1972**	**1975**
Year to	**1970**	**1972**	**1975**	
Ignition timing °	38	38	38	38
Ignition timing piston (in)	0·355	0·355		
Points gap (in)	0·015	0·015	0·015	0·015
Drive main ID (in)	1·125	1·125		
Drive main OD (in)	2·812	2·812		
Drive main width (in)	0·812	0·812		
Timing main ID (mm)	25	25		
Timing main OD (mm)	52	52		
Timing main width (mm)	15	15		
Centre main clearance	0·0005–0·0022	0·0005–0·0022		
Big end rod dia. (in)	1·624	1·624		
Big end clearance (in)	0·0005–0·002	0·0005–0·002		
Big end width (in)	0·904	0·904		
Big end rod side play (in)	0·008–0·014	0·008–0·014		
Big end pin dia. (in)	1·624	1·624		
Big end under sizes (in)	−0·01, −0·02, −0·03, −0·04	−0·01, −0·02, −0·03, −0·04		
Crank end float (in)	0·0015–0·0145			
Cam bush dia. (in)	1·061	1·061		
Small end bush dia. (in)	0·689	0·689		
Oil pressure (psi)	70–90	70–90		
Primary drive (in)	$\frac{3}{8}$ Triplex	$\frac{3}{8}$ Triplex	$\frac{3}{8}$ Triplex	$\frac{7}{16}$ Duplex
No. of pitches	82	82	82	
Rear chain size (in)	$\frac{5}{8} \times \frac{3}{8}$	$\frac{5}{8} \times \frac{3}{8}$	$\frac{5}{8} \times \frac{3}{8}$	$\frac{5}{8} \times \frac{3}{8}$
No. of pitches	107	108		
Sprockets: engine (T)	28	28	28	23
Sprockets: clutch (T)	50	50	50	43
Sprockets: gearbox (T)	19	19 **1**	18	19
Sprockets: rear wheel (T)	52 **1**	53	53 **1**	50
Box ratios: top	1·0	1·0	5th 1·0	5th 1·0
Box ratios: 4th			4th 1·19	4th 1·19
Box ratios: 3rd	1·19	1·19	1·40	1·40
Box ratios: 2nd	1·69	1·69	1·84	1·84
Box ratios: 1st	2·44	2·44	2·60	2·60
O/A ratios: top	4·89 **2**	4·98 **2**	5th 5·26 **2**	5th 4·92
O/A ratios: 4th			4th 6·26	4th 5·85
O/A ratios: 3rd	5·83	5·95	7·36	6·89
O/A ratios: 2nd	8·3	8·42	9·66	9·05
O/A ratios: 1st	11·95	12·15	13·59	12·72
	2 1970—as 1970/71	**2** 1972—5·26 6·52, 8·88, 12·83	**2** 1975—4·98	
	1 1970—53	**1** 1972—18	**1** 1975—50	
Front tyre (in)	3·25 × 19	4·10 × 19	4·10 × 19	4·10 × 19
Rear tyre (in)	4·10 × 19	4·10 × 19	4·10 × 19	4·10 × 19
Pressure solo (psi)	26/28	22/28		
Rim—front	WM2	WM2		
Rim—rear	WM3	WM3		
Brake—front dia. (in)	8	8	10 disc	10 disc

Appendix

Model	Trident T150	T150	T150V	T160
Year from	1968	1970	1972	1975
Year to	1970	1972	1975	
Brake—front width (in)	1·625	1·5		
Brake—rear dia. (in)	7	7	7	10 disc
Brake—rear width (in)	1·125	1·125		
Front spring rate (lb/in)	32·5	25		
Front movement (in)		6·75		
Rear spring rate (lb/in)	110	110		
Rear movement	2·5	3		
Petrol tank (Imp. gal)	4·25	4	4·5	4·8
Petrol tank (US gal)	5·1	4·8	5·4	5·8
Petrol tank (litre)	19·3	18·1	20·4	21·8
Oil tank (Imp. pint)	6	5·8	5·8	6
Oil tank (US pint)	7·2	7·0	7·0	7·2
Oil tank (litre)	3·41	3·29	3·29	3·41
Box capacity (Imp. pint)	2	2	2	2
Box capacity (US pint)	2·4	2·4	2·4	2·4
Box capacity (litre)	1·36	1·36	1·36	1·36
Chaincase (Imp. pint)	0·5	0·5	0·5	0·5
Chaincase (US pint)	0·6	0·6	0·6	0·6
Chaincase (cc)	284	284	284	284
Front forks/leg (Imp. pint)	0·33	0·33	0·33	0·33

Oh dear! John Hobbs' sprint engine at Elvington in 1970

Model	Trident T150	T150	T150V	T160
Year from	**1968**	**1970**	**1972**	**1975**
Year to	**1970**	**1972**	**1975**	
Front forks/leg (US pint)	0·4	0·4	0·4	0·4
Front forks/leg (cc)	190	190	190	190
Petrol grade	4 star	4 star		
Oil grade	SAE20/50	SAE20/50	SAE20/50	SAE20/50
Box oil grade	EP90	EP90	EP90	EP90
Case oil grade	SAE20/50	SAE20/50	SAE20/50	SAE20/50
Fork oil grade	TQF	TQF	TQF	TQF
Ignition system	Coil	Coil	Coil	Coil
Gen. type	Alternator	Alternator	Alternator	Alternator
Output (watt)	120	120		
Battery (volt)	12	12	12	12
Earth	Pos.	Pos.	Pos.	Pos.
Wheelbase (in)	58	57	58	58
Ground clear. (in)	6·5	6·5	6·5	6·5
Seat height (in)	32	31	31·5	31
Width (bars) (in)	32·5	33	29	29
Length (in)	86·75	86·25	88	88
Height (in)	44	42		
Fork angle °		61		62
Dry weight (lb)	468	460	460	503
Power: bhp	58	58	58	58
@ rpm	7250	7250	7250	7250
Torque (lb ft)		45		
@ rpm		6900		

Colours

1937
Speed Twin General finish of amaranth red for frame, forks, mudguards, toolbox and oil tank. Petrol tank chrome plated with red side and top panels, which were lined. Triumph logo on tank sides. Wheel rims were chrome plated with red, lined, centres. Chrome plated exhaust system, headlamp rim, headlamp shell and minor parts.

1938
Tiger 100 Black frame, forks, toolbox and oil tank. Mudguards in silver with black centre line. Petrol tank chrome plated with silver sheen top and side panels lined in blue. Wheel rims chrome plated with silver centres, blue lined. Chrome plated exhaust system, headlamp shell and rim, and minor parts.
Speed Twin continued as in 1937.

1939
Both models as in 1938.

1946
Speed Twin and **Tiger 100** in pre-war colours with telescopic forks and headlamp shell in machine colour. Wheels chromed or plated, depending on supply position.
350 cc model 3T Black frame, forks, oil tank, toolbox, mudguards, wheels and headlamp shell. Petrol tank chrome plated with black panels lined in ivory. Chrome plated exhaust system, headlamp rim and minor parts. Ivory mudguard stripes.

1947
All models as in 1946. Chrome supply difficult so variations depending on availability.

October 1948
Colours as in 1946. Nacelle introduced in machine colour with chrome plated side flashes. Model 3T rims chrome plated with black centres, lined in ivory.

November 1948
TR5 Black frame, forks, oil tank, toolbox and headlamp shell. Mudguards in silver with black centre line. Petrol tank chrome plated with silver panels lined in blue. Wheel rims chrome plated with silver centres, blue lined.
5T gold lining as before.

October 1949
New petrol tank style and finish for road models. Tank now painted all over with styling strip on each side comprising four horizontal chrome plated bars with Triumph logo incorporated. All wheel rims chrome plated with lined, painted centres in machine colours.
Thunderbird Colour scheme as **Speed Twin** in blue grey.
3T, 5T, T100, TR5 Colours as in 1948. **TR5** retained chrome plated tank with lined panels.
500 cc GP racer Alloy mudguards and wheel rims. Petrol tank silver with blue lining, remainder black. Chrome plated exhaust pipes and megaphones. Mudguards in silver sheen with black centre stripe.

November 1950–1953
Thunderbird Colour changed to a lighter shade of blue with polychromatic finish.
Other machines as in 1949.

October 1953
Tiger 100 and Tiger 110 Petrol tank and mudguards in shell blue sheen with black line on guards. Wheels chrome plated with shell blue centres, lined black. Frame, forks, nacelle, oil tank and battery cover in black.

1954
TR5 Trophy Petrol tank changed to same style as other models.

1955
TR5 as **T100** except wheel rims just chrome plated. Other models as 1954.

October 1955
Frame, forks, mudguards, nacelle, petrol tank, oil tank and toolbox crystal grey for **Thunderbird**.
TR6 as **TR5**, **T100** and **T110** with chrome plated wheel rims.

October 1956
New tank badge design for all twins, with chrome plated grille carrying Triumph logo. Frame, forks, oil tank and battery cover black for all models. Petrol tank and mudguards in machine colours which were **Speed Twin** in red, **Thunderbird** in bronze gold, **Tiger** and **Trophy** models in silver grey. Chrome plated wheel rims for **5T** and **6T**.
Two-tone option for the **Tiger** models was available and applied to tank and mudguards. The upper section of the petrol tank was in ivory and the lower in blue. The mudguards were ivory with a light blue centre stripe, gold lined.

1957
All machines carried transfer 'World Motorcycle Speed Record Holder'.
350 cc Model 21 For launch the whole machine was finished in metallic silver grey applied to frame, forks, mudguard, nacelle, tank and rear enclosure. Production machines finished in shell blue with black frame.

October 1957
Tiger model option with tank top black and tank lower and mudguards ivory.
Thunderbird Available with gold tank top and black lower, ivory mudguards, and other painted parts in black. Other machines unchanged.

September 1958
500 cc model 5TA As **Model 21** but in amaranth red for all painted parts.
T120 Bonneville Black frame, forks, nacelle, oil tank and battery box. Petrol tank pearl grey top and tangerine lower, mudguards pearl grey with tangerine centre stripe.
T100, T110, silver grey tank and mudguards plus option with tank top and m/guards ivory and tank lower black.
TR6 as **T100** with export option in ivory and red lower tank. **6T** in charcoal for tank, forks and mudguards with frame, oil tank and battery cover in black.

1959
Bonneville Changed petrol tank lower part and mudguard stripe to royal blue. Oil tank and battery box became pearl grey, remainder unchanged.

October 1959
Unit construction **Tiger 100A** All black finish, lower petrol tank ivory, usual parts chrome plated.
5TA bright red, **T110** as **T100A**.

October 1960
Model 21 and **3TA** Continued in shell blue with black frame. The **5TA** continued bright red while the **Tiger 100A** was finished with black petrol tank top and silver lower, the silver also being applied to the front mudguard and rear enclosure. The frame and forks were in black and this finish was used for all three 650 cc models, although the lower fork leg of the **6T** was polished. Otherwise the **6T** was as the **T100A**, with black tank top and silver lower tank, front mudguard and rear enclosure. **Tiger 110** was as **6T** but with blue tank top and upper forks, while retaining the silver.
The **Bonneville** had a sky-blue tank top and silver mudguards with a sky-blue stripe, gold lined. The lower petrol tank, oil tank and battery box were also in silver.

January 1961
New version of **TR6 Trophy** Black frame, forks, oil tank and battery box. Petrol tank top and mudguard stripe in ruby red, tank lower and mudguards in silver. Chrome plated headlamp shell and wheel rims.

October 1961
Model 5TA continued in ruby red, while **3TA** continued in shell blue, with black frame.
Tiger 100 SS Petrol tank top, mudguard strip and partial rear enclosure in kingfisher blue, tank lower and mudguards in silver. Chrome plated headlamp.
Thunderbird As October 1960, but silver now called silver sheen.
Trophy TR6 As January 1961 except ruby red changed to polychromatic burgundy.
Bonneville As October 1960 except that oil tank and battery box reverted to black. Export option in flame and silver.

October 1962
3TA available in silver bronze as an option to shell blue.
Tiger 90 Alaskan white petrol tank, mudguards and partial rear enclosure. Black frame, gold and black lining on mudguards, chrome plated headlamp shell.
Tiger 100 SS As October 1961 except blue now regal purple.
Thunderbird As October 1960 and **TR6 Trophy** same finish as **T100 SS**. **Bonneville** with alaskan white petrol tank and mudguards, the latter with black stripe lined in gold. Black frame, forks, oil tank and battery cover.

October 1963
3TA In silver beige for petrol tank, mudguards, partial rear enclosure, nacelle and forks, black frame. Frame, forks and nacelle black on **5TA** together with tank top. Tank lower, mudguards and partial rear enclosure in silver.
Tiger 90 With gold tank top and white tank lower and mudguards, the latter gold lined. Black frame, forks, oil tank and battery box.
Tiger 100 SS With scarlet tank top and silver tank lower and mudguards, remainder as **T90**.
Thunderbird As October 1962 and **TR6** as at January 1961 except ruby red changed to scarlet.
Bonneville With gold tank top and mudguard stripe, with white tank lower and mudguards. Rest as **TR6**.

October 1964
3TA and **5TA** as October 1963.
Tiger 90 With pacific blue tank top and mudguard stripe with silver tank lower and mudguards. Remainder as before.
Tiger 100 as October 1963 **Tiger 90**.
Thunderbird as before, **Trophy** same as **Tiger 100** and **Bonneville** as **Tiger 90** in blue and silver.

September 1965
New tank badges for all twins of simpler style with Triumph logo beneath. All machines had black frames, forks, oil tanks, battery boxes and nacelles where fitted. Two-tone finishes used in all cases with first colour applied to tank upper section and mudguard centre stripe. Second colour used for mudguards and lower tank.
3TA and **TR6** First colour in pacific blue, **T90** and **Bonneville** in grenadier red, **5TA** and **Thunderbird** in black, and **Tiger 100** in sherbourne green. Second colours for **3TA**, **T90**, **T100**, **TR6** and **T120** in alaskan white, for **5TA** and **6T** in silver.
Chrome plated headlamp shell fitted to **T90**, **T100**, **TR6** and **T120**, that is all models without nacelle.

November 1966
Generally as in September 1965, no nacelle models so all headlamp shells chrome plated.
First colour for **T90** in hi-fi scarlet, **T100 SS** and **T100T** in

pacific blue, **TR6** in mist green and **T120** in aubergine (purple). Second colour white for all models.

November 1967
Generally as November 1966. First colour for **T90** and **TR6** in riviera blue, for **T100 SS** and **T100T** in aquamarine green, and for **T120** in hi-fi scarlet. Second colour for all models in silver.

November 1968
As for November 1966. First colour for **T100 SS** and **T100T** in lincoln green, **TR6** in trophy red and **T120** in olympic flame. Second colour for all models in silver.

1970
General finish as in November 1966. First colour for **T100** models in jacaranda purple and second silver sheen. **TR6** tank gold with black centre stripe, **T120** in astral red with silver side panels.

1971
New style for 650 cc models with slim forks and conical hubs. Black frames, air filter boxes and side panels. **TR6** models in pacific blue and white for petrol tank and mudguards. Tank badge plain metal Triumph logo. **T120** tank in Tiger gold with central black stripe, mudguards in gold with black stripe.
T100 models as November 1966 in olympic flame and black.

1972
As for 1971. Tank badge plain metal Triumph logo without any surround. Chrome plated headlamp. First colour for **T100R** in cherry, for **TR6R** in polychromatic blue, and for **T120** in tiger gold. Second colour in white for all models.

1973
As for 1971 in general. **T100R** with white tank upper and vermilion lower, chrome plated mudguards. **TR6** and **T120R** in 1972 colours. **T120V** and **T140V** with hi-fi vermilion tank with gold panels. Chrome plated mudguards and headlamp, frame and other cycle parts black. **TR7RV** in pacific blue and white as **TR6**.
TR5T fitted with alloy petrol tank with hunting yellow side panels. Chrome plated mudguards and headlamp, black frame and side covers.

1974
As for 1973. **T120V** with purple and **T140V** with cherokee red tank, both with cold white panels. **TR7RV** in jade green and white.

1975
As for 1974.

1976
T140V available with red or blue tank with white side panels. Chrome plated mudguards, fork covers and headlamp. Black frame, headlamp brackets, air box and side covers.
TR7RV generally as **T140V** in jade green and white.

1977
T140V and **TR7RV** as in 1976.
Jubilee model Frame and forks as **T140V**. Petrol tank, side covers, chainguard and mudguards in basic silver colour. Petrol tank has blue side panels lined with red border, itself lined with narrow white lining. Mudguards have blue centre stripe with outer red and inner white lines. Chain guard has blue styling stripe lined as mudguards. Side panels carried 'Bonneville 750' in blue and lined in blue with white panel beneath lined in red on lower edges. This panel carried 'Silver Jubilee 1977' and 'Limited Edition' in red together with a Union Jack flag in correct colours. Wheel rims were chrome plated with blue centres and lined in white and red. The seat was in powder blue with red piping and a chrome trim strip along its lower edge.

1978
General finish as in 1977 but with more variations on colour for petrol tank, mudguards and side panels. Colours used were tawny brown and gold or aquamarine and silver. **T140E** model was available in the first of these, astral blue and silver or candy apple red and black.

1979
Colours as in 1978 with variations on tank styling and pin-striping in two basic forms.

May 1979
T140D Tank and side covers black, gold lined. Wheel spoke recesses in black, rims polished. Chrome mudguards and headlamp.

1980

T140 flame or grey and black, or black or grey and red, or black with white lining. **TR7** in blue, rest as 1979.

1981

T140 and **TR7** as 1980. Executive maroon shaded to ruby. **TR65** cherry red. **TR7T** yellow tank, mudguards, side panels.

1982

TR7, TR65, Executive as 1981. **TR65T** as **TR7T**. **T140** in black with red flashes. TSS black, gold lined. TSX red tank, mudguards side covers.

1983

All in burgundy, black or blue with lining.

Trident

Late 1968 1969

Tank and mudguards in aquamarine. Triumph logo on white tank panel in front of kneegrip. Black side covers with Trident motif in black outline letters on aluminium coloured panel. Black frame and forks, chrome plated headlamp shell.

1971

New style machine with black frame and chromed headlamp shell. Petrol tank and mudguards black with styled white side panels on tank and centre stripe on mudguards. Black side covers with Trident motif. Option of spring gold and black.

1972

Generally as 1971, but with chrome plated mudguards. Petrol tank and side covers in regal purple, tank logo on white panel, Trident motif in white on side covers.

1973

As 1972 with petrol tank in jet black with red side panels. Black side covers with nameplate held by screws.

1974

As 1973 with petrol tank in black with deep yellow side panels.

1975

As 1973 with petrol tank in black with gold side panels.

March 1975

T160 Generally as **T150V** with tank in cherokee red with white flashes or in white with sunflower flashes.

Scooter

1958

Introduced in 1958 in shell blue.

1961

Also available in primrose or grey. All three finishes as single colours or with ivory weathershield panels.

Engine and frame numbers

1934 to 1936

Model 6/1 engine prefix   1934   1V4
                          1935   1V5
                          1936   1V6

1937 to 1949

The year and model were used as a prefix to the engine number. From 1937 to 1939 the final digit (7, 8 or 9) was used and from 1946 to 1949 the final two figures (46, 47, 48 or 49). The model numbers were T or 5T for the Speed Twin, T100 for Tiger 100, 3T for 350 twin and TR5 for Trophy.

Typical numbers were thus:

8-T-12345   (1938 Speed Twin)
47-5T-23456   (1947 Speed Twin)
48-3T-34567   (1948 350 cc Twin)
9-T100-45678   (1939 Tiger 100)

Pre-war frames (1937/39) used the prefix TH for the 500 cc models (5T and T90) and TF for the Tiger 100.

Engine numbers commenced at:

Year	Number
1946	72000
1947	79046
1948	88782
1949	100762

1950 to 1968

Engine numbers had a prefix indicating the model type along the lines above such as 3T, 5T, 6T, T100, T110, 3TA, 5TA etc. This was followed by a number from the list below.

Year	Unit 350 and 500 cc	Pre-unit 500 and 650 cc
1950		From 100N
1951		101NA-15808NA
1952		15809NA-25000NA
		then 25000-32302
1953		32303-44134
1954		44135-56699
1955		56700-70929
1956		70930-82799
		then 0100-0944
1957	H101-H760	0945-011115
1958	H761-H5484	011116-020075
1959	H5485-H11511	020076-029363
1960	H11512-H18611	029364-030424
		then D101-D7726
1961	H18612-H25251	D7727-D15788
1962	H25252-H29732	D15789 on
		Unit 650 cc
1963	H29733-H32464	DU101-DU5824
1964	H32465-H35986	DU5825-DU13374
1965	H35987-H40527	DU13375-DU24874
1966	H40528-H49832	DU24875-DU44393
1967	H49833-H57082	DU44394-DU66245
1968	H57083-H65572	DU66246-DU85903
1969	H65573-H67331	DU85904-DU90282

Frame Number Prefix

Rigid	3T	TC
	5T, T100, 6T, TR5	TF
Swinging fork	all pre-unit	S
	'21'	H

1969 onwards

New coding system for all models using two-letter prefix for month and season/year of manufacture. Note that season/year begins in August of previous year so that JB is August 1979 not 1980.

Production numbers start at 00100 each season/year and run on irrespective of the model on which they are used. Model type code continued as before.

Letter code used is:

Letter	Month	Year
A	January	1979
B	February	1980
C	March	1969
D	April	1970
E	May	1971
G	June	1972
H	July	1973
J	August	1974
K	September	1975
N	October	1976
P	November	1977
X	December	1978
KDA	1981 models	Sept. 1980–April 1981
EDA	1982 models	May 1981–Jan. 1982
BEA	1983 models	Feb. 1982–Jan. 1983
T140V	AEA34393	Last models Jan. 21, 1983

Scooter numbers

Engines for model TW2S with electric start have letter 'E' at end of number.

Year	Engine	Frame
1959	W101	101T
1960	W3201	4001T
1961	W11790	18800T
March 1961 (new exhaust)	W16582	27407T
1962	W17800	30140T
1963	W18485	31825T
1964 last TW2	W19792	34286T
last TW2S	W19793	34249T

Model recognition points

This section has been compiled for use with the data on engine/frame numbers and machine colours. It represents a précis of the main text as applicable.

1938
5T 6 stud barrel, girders, magdyno. Pre-production chaincases had non-faired boss over engine sprocket.

1939
5T 8 stud barrel. **T100** introduced. Bead surround on front number plate.

1946
5T and **T100**. Teles. Separate dynamo. 19-inch front wheel. Speedo drive from rear wheel.
3T New model.

1947/48
Sprung hub available. All models with tank top instrument panel. Speedo drive from gearbox when sprung hub fitted.

1949
Nacelle introduced. Tank top panel deleted and parcel grid offered as option. Oil pressure tell-tale on timing chest. Speedo drive from gearbox standard. 60 watt dynamo. **TR5** added to range.

1950
6T added to range. Painted petrol tanks with horizontal chrome styling bars, except for **TR5**. Gearbox redesign. Barrel shaped saddle springs. Mk 2 sprung hub.

1951
T100 and **TR5**. Gravity die cast head and barrel with splayed exhaust ports. Race kit available for **T100**. All models fitted with new front brake with cast iron drum. Filler caps changed. Parcel grid standard.
T100 Dualseat standard.
3T dropped from range.

1952
6T fitted with SU.

1953
5T Alternator
T100c replaced race kit, dropped at year end.

1954
6T Alternator.
T110 added to range. 8-inch front brake, swing arm frame, stepped dualseat.
T100 Swing arm frame, 8-inch front brake.

1955
All models in swing arm frame, introduction of big main bearing and shell big ends.
T100 and **TR5**. Raised compression ratio.

1956
T110 Light alloy head. Ventilated front brake.
TR6 added to range.

1957
Tank motif changed to grille carrying Triumph logo. Allowed the use of two-tone colour.
5T, **6T**, **TR5**. Full width front hub.
T100 Twin inlet port head.
TR6 8-inch front brake.
3TA Introduced with full bathtub, distributor and no primary chain adjustor.

1958
3TA Parcel grid fittings.
All 500 and 650 models—slickshift gearchange.
5T and **6T** Deep section front mudguard.
T100 and **T110** As **5T** plus 8-inch full width front brake.
TR6 Full width front brake.
T110 Twin splayed inlet port head.
5T and **TR5** dropped from range in August.

1959
5TA added to range.
All 500 and 650 models—new crankshaft.
T120 added to range, fitted with nacelle.
T100 discontinued in June.

1960
5TA Primary chain adjustor added.
T100A added to range.
650 models—new frame and forks.

6T and **T110** Bathtub fitted, deep front mudguards.
T110 and **T120** Retained magneto, alternator for charging.
T120 No nacelle, q d headlamp.
TR6 Discontinued in September.

1961
All unit models—modified head angle, floating brake shoes.
3TA Primary chain adjustor added.
T100A Sports camshaft. Discontinued in August.
T110 Discontinued in August.
TR6 Reintroduced in one-carb T120 form.
650 models—modified frame with lower tank rail, floating brake shoes.
6T Alloy head, 8-inch front brake.
T120 Tacho drive on timing cover, 3-gallon tank.

1962
3TA and **5TA** New clutch operation, Siamezed exhaust, RM 19, no steering damper.
T100 SS Introduced as **T100A** with new cams, Siamezed exhaust. Partial rear enclosure, no nacelle.
6T No slickshift, Siamezed exhaust.
T120 Heavier flywheels, balance factor changed.

1963
3TA and **5TA** 3-vane clutch, smaller rectifier, twin exhausts.
T90 Introduced similar to T100SS with partial rear enclosure, Siamezed exhaust, points in timing cover.
T100 SS Points in timing cover.
All 350 and 500 twins—new, locked, rocker box caps.
All 650 twins—unit construction with new alloy 9-bolt head.
Continued on page 186.

Production flow chart

(Figures in brackets are months)

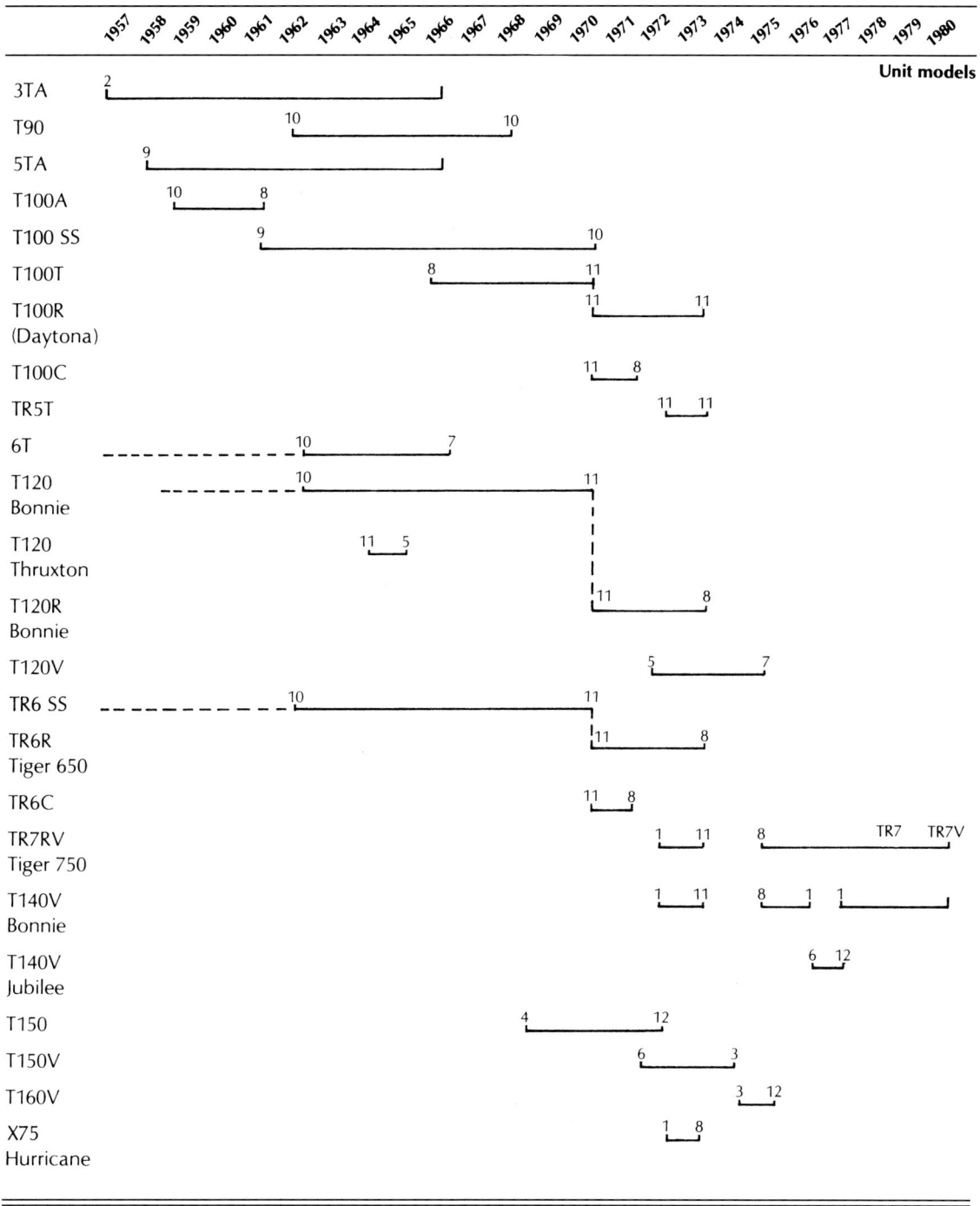

6T Nacelle, partial rear enclosure, one carburettor.
TR6 One carburettor, Siamezed exhaust.
T120 Two carbs, two exhausts.

1964
3TA and **5TA** Partial rear enclosure, new forks, points in timing cover, magnetic speedo.
T90 and **T100 SS** No partial rear enclosure, new forks, separate exhausts, magnetic speedo.
All 650 twins—new forks, magnetic speedo.
6T 12-volt electrics.
T120 Induction balance pipe.

1965
3TA and **5TA** Partial rear enclosure, new forks.
T90 and **T100 SS** New forks
All 650 twins—new forks, modified rear brake.

1966
All models—new tank badges.
3TA and **5TA** No partial rear enclosure, frame changes, 18-inch wheels, 12-volt electrics.
T90 and **T100 SS** Frame changes, 12-volt electrics.
All 650 twins—frame changes, oil supply to exhaust tappets.
6T No partial fairing, 18-inch wheels.
3TA, **5TA** and **6T** Discontinued in July.

1967
T90 and **T100 SS** New frame as **T100T**.
T100T Introduced similar to **T100 SS** but with two carburettors, new head, 8-inch front brake.
All 650 twins—improved oil pump.

1968
T90 and **T100T** Modified front forks, separate points.
T100 SS Fitted with **T100T** head, modified forks, separate points.
TR6 and **T120** Modified front brake and forks, separate points.
T90 Discontinued in October.

1969
All models—modified silencers, exposed rear springs, exhaust balance pipes.
T100 SS 7-inch 2LS front brake.
T120 Twin windtone horns, air cleaners.
T150 Introduced to home market, vertical cylinders.

1970
All models—minor changes to carburettor mountings, ignition coil, engine breather, suspension units. Complete range replaced in November.

1971
New range.
T100R As **T100T**, new switches, rubber mounted instruments and headlamp, indicators.
T100C Street scrambler as **T100R** but only one carburettor, raised exhaust, both pipes on left.
All 650 twins—new frame containing engine oil, new forks, brakes, conical hubs, indicators.
T120R Two carburettors.
TR6R (or **Tiger 650**) One carburettor, otherwise as **T120**.
TR6C Street scrambler version of **TR6R** with upswept exhaust as **T100C**.
T150 Megaphone style silencers, new forks, conical hubs, indicators, revised side covers.
T100C and **TR6C** Became export only in August.

1972
During year 5-speed gearbox became available for **T120** and standard on **T150**.
T140 Added to range in autumn. 10-stud head, new crankcases, triplex primary drive.

1973
TR5T Adventurer introduced. Trail bike format.
T140 10-inch disc front brake.
TR7RV Introduced as street scrambler version of **T140**.
T100R Some built with disc front brake.
T150 10-inch disc front brake.
X75 Introduced. Chopper style **T150** using BSA engine with sloping cylinders. 5-speed gearbox. Exhausts all on right.
Late 1973 all models except **T120** discontinued.

1974
Few machines produced due to blockade.

1975
T120 Discontinued.
From June, left side gear pedal.
T150 changed to **T160** with BSA sloping style cylinders, duplex primary chain, left side gear pedal, electric starter, 4-into-2 exhaust, rear disc brake.
T160 Discontinued at end of year.

1976
T140V and TR7V only models.
1977
Silver Jubilee models.
1978
New cylinder head, Mk 2 Concentrics.
1979
Electronic ignition, T140D
1980
Electric starter, T140ES based on T140E, Executive model.
1981
TR7T Tiger Trail off-road model. TR65 Thunderbird economy model. Royal models for UK and USA.
1982
TSS with 8 valves, TSX Custom model, TR65T off-road.
late 1982
Reduced range. T140ES revised. Daytona 600 for UK and Thunderbird 600 for USA.
1983
Production ceased.
1985–88
Devon-built Bonneville to UK and USA forms.

Carburettor settings
Amal

Year	Model	Type	Size	Main	Pilot	Slide	Needle Pos.	Needle Jet
Pre-unit construction models								
1934/35	6/1	75	$\frac{7}{8}$	120	—	3	3	
1937/39	5T	76	$\frac{15}{16}$	140	—	3	3	·106
1938/39	T100	76	1	160	—	3	3	·107
1946/52	3T	275	$\frac{7}{8}$	120	—	4	3	·107
1953	3T for AA	274	$\frac{21}{32}$	75	—	4	1	std.
1946/49	T85	275	$\frac{7}{8}$	120	—	4	3	·107
1946/53	5T	276	$\frac{15}{16}$	140	—	$3\frac{1}{2}$	3	·107
1955/60	5T	376	$\frac{15}{16}$	200	30	$3\frac{1}{2}$	4	·106
1946/48	T100	276	1	160	—	$3\frac{1}{2}$	3	·107
1949/54	T100	276	1	150	—	$3\frac{1}{2}$	2	·107
1949/50	T100 racing	76	1	130	—	4	3	·109
1951/52	T100 racing	76	1	190	—	4	3	·109
1953	T100c	76	1	150	—	4	2	·107
1955/61	T100	376	$\frac{15}{16}$	220	25	$3\frac{1}{2}$	4	·106
1957/60	T100 export	376	1	200	25	$3\frac{1}{2}$	3	·106
1955	T100 Daytona	15GP	1	250	—	6	1	·107
1957	T100 (Comp)	15GP	1	250	—	6	2	·107
1950	TR5	276	$\frac{15}{16}$	140	—	$3\frac{1}{2}$	3	·107
1951/54	TR5	276	1	150	—	$3\frac{1}{2}$	2	·107
1955/61	TR5	376	$\frac{15}{16}$	220	25	$3\frac{1}{2}$	4	·106
1961	TR5 A/R/C	376	1	190	25	$3\frac{1}{2}$	3	·106
1948/50	GP	6	1	A/R	—	6/4	—	·109
1948/50	GP (on alcohol)	6	1	A/R	—	6/4	—	·113
1950	6T	276	1	170	—	$3\frac{1}{2}$	2	·107
1950/53	6T	276	$1\frac{1}{16}$	140	—	$3\frac{1}{2}$	2	·107
1955/60	6T export	376	$1\frac{1}{16}$	270	25	$3\frac{1}{2}$	4	·106
1959/61	6T home	376	$1\frac{1}{16}$	270	25	$3\frac{1}{2}$	4	·106
1962	6T	376	$1\frac{1}{16}$	220	25	4	4	·106
1954	T110	289	$1\frac{1}{8}$	200	—	4	3	·107
1955/61	T110	376	$1\frac{1}{16}$	250	25	$3\frac{1}{2}$	3	·106
1960/61	T110	376	$1\frac{1}{16}$	250	25	$3\frac{1}{2}$	4	·106

1959/61	T120	376	$1\frac{1}{16}$	240	25	$3\frac{1}{2}$	2	·106
1960	T120	389	$1\frac{3}{16}$	310	30	3	3	·106
1955/60	TR6	376	$1\frac{1}{16}$	270	25	$3\frac{1}{2}$	4	·106

Unit construction models

1957	T21	375	$\frac{13}{16}$	110	25	$3\frac{1}{2}$	3	·105
1957/61	T21	375	$\frac{25}{32}$	100	25	$3\frac{1}{2}$	3	·105
1962/66	T21 and 3TA	375	$\frac{25}{32}$	100	25	$3\frac{1}{2}$	3	·106
1959/65	5TA	375	$\frac{7}{8}$	160	25	3	3	·105
1963/67	T90	376	$\frac{15}{16}$	180	20	3	3	·106
1968	T90	624	24 mm	140	—	$3\frac{1}{2}$	2	·106
1962/67	T100 SS	376	1	190	25	$3\frac{1}{2}$	3	·106
1968	T100 SS	626	26 mm	190	—	4	2	·106
1969	T100 SS	626	26 mm	180	—	4	2	·106
1970	T100 SS	626	26 mm	170	—	4	2	·106
1973	T100 SS	626	26 mm	150	—	$3\frac{1}{2}$	1	·106
1967	T100 T	376	$1\frac{1}{16}$	200	25	$3\frac{1}{2}$	3	·106
1968	T100 T	626	26 mm	150	—	$2\frac{1}{2}$	2	·106
1969	T100 T	626	26 mm	160	—	3	2	·106
1970	T100 T	626	26 mm	150	—	3	1	·106
1971/72	T100 C	626	26 mm	170	—	4	2	·106
1971/72	T100 R	626	26 mm	150	—	3	1	·106
1973	P.51 500	928	28 mm	210	—	3	2	·106
1963/66	6T	376	$1\frac{1}{16}$	220	25	4	4	·106
1964/66	6T USA	376	$1\frac{1}{16}$	270	25	4	4	·106
1962/63	T120	376	$1\frac{1}{16}$	240	25	$3\frac{1}{2}$	2	·106
1963/67	T120 USA	389	$1\frac{3}{16}$	330	25	4	2	·106
1964/67	T120 R USA	389	$1\frac{1}{8}$	260	20	3	3	·106
1967/68	T120	930	30 mm	220	20	$2\frac{1}{2}$	2	·106
1969/70	T120	930	30 mm	190	—	3	2	·106
1971/73	T120	930	30 mm	180	—	3	1	·106
1962/63	TR6 SS	376	$1\frac{1}{16}$	250	25	$3\frac{1}{2}$	3	·106
1964/67	TR6 Police	389	$1\frac{1}{8}$	310	25	$3\frac{1}{2}$	1	·106
1964/67	Met. Police Mk 3	389	$1\frac{3}{16}$	320	25	$3\frac{1}{2}$	2	·106
1967	TR6	389	$1\frac{3}{16}$	330	25	4	2	·106
1968	TR6	930	30 mm	230	—	4	2	·107
1969/73	TR6	930	30 mm	230	—	$3\frac{1}{2}$	2	·106
1973	T140	930	30 mm	190	—	3	1	·106
1975/78	T140	930	30 mm	190	—	3	2	·106
1978/80	T140	930	30 mm	200	25	3	2	·105
1973	TR7	930	30 mm	260	—	$3\frac{1}{2}$	1	·106
1975/80	TR7	930	30 mm	270	—	$3\frac{1}{2}$	1	·106

1969/70	T150	626	26 mm	150	—	3	2	·106	
1971/74	T150	626	26 mm	150	—	3½	2	·106	
1973	X75	626	26 mm	150	—	3½	2	·106	
1975	T160	626	26 mm	150	—	3½	2	·106	
1948	TRW	Solex	Choke	110	—	—	—	—	
1952/58	Thunderbird	SU	M9	—	—	—	—	—	
1958/64	Scooter 250 cc twin	Zenith 17MXZ	—	82	45	—	fixed	200 starter slide	
1971	Bandit 350 cc twin	626	26 mm	—	—	—	—	—	

Prices

The price of the first 650 cc model 6/1 in September 1933 was £70.0s.0d. This rose to £77.0s.0d in January 1935.

The Speed Twin was launched in August 1937 at £75.0s.0d. plus £2.15s.0d. for the speedometer. In November 1938 it was down to £74.0s.0d., with the Tiger 100 at £80.0s.0d., in each case the speedometer being an extra at £2.15s.0d.

After the war the 3T was introduced at £139.14s.0d. including £29.14s.0d. purchase tax and its speedometer at £4.8s.11d. including 18/11d. tax. The Speed Twin cost a total of £163.3s.11d. with tax and speedometer, The Tiger 100 £180.6s.10d., and the Tiger 85 would have sold at £160.0s.5d.

The prices of the various models over the years are set out in the following lists together with tables of some of the accessories.

Certain machines and parts have not been included as they were only produced and sold for very short periods. Such an item was the parcel grid sold as an option for £1.11s.9d. in 1949, before being fitted as standard. A machine not included is the 1965 Thruxton Bonneville which was listed at £357.9s.3d. less fairing. However, they were normally bought with fairing and a good number of other options so no list price ever meant very much. Further rare options were the 1961 remote float chamber at £15.12s.5d. which was used on the high performance Bonneville fitted with twin Monoblocs with chopped float chambers.

Pre-unit construction models

Date	3T	5T	6T	TR5	T100	T110	GP
4. 4.46	£139.14s. 0d.	£163. 3s.11d.					
5. 9.46	£149.17s. 3d.	£167.12s.10d.			£180. 6s.10d.		
1947	£162.11s. 3d.	£180. 6s.10d.			£193. 0s.10d.		
12. 2.48							£342.18s. 0d.
7.10.48	£162.11s. 3d.	£180. 6s.10d.			£193. 0s.10d.		£342.18s. 0d.
30.12.48	£162.11s. 3d.	£180. 6s.10d.		£195.11s. 8d.	£193. 0s.10d.		£342.18s. 0d.
24. 3.49	£167.12s.11d.	£185. 8s. 6d.		£200.13s. 4d.	£198. 2s. 6d.		£342.18s. 0d.
27.10.49 / 9.11.50	£167.12s.10d.	£185. 8s. 5d.	£194. 6s. 3d.	£200.13s. 3d.	£198. 2s. 5d.		£342.18s. 0d.
8.11.51 / 3. 4.52		£209.11s. 2d.	£219.15s. 7d.	£227. 8s.11d.	£223.12s. 3d.		

Appendix

	T100C	5T	6T	TR5	T100	T110
Dec. 1952	£233.16s. 8d.	£203. 3s. 4d.	£219.15s. 7d.	£227. 8s.11d.	223.12s. 3d.	
23. 4.53	£221. 2s. 6d.	£192. 2s. 6d.	£207.16s. 8d.	£215. 1s. 8d.	£211. 9s. 2d.	
7. 1.54		£190.16s. 0d.	£200. 8s. 0d.	£210. 0s. 0d.	£228. 0s. 0d.	£240. 0s. 0d.
Sept. 1954		£210. 0s. 0d.	£219.12s. 0d.	£234. 0s. 0d.	£228. 0s. 0d.	£240. 0s. 0d.

	TR6	5T	6T	TR5	T100	T110	T120
27.10.55		£249. 0s. 0d.	£217. 4s. 0d.	£227. 8s. 0d.	£240. 0s. 0d.	£237.12s. 0d.	£246.12s. 0d.
8. 3.56		£265. 7s. 3d.					
25.10.56 }		£267.16s.10d.	£235.12s. 0d.	£244.18s. 0d.	257.18s. 5d.	£255. 8s.10d.	£265. 7s. 3d.
4. 4.57 }							
31.10.57 }		£280.13s. 9d.	£253. 4s.11d.	£258. 4s. 8d.	£274. 9s. 0d.	£269. 9s. 3d.	£278. 3s.11d.
6. 3.58 }							
23. 4.59		£271. 8s. 2d.		£249.13s.11d.		£260.11s. 0d.	£268.19s.11d.	£284.13s. 6d.
21. 1.60		£271. 8s. 2d.		£249.13s.11d.			£268.19s.11d.	£284.13s. 6d.
5.10.60				£255.14s. 6d.			£272.12s. 3d.	£288. 5s.11d.
26. 1.61		£276. 4s. 8d.		£255.14s. 6d.			£272.12s. 3d.	£288. 5s.11d.
19.10.61 }		£280.19s. 1d.		£265. 0s. 2d.				£295. 1s. 4d.
8. 3.62 }							
22. 3.62		£295. 1s. 3d.		£278. 9s. 0d.				£309.15s. 8d.

Unit construction models

	3TA	5TA	T100A	T100 SS	T90		
4. 4.57	£217. 0s. 0d.						
31.10.57 }	£228. 5s.11d.						
6. 3.58 }							
15. 4.59		£245.15s. 2d.					
23. 4.59	£220.14s.11d.	£237.12s. 8d.					
21. 1.60	£227.19s. 8d.	£237.12s. 8d.	£247.17s. 9d.				
5.10.60	£234. 0s. 3d.	£243.13s. 3d.	£250.18s. 0d.				
19.10.61 }	£241.13s.11d.	£253.19s. 4d.		£258.17s. 5d.			
8. 3.62 }							
22. 3.62	£253.19s. 3d.	£266.16s.11d.	6T	£271.15s. 1d.		TR6 SS	T120
15.11.62 }	£261. 0s. 0d.	£274. 4s. 0d.	£286. 4s. 0d.	£279. 0s. 0d.	£274. 4s. 0d.	£303. 0s. 0d.	£318. 0s. 0d.
24. 1.63 }							
30.10.63	£261. 0s. 0d.	£274. 4s. 0d.	£295. 4s. 0d.	£279. 0s. 0d.	£274. 4s. 0d.	£307. 4s. 0d.	£320. 8s. 0d.
12. 3.64 }	£279. 9s. 8d.	£283. 1s. 5d.	£308. 3s. 0d.	£286.13s. 0d.	£283. 1s. 5d.	£320.13s.10d.	£326.13s. 3d.
3. 4.65 }							
2. 9.65 }	£279. 9s. 8d.	£283. 1s. 5d.	£308. 3s. 0d.	£291. 8s. 7d.	£286.13s. 0d.	£336.16s. 4d.	£349. 7s. 1d.
24. 3.66 }							

	T90	T100 SS	T100T	TR6 SS	T120
3.11.66	£291. 6s. 4d.	£296. 3s. 5d.	£331. 7s. 6d.	£342. 6s. 0d.	£355. 0s.10d.
16. 3.67 / 8.11.67	£291. 6s. 4d.	£296. 3s. 5d.	£333. 7s. 7d.	£342. 6s. 0d.	£355. 0s.10d.
10. 4.68	£302. 4s. 0d.	£307. 4s. 9d.	£345.16s. 8d.	£355. 1s. 9d.	£368. 6s. 2d.
Jan. 1970		£346. 5s. 3d.	£380. 5s. 3d.	£404. 5s. 3d.	£420. 5s. 3d.

	T100R	T100C	T120R	TR6R	TR6C	TR5T	T120V
1971	£465	£468	£525	£488			
1972	£528		£616	£573			£650
1973	£515		£519	£499		£519	£545
1974							£714

	TR7RV	T140V	Jubilee Bonnie	T140E	T140D	T140ES
1973	£ 649	£ 649				
1974	£ 616	£ 649				
1975	£ 805	£ 805				
1976	£ 805	£ 885				
1977	£1012	£1012				
6.78	£1011	£1011				
11.78	£1123	£1134				
1.79	£1247	£1269				
3.79	£1385			£1399		
6.79	£1385			£1399	£1595	
7.79	£1385			£1399	£1660	
8.79 / 5.80	£1545			£1560	£1768	
6.80	£1679			£1699	£1768	£1868
4.81				£1965		£2035

Jubilee Bonnie 1977: £1149

Scooter Prices
Standard model—type TW2
With electric start—type TW2S

	TW2	TW2S
1958	£187. 2s.6d.	£200.17s.0d.
1959/60	£180.18s.9d.	£194. 4s.2d.
June 1961	£184. 0s.7d.	£197.10s.7d.
April 1962	£180.18s.9d.	£194. 4s.2d.
September 1962/64	£184.10s.0d.	£198. 0s.0d.

Final price list dated April 1983 had the **T140ES** listed at £2204 at home and £2268 for the USA. Other model prices were £2137 for the Daytona 600, £2181 for the Thunderbird 600, £2359 for the **TSX4** and £2499 for the **TSX8** and the **TSS**. Where the TSS had the frame with anti-vibration engine mounts the price was £2549,. When the Bonneville appeared again for 1985 the price was £2760.

Scooter accessories in September 1962

Front carrier	£3. 2s.6d.
Rear carrier	£3. 7s.6d.
Wheel disc	£1.10s.0d.
Spare wheel and tyre	£5.12s.0d.
Spare wheel cover	£1.17s.6d.
Spare wheel cover plate	11s.0d.
Pannier bag	£2.12s.3d.
Pannier bag carrier	£2. 0s.0d.
Windscreen	£5. 0s.0d.
250 cc model touring kit	£4.17s.6d.

Trident Prices

Introduced at £614.3s.5d. including purchase tax, and rose to £670 in November 1970 and to £714 in August 1971. It remained at this point until the five-speed gearbox was introduced that year, when it rose to £746. For 1973 it was £749, for 1974 it rose slightly to £779, and in 1975 jumped to £971.

The X75 Hurricane was listed at £895 during its short life in 1973.

The final Trident, the T160, was listed at £1215 in 1975. It is shown at £1100 in a March 1976 list and £1200 in a November 1976 one, neither of which meant much in the circumstances.

The TR6 Thunderbird introduced in 1981 and reduced to a 600 in 1983

The Phoenix 900 with new, water-cooled, twin engine shown early in 1983

Engine unit of the TSS with eight valves and derived from the earlier Weslake kit